THE PELICAN CLASSICS

AC 6

HALIFAX

COMPLETE WORKS

GEORGE SAVILE, MARQUESS OF HALIFAX, the seventeenth-century statesman and pamphleteer, was the son of a Yorkshire baronet, born in 1633 and educated at Shrewsbury School. After a period of foreign travel he went to Court at the Restoration of Charles II and was created Viscount Halifax in 1668. For most of the 1670s he was in opposition, but during the Exclusion Crisis of 1678–81 he emerged as one of the most respected supporters of the monarchy, and his conduct earned him an earldom in 1679 and a marquessate in 1682, when he was also appointed Lord Privy Seal. The antipathy between him and James II sent him into opposition in 1685, and he played a distinguished and influential part in the Revolution of 1688. He was reappointed Lord Privy Seal in 1689, and enjoyed the respect and trust of William III. But he resigned in 1690, again went into opposition, and died an embittered and disillusioned man in 1695. All his writings were either *pièces d'occasion*, of which the most famous is *The Character of a Trimmer* (1674), or essays and epigrams not intended for immediate publication, notably his exquisite *Character of King Charles II*, which did not see the light of day until 1750. His reputation as a statesman and writer suffered an eclipse until the late nineteenth century, but in the sphere of political thought he is now recognized as one of the most distinguished predecessors of Burke, and in the sphere of literature as a prose writer who is the equal of the great Augustans.

J. P. KENYON has been Professor of Modern History in the University of Hull since 1962. Before that he was a Fellow of Christ's College, Cambridge, and University Lecturer in History. He was also a visiting professor at Columbia University, New York, in 1959. His publications include *Robert Spencer Earl of Sunderland* (1958), *The Stuarts* (1958) and *The Stuart Constitution* (1966). He is now writing a new study of the Popish Plot.

HALIFAX

COMPLETE WORKS

EDITED WITH
AN INTRODUCTION BY

J. P. Kenyon

PENGUIN BOOKS

Penguin Books Ltd, Harmondsworth, Middlesex, England
Penguin Books Inc., 7110 Ambassador Road, Baltimore, Maryland 21207, U.S.A.
Penguin Books Australia Ltd, Ringwood, Victoria, Australia

—

Published in Penguin Books 1969

—

Made and printed in Great Britain
by Hazell Watson & Viney Ltd,
Aylesbury, Bucks
Set in Monotype Fournier

CONTENTS

Introduction 7

Outline of Events 41

A Note on this Edition 43

The Character of a Trimmer [*CT*][1] 49

A Letter to a Dissenter [*LD*] 105

The Anatomy of an Equivalent [*AE*] 121

Maxims of State [*MS*] 147

A Rough Draft of a New Model at Sea [*RD*] 153

Some Cautions Offered [*SCO*] 167

Political Thoughts and Reflections [*PTR*] 193

Moral Thoughts and Reflections [*MTR*] 215

Miscellaneous Thoughts and Reflections [*Misc.TR*] 231

A Character of King Charles the Second [*KCII*] 247

Advice to a Daughter [*AD*] 271

Selected Letters 317

Appendix: 'Observations upon a Late Libel.' 345

1. The pamphlets are cited in the footnotes that follow by the abbreviations placed after their titles here.

INTRODUCTION

> A man that steps aside from the world, and hath leisure to observe it without interest or design, thinks all mankind as mad as they think him, for not agreeing with them in their mistakes.[1]

No one would think that the man who wrote this passage, and scores like it, was actively involved in high politics for at least twenty-five years in one of the stormiest periods of English history. George Savile, Marquess of Halifax, was one of those intellectuals who found the practice of politics odious and uncomfortable, who found no satisfaction in political association. But he was so interested in the pursuit and exercise of power, and so convinced that his were the only right answers to the public questions of the moment, that though he found it absolutely necessary to 'step aside from the world' every few years for repose and recuperation, he always returned to Whitehall or Westminster for further punishment.

His comments on politics are therefore unique. Men like Hobbes and Locke (to mention only contemporaries of his) shared his cynicism but not his practical experience; however closely they observed politics, they remained outside it. On the other hand, a man like Clarendon, who did write with first-hand experience of politics and government, was deeply committed to a certain view of politics which inhibited, or even prohibited, intellectual speculation. Halifax was at the centre of politics, but he remained uncommitted; not only did he never join any political association, party or group, he was never in close alliance with any individual politician of his own class or status – such confidences as he gave were always to his inferiors. Even his attachment to monarchy cannot be taken entirely for granted.[2] He came of a royalist family, but his principles were never fixed by residence at Oxford or Cambridge – instead he spent several years abroad, mainly in the Huguenot south of France – and he retained a strong sympathy for republicanism to the end.

1. *MTR*, p. 216 below. 2. See p. 29 below.

Intellectually he was head and shoulders above most contemporary statesmen. His nearest rival was Anthony Ashley Cooper, Earl of Shaftesbury; but Shaftesbury never perceived the danger from France, never appreciated that there could be a non-violent solution to the problem of a Catholic succession. An owl amongst crows, Halifax found politics a painful and laborious business, and though his career was on the whole successful and distinguished, the tone of his *Political Thoughts and Reflections*, which were probably not intended for publication, does not suggest that he derived any satisfaction from it.

But behind the cynicism and the mordant wit lies a humane, sensitive and tolerant man. His prose, elegant yet light, was ideally suited to his purpose, and as a writer alone he would still deserve to be read. He would also deserve to be read as one of the few non-partisan observers of a period which was of decisive importance in the formation of the British Constitution. But Halifax is more than that. Though most of his writings were keyed to contemporary crises of one kind or another, he always tried to strike down to first principles; he wrote about politics in general, not just seventeenth-century politics, and this is true even of his political testament, *The Character of a Trimmer*. It is this detachment, near-miraculous in the hurly-burly of later Stuart politics, that gives his work its permanent value.

*

Halifax came to Court at the Restoration in 1660. Twenty-seven years old, intelligent, well-connected and wealthy, he was strikingly eligible for office. Whether his failure to obtain it was his personal choice or not it is impossible to say, but the fact that he was given a peerage in 1668 for no apparent reason is an indication of his high standing. He was already noted for his antipathy to the Church of Rome and the France of Louis XIV,[3] and on the face of it it is surprising that he should be asked to join the Privy Council in April 1672, when Charles II had just declared war on Holland in

3. This is evident in his first extant letter, of 1666, printed in H. C. Foxcroft, *A Character of the Trimmer; A Short Life of the 1st Marquis of Halifax*, (Cambridge University Press, 1946), pp. 20–1.

alliance with France and suspended the penal laws against the Catholics. It is equally surprising that he should have accepted, but he may have listened to the advice of his uncle, the Earl of Shaftesbury, who was appointed Lord Chancellor at the same time. He left this 'prerogative government' in 1674, with Shaftesbury, and for five years he was a member of the opposition in the House of Lords. His chance came in April 1679, when the crisis of the 'Popish Plot' so weakened the King's position that he was forced to broaden his administration by bringing the principal opposition leaders, Halifax amongst them, into a reconstituted Privy Council.

In view of his known hostility to the Roman Catholic heir-presumptive, James, Duke of York, Halifax might have been expected to stand by Shaftesbury in demanding the Duke's exclusion from the succession by statute. Instead he parted company with him on this issue in the summer of 1679 – for which he duly received an earldom – and despite prolonged absences from London he remained firm, even to the extent of successfully opposing the second Exclusion Bill in the House of Lords in November 1680.

From this watershed his career ran down. He was often at Court, but he did not seek office, and his prejudice against France made it inevitable that he be kept ignorant of the secret agreement between Louis XIV and Charles II in March 1681, which governed England's foreign policy, and strongly influenced her domestic policy, over the next four years. When the Duke of York returned from exile in Scotland in 1682 he might have been expected to retire; James was his *bête-noire*, and the feeling was heartily reciprocated.[4] Instead he accepted a marquessate, and in October 1682 he took office for the first time, as Lord Privy Seal. In so doing he allowed himself to be associated in the public mind with the aggressive and reactionary policy of Charles's declining years – the period of 'The Stuart Revenge' – particularly the remodelling of the parliamentary corporations and the judicial murder of leading Whigs like William

4. According to James, Halifax 'was an atheist, and had no bowels', (James Macpherson, *Original Papers* (1775), i. p. 105). On another occasion he wrote, 'I never could understand his politics, and am sure they were never calculated for the meridian of a monarchy' (*HMC Dartmouth*, i, 40–41).

Lord Russell and Algernon Sydney. His innocence of any complicity in these events (he had in fact tried to save Russell from the scaffold) did not appear until 1689. He gave his enemies another handle by his patronage of the King's illegitimate son, Monmouth, though he had been the first to criticize Shaftesbury for similar conduct in 1680. Conscious of his waning influence, in the last months of 1684 he took the extraordinary step of publishing in manuscript his *Character of a Trimmer*; an impassioned appeal to the King to jettison his brother, take a firm stand against French aggression in Flanders and summon another Parliament. The King was dead within two months, but it was an ineffectual gesture anyway.

It was difficult for Halifax's colleagues to understand why a man of his undoubted gifts, his great ambition (for his family, if not for himself) and his positive opinions on policy matters had delayed his acceptance of government office so long, and why he was apparently content to remain on the fringes of power.[5] From 1681 to 1685 his influence on day-to-day policy was always 'apparent rather than effective', and he took part of the blame for its failures without sharing any of the advantages of its success.[6] It is always said that Charles II delighted in his company, and as a result he was influential in the closet, but there are no signs of this influence. Dryden unintentionally applied an important distinction when he remarked: '[The King] was master of too much good sense to delight in heavy conversation, and whatever his favourites of state might be, yet those of his affection were men of wit. He was easy with these, and complied only with the former.'[7]

In any case, though he is credited with some good sallies – he remarked to the Earl of Danby, who had just declined a handsome bribe, that he wondered if he would reply as courteously to a man who asked for the use of his wife – his wit was clearly based on

5. According to Halifax he was offered the post of First Lord of the Treasury in November 1679, with a promise of the Lord Treasurership later (MS Notebook, Chatsworth, *sub* 'Hyde'). At the same time, and again in 1680, he was strongly 'tipped' for the Lord Lieutenancy of Ireland.

6. H. C. Foxcroft, *The Life and Letters of Sir George Savile, Bart., first Marquis of Halifax*, 2 vols, 1898, i, p. 300 (Hereafter cited as 'Foxcroft').

7. Dedication to *King Arthur, Works* (1808), viii, p. 116.

sarcasm rather than humour, and he himself admits that he would not stoop to the kind of bawdry Charles II preferred:

> [The King's] aversion to formality made him dislike a serious discourse, if very long, except it was mixed with something to entertain him. Some, even of the graver sort, too, used to carry this very far, and rather than fail, use the coarsest kind of youthful talk.[8]

The disproportionate amount of space in his *Character of King Charles II* which is devoted to an analysis of the King's wit suggests that he attached far too much importance to it, and his friend Gilbert Burnet says as much:

> When after much discourse a point was settled, if he could find a new jest, to make even that which was suggested by himself seem ridiculous, he could not hold, but would study to raise the credit of his wit though it made others call his judgment in question.[9]

Burnet found him difficult to understand on other scores – on titles, for instance:

> When he talked to me, as a philosopher, of his contempt for the world, I asked him what he meant by getting so many new titles, which I called the hanging himself about with bells and tinsel. He had no other excuse for it but this, that since the world were such fools as to value these matters, a man must be a fool for company; he considered them but as rattles, yet rattles please children, so these might be of use to his family.[10]

His career was one long dilemma. He was a parliamentary statesman of consummate skill, but in an age when Parliament met infrequently, and then not for constructive deliberation. He loved power, but hated the drudgery of administration – which was why he always chose to be Lord Privy Seal. He deprecated the increasing bitterness of politics in his lifetime; and the unscrupulousness and savagery of his enemies in 1679, which led them even to impugn his wife's honour,[11] were a profound shock. In his letters the rather

8. *KCII*, p. 257 below.
9. *History of My Own Time* (1833 edn.), i. p. 492.
10. ibid, i, p. 493. See his remarks on the earldom, Letter II, p. 318 below; and his description of monarchy as 'milk for the babes', *CT*, p. 55 below.
11. *Poems on Affairs of State* (Yale University Press, 1966), i, p. 407.

naïve delight with which he greeted his appointment to the Council in April 1679 soon gave way to disillusionment and disgust, and in January 1680, at the height of the Exclusion Crisis, he retired to his country seat at Rufford, in Nottinghamshire.[12] Similar attacks in 1689 drove him out of office, and strengthened his animus against party politics.

So, despite his reputation as a moderate, or a 'trimmer', he found that he could exercise little influence on government; like his friends Sir William Temple and Sir William Coventry, he was an oracle whose advice was never heeded. Finally he pinned his hopes on converting the monarch, face to face, and it is significant that the pamphlet to which he attached most significance, *The Character of a Trimmer*, was a direct personal appeal to Charles II, not to the country. Of similar significance is the care with which he noted every word which fell from King William's lips in 1689.[13] He was certainly not a 'courtier' in the vulgar sense, but it is not surprising that many contemporaries took him for one – or were at a loss to understand what he was.

> He was punctual in all his payments [wrote Burnet], and just in all his private dealings, but with relation to the public he went backwards and forwards, and changed sides so often that in conclusion no side trusted him. He seemed full of commonwealth notions, yet he went into the worst part of King Charles's reign. He was out of measure vain and ambitious.[14]

*

Halifax's fame rests on two episodes: his opposition to the Exclusion Bill, and his part in the Revolution of 1688–9. First, the Exclusion Bill.

Charles II's fourth Parliament was elected in the autumn of 1679, but it was not allowed to meet until October 1680. As the King had feared, the Opposition at once brought in a bill to exclude the Duke of York from the succession; it speedily passed the Commons, and came up to the Lords on 15 November. Halifax opposed

12. Letters I–IV, p. 317 below.
13. These notes were printed by Foxcroft, ii, pp. 201–52.
14. *History of My Own Time*, *loc. cit.*

it with the utmost vigour, speaking at least sixteen times, and after a debate lasting most of the day it was thrown out by 63 votes to 30.

Given the weight of conservative opinion in the Lords, and the firm attitude adopted by the King, it is doubtful if this bill would have passed anyway.[15] But contemporaries were unanimous in awarding Halifax the credit; James himself acknowledged it, then and later, and an infuriated House of Commons promptly requested the King to remove him 'from his presence and counsels for ever'. His popular reputation is summed up in half a dozen lines from *Absalom and Achitophel*:

> Jotham of pregnant wit and piercing thought,
> Endowed by nature, and by learning taught
> To move Assemblies, who but only tried
> The worse awhile, then chose the better side;
> Nor chose alone, but turned the balance too;
> So much the weight of one brave man can do.[16]

It certainly required courage of a high order to do what Halifax did. After all, he had retired to the country that winter because he could not stand the ferocious personal abuse heaped upon him, and because he disliked being at loggerheads with his old associates in Opposition, like Shaftesbury. If he took a stand against Exclusion now he would court much greater abuse, he would have to break with his old associates for good, and he would lose some of his old friends, like Sir William Temple and the Earl of Sunderland, who were now converts to the Whig opposition on this issue. It must have been tempting to cross to the other side and let James bleed to death; he doubted his capacity to rule – did not, in fact, believe he would ever come to the throne – and he despised the religion he represented. Moreover, a man who believed as he did that constitutions were not immutable and should be adapted to changing circumstances can have had no theoretical objection to the alteration of the (unwritten) Law of Succession. Why did he act as he did, knowing that, win or lose, he would suffer by it?[17]

15. J. P. Kenyon, *Robert Spencer, Earl of Sunderland* (Longmans, Green & Co. Ltd, 1958), p. 64; K. H. D. Haley, *Shaftesbury* (Clarendon Press, 1968), p. 601.
16. *Dryden's Poems* (Oxford University Press, 1962), p. 212.
17. His suffering is indicated by Letters X–XV, pp. 326–32 below.

Contemporaries were probably aware of his reasons, but they did not state them; his own letters are evasive or non-committal;[18] and of the Lords debate itself we still know little more than Macaulay's legendary old men.[19] However, some fragmentary notes published by E. S. de Beer in 1943 do offer a few important clues.[20] Typically, Halifax rejected the face-saving argument that the bill was unconstitutional; he admitted that it was perfectly proper for Parliament to alter the succession if it wished to do so. The burden of his argument was that James simply would not accept exclusion, that he would appeal to arms, and that with the probable assistance of Scotland and Ireland he could do so with success. This alone was enough to sway the men of his own generation, who had lived through the civil wars of the 1640s, even if they had been too young to take part; the fear of a recurrence of civil war was one of the strongest emotions in late seventeenth-century politics, and he carried moderate opinion with him when he accused Shaftesbury, who *had* fought in the civil wars, of criminal irresponsibility.[21] The courtiers were used to getting the better of the vote; the importance of Halifax's intervention was that it made them feel that for once they had the better of the argument, too.[22] In 1691 John Dryden still remembered the perils of those days, and the moderating influence of Halifax's 'wholesome counsels',

which, wisely administered and as well executed, were the means of preventing a civil war, and of extinguishing a growing fire which was just ready to have broken forth among us. So many wives, who have yet their husbands in their arms; so many parents, who have not the number of their children lessened; so many villages, towns and cities, whose inhabitants are not decreased, their property violated, or their

18. See Letter IX, p. 324 below.

19. 'Old men who lived to admire the eloquence of Pulteney in its meridian, and that of Pitt in its splendid dawn, still murmured that they had heard nothing like the great speeches of Lord Halifax on the Exclusion Bill', *Essays*, (Everyman edn.), i, p. 255.

20. *Bulletin of the Institute of Historical Research*, xx (1943), pp 32-6, particularly p. 35.

21. This I take to be the meaning of the note: 'Lord Shaftesbury has been in so many changes that it is charity to fear [?for him] for he fears not', ibid., p. 35.

22. A point put by Haley, *op. cit.* p. 602.

wealth diminished – are yet owing to the sober conduct, and happy results of your advice.[23]

*

James II owed it in part to Halifax that he succeeded to the throne in February 1685 without opposition; and he told him when he made him Lord President of the Council that all he chose to remember of his past conduct was his opposition to the Exclusion Bill.[24] For his part Halifax told Sir John Reresby 'that he used his constant endeavours to serve the King, and would continue them'.[25] But it was a short-lived honeymoon, and in October he was abruptly dismissed in favour of his arch-enemy Lord Sunderland.

After a brief session in November, Parliament was not summoned again, and for two or three years Halifax remained in retirement; like many other Protestant peers, he did not even come to Court. But towards the end of 1686 he seized the excuse of his younger son's visit to The Hague to open a correspondence with William Prince of Orange, who had married James's elder daughter Mary and would almost certainly succeed him on the throne. They had corresponded occasionally during the Exclusion Crisis, and they had met in England in 1681; now William sought his advice on English affairs, and over the next eighteen months Halifax wrote whenever he could find a safe messenger going into Holland.

His advice was perfectly consistent, and in keeping with one who was the spokesman of moderate opinion. He did not believe that James could persuade his present Parliament to repeal the penal laws against Catholics, and still less the Test Act of 1673, which kept them out of office.[26] When James suspended all this legislation in April 1687, and made a sustained bid for the political support of

23. *Works*, viii, p. 115. (He refers to the Lords debate as 'advice' in deference to parliamentary privilege.)

24. 'A handsome expression, which has been the more noticed, as well because it is almost the single instance of this Prince's showing any disposition to forget injuries, as on account of a delicacy and propriety in the wording of it by no means familiar to him' (Charles James Fox, *History of the Reign of James II*, 1808, pp. 83–4).

25. *Memoirs of Sir John Reresby* (Glasgow, 1936), p. 360.

26. Letters XVII–XIX, pp. 333–8 below.

the Dissenters, he was still sanguine; though the flood of Addresses from Dissenters giving thanks for the King's Indulgence provoked him to write his famous *Letter to a Dissenter*, which one historian has called 'the perfect model, perhaps, of a political tract'.[27]

This *Letter* stressed with biting logic that James was only turning to the Dissenters as second best, after failing to win over the Church of England. Most important, Halifax reminded his readers of Rome's reputation:

> Wine is not more expressly forbid to the Mahometans, than giving heretics liberty to the Papists; they are no more able to make good their vows to you than men married before, and their wife alive, can confirm their contract with another. The continuance of their kindness would be a habit of sin, of which they are to repent, and their absolution is to be had upon no other terms than their promise to destroy you. You are therefore to be hugged now, only that you may be the better squeezed at another time.[28]

He closed with a reasoned appeal for passivity and non-aggression which was an echo of his advice to William:

> If we give no advantage by the fatal mistake of misapplying our anger, by the natural course of things this danger will pass away like a shower of hail; fair weather will succeed, as lowering as the sky now looketh, and all by the plain and easy receipt: *Let us be still, quiet and undivided, firm at the same time to our religion, our loyalty and our laws.*[29]

And King James's violent activity in the winter of 1687–8; the remodelling of parliamentary corporations, the dismissal of Lord Lieutenants by the score and Justices of the Peace by the hundred; still left him unmoved. He told William soothingly:

> In some particulars, to men at a distance, the engine seemeth to move fast, but by looking nearer one may see that it doth not stir upon the whole matter, so that here is rapid motion without advancing a step, which is the only miracle that Church hath yet showed to us.[30]

He refused to be panicked even by the birth of a son to James on

27. Sir James Mackintosh, *History of the Revolution* (1834), p. 174.
28. p. 106 below.
29. p. 116 below.
30. Letter XX, p. 338 below.

10 June 1688, which led to the dispatch on the 30th of the famous document inviting William of Orange to bring an army to England and force James to summon a new Parliament. The signatories made a tentative approach to him, but 'he did not encourage a further freedom'; 'he expressed his dislike of the design as impracticable, and depending upon so many accidents that he thought it was a needless putting of all things upon so dangerous an issue'.[31] He was immensely heartened by the acquittal of the Seven Bishops on the very day the Invitation was sent off;[32] it confirmed his belief that James's regime would soon collapse of its own accord. On 25 July, in his last surviving letter to the Prince, he still urged him not to interfere in English affairs:

> I still remain persuaded that there is no effectual progress made towards the great design; and even the thing that party relieth upon[33] is subject to so many accidents and uncertainties that according to human probability we are secure, notwithstanding the ill appearances, which fright most when they are least examined.[34]

Halifax's attitude has often been condemned, particularly by Macaulay, who dismissed him as 'a sceptic, a voluptuary, not likely to venture his all on a single hazard, or to be a martyr in any cause'.[35] Maybe so, but Daniel Finch, Earl of Nottingham, who also corresponded with William in 1687 and 1688, adopted precisely the same attitude, and he was certainly not lacking in moral courage. In merely physical terms William's expedition was a frightful risk, and it only succeeded through luck, and because James's regime, when put to the test, proved as rotten and ricketty as Halifax always said it was. Halifax, Nottingham and many more thought that James II was an incompetent and improvident fool who did not

31. *Supplement to Burnet's History*, ed. H. C. Foxcroft (Oxford University Press, 1902), p. 291.

32. The Archbishop of Canterbury and six bishops were prosecuted for seditious libel after they had published a petition to the King requesting him to withdraw his order that his Edict of Toleration be read from the pulpits of the Established Church.

33. The birth of the Prince of Wales.

34. Letter XXI, p. 342 below.

35. *History of England* (Everyman edn.), ii, p. 18.

pose any permanent threat to their interests, whatever temporary inconvenience he might cause. On the other hand, to bring in a prince of proven ability and marked authoritarian tendencies might be to exchange King Log for King Stork.[36] Moreover, as in 1680, there was a very real threat of civil war, and he took pains to warn William against 'unseasonable stirrings', provoked by 'unskilful agitators, warm men, who would be active at a wrong time'.[37] No doubt the 'Immortal Seven' were of this number.

So, once William had landed, on 5 November, Halifax's main concern was to prevent any actual fighting. In conjunction with other peers he proposed an immediate summons of Parliament in November, and tried to delay James's departure to Salisbury on the 18th to take command of the army. When James abandoned any pretence of military resistance and returned to London on 27 November Halifax advised him to negotiate, and he was sent with Nottingham and Godolphin to seek terms from the Prince.

His studied loyalty to the King did not crack until 11 December, when he returned from the Prince's camp – where he must have experienced many petty insults and humiliations from cock-a-hoop Whigs – to find that James had apparently fled the country the night before. To his mind this act of criminal irresponsibility at a time of crisis dissolved the bonds of allegiance. He was elected chairman of an *ad hoc* committee of peers and bishops which met at the Guildhall to assume responsibility for the government of London, but as soon as it became known that James had in fact been detained in Kent and was returning to the capital he left to join William at Windsor. There he effortlessly assumed command of the informal council advising the Prince on English affairs, though many of its members had sailed with William, and it was perhaps because of his influence that it rejected such extreme proposals as James's immediate disposition. It advised William simply to request James to leave London, and Halifax stoically accepted

36. As early as 1680, in his speech against Exclusion, Halifax had referred to William's attempt on the province of Guelderland in 1675. de Beer, *op. cit.*, p. 35; S. B. Baxter, *William III* (Longmans, Green & Co. Ltd, 1966), p. 123.
37. Letter XX, p. 339 below.

the distasteful task of taking this message to the King. James retired to Rochester, and slipped away to France for good on the night of the 22nd. Halifax entered London with William, and on 21 December he was again elected chairman of the Guildhall Committee, which now had the responsibility of administering the whole of England, and not just London. When news came on the 23rd that James had gone Halifax refused to allow a letter of explanation he had left behind to be read out, and the committee handed back its powers to the Prince, with a request that he summon a Convention as soon as possible.[38]

In all these vicissitudes Halifax had maintained and improved his position as a spokesman of moderation. He had stood by James as long as any reasonable man could, and defected to William only when this presented the best chance of peace, and it was expected that he would support the most moderate solution possible; the installation of the Princess Mary as Regent for her father, or possibly as sole monarch in his stead. Subsequent events suggest that he may have said as much at the time, and when the Convention met on 22 January 1689, he was at once elected Speaker of the House of Lords. Instead, on 25 January he exerted all his considerable influence against a Regency, and had the proposal thrown out by the narrow majority 51 to 49. He was defeated on a proposal that the Crown be offered to William alone, and he caused even greater offence when he pressed for the inclusion in the new Oath of Allegiance of a statement that William and Mary were 'rightful and lawful' monarchs, a step that Parliament was not prepared to take until 1696, and then not unanimously.[39]

Halifax had grave doubts of the permanence of any settlement,[40] which is why he argued that it was essential to erect a legal and stable government to which allegiance could properly be given under the terms of Henry VII's Treasons Act; otherwise the sudden return of James II would expose them all to the most severe penalties. Again, he was probably only expressing moderate

38. A convention was simply a parliament not summoned by royal writ.

39. Reresby *op. cit.*, p. 558.

40. He often spoke to Reresby with startling frankess, ibid., pp. 560–61, 564–5, 566, 572, 577–8.

opinion: when the diehard Earl of Clarendon remonstrated with one of his supporters for deserting him, he got the reply, 'There was an absolute necessity of having a government, and he did not see it likely to be any other way than this.'[41] But moderate opinion was disgusted with itself, and Halifax was the scapegoat; the inconsistency in his conduct was only apparent, but it was one inconsistency too many. The Tories would not forgive him for making the monarchy elective; the Whigs remembered his support for Charles II and James in the Exclusion Crisis, and they were sharpening their long knives against the 'prerogative men' of the two previous reigns. Halifax's aloofness had never fostered political alliances or friendships, and in the tense, bitter months of 1689 none of his colleagues stood by him.

As soon as he came to the throne William made him Lord Privy Seal, and gave him a degree of confidence he withheld from most of his English ministers. But criticism was unrelenting, inside and outside Parliament: he was most unfairly blamed for the disastrous campaign in Ireland; the Whig Duke of Bolton tried to force him from the Speakership of the House of Lords; and on 10 June a motion was put in the Commons 'that it is inconvenient to his Majesty's affairs that the Marquis of Halifax is in his Majesty's Council'.[42] It was defeated, but the parallel with 1680 was there, and during the autumn recess that followed Halifax began his retreat by resigning the Speakership.

But his enemies were not appeased, and on 2 November they secured the appointment of a Lords' Committee to investigate the 'murders' of Lord Russell and Algernon Sydney in 1683, as well as the resumption of borough charters by writs of *quo warranto* in the same year. It was avowedly an attack on Halifax, and as the only member of Charles II's Government who had tried to save Lord Russell, and the only one who had taken no part in the attack on the corporations, he had every right to feel bitter. He cleared his name with ease, but as soon as the Committee's report exonerating him was presented, on 20 December, he sought permission to resign

41. *Clarendon's Diary & Correspondence*, ed. S. W. Singer (1828), ii, p. 262.
42. Henry Horwitz, *Revolution Politicks* (Cambridge University Press, 1968), pp. 95–6.

the Privy Seal. William was reluctant, but he finally gave way on 8 February 1690 to a plea of ill health.[43]

They parted on the best of terms, but it was not long before Halifax returned to open opposition in Parliament, for the first time since the 1670s. The vague fears which had led him to discourage William's intervention in 1688 now came to dominate his mind, and he saw that the war with France, conducted on an unprecedented scale, could give William the financial and military resources to make himself as absolute as Louis XIV.[44] He was particularly concerned at the apparent ease with which the Treasury could manipulate the House of Commons, and furious that some of James II's most disreputable servants – notably Lord Sunderland – were now back in power. In the summer of 1692 he was dismissed from the Privy Council. The following winter he lent his support to a bill to remove office-holders from Parliament, and in 1693 to a Triennial Bill, to force the King to hold a general election every three years. Needless to say, these were both 'country' measures, fiercely resisted by Court and King.

He also turned to the press. His *Maxims of State*, in 1693, were read as an oblique attack on the King and Lord Sunderland, and in *A Rough Draft of a New Model at Sea* the following year he ostentatiously reaffirmed his belief in limited monarchy and his dismissal of absolutism. He died quite suddenly on 5 April 1695, but his parting shot came a few months later with *Some Cautions Offered to the Consideration of those who are about to choose Members to serve in the ensuing Parliament*, which though flippant in tone, expressed his serious concern at the decay of Parliament since the Revolution.

*

43. 'Tush,' said the sickly William, 'you have health enough' (Foxcroft, ii, p. 249).

44. As early as December 1690 he was jotting down snippets of information from the Dutch ambassador: 'That Dykeveldt put the King upon arbitrary counsels. Said that the late mutinies at Harlem and Rotterdam arose in part from jealousies of that kind' (MS Notebook, Chatsworth, *sub* 'D'). See also a violent speech from the session 1692–3, printed in Foxcroft, *Character*, pp. 318–19.

It is not difficult to make out a defence for Halifax's conduct in the last five years of his life – he was not the only man who was concerned at the state of Parliament, or alarmed at certain tendencies in William's Government – but to many contemporaries, even his friends, it seemed an irresponsible and destructive end to a great career, and in the next generation, which was deeply divided by party questions and positively delighted in extremism, his policy of 'trimming' could only be dismissed as irrelevant. Under Queen Anne, as at no other time in our history, moderation and compromise were at a discount.

Certain accidental factors also conspired to bury him. His line died out with his son, the second marquess, in 1700, and the vacant title was almost at once assumed by Charles Montague, the Junto leader. None of his great parliamentary speeches were extant, of course, and though his works were collected and published in 1700, with an execrable elegy by Elkaniah Settle,[45] and ran to two editions, interest then died out. When his granddaughter published his incomparable *Character of King Charles II* in 1750 it seems to have excited little comment, and it was not reprinted until 1898.

Of course, the verdict of Gilbert Burnet, whose influential *History of My Own Time* was published in two volumes in 1723 and 1734, was far from favourable,[46] and it was endorsed by that great oracle of the eighteenth century, David Hume:

This man, who possessed the finest genius and most extensive capacity of all employed in public affairs during the present reign, affected a species of neutrality between the parties, and was esteemed the head of that small body known by the denomination of Trimmers. This conduct, which is more natural to men of integrity than of ambition, could not, however, procure him the former character, and

45. 'In SENATES, There, with all his *Brightest Beams*,
Not *Michael*, to th'Embattl'd *Seraphims*,
A Mightier *Leading* CHIEF: Oraculous *Sense*:
Victorious *Right*! Amazing *Eloquence!*
All from that clearest *Organ* sweetly Sung;
From that bold *English* CICERO'S Silver Tongue,
Well might Great TRUTH, and Genuine *Justice* flow;
For he look'd *Upward*, when he talk'd *Below* . . .' (etc.)

46. p. 12 above.

he was always, with reason, regarded as an intriguer rather than a patriot.[47]

The influential historians of the early nineteenth century, like Henry Hallam[48] and Sir James Mackintosh,[49] were content to echo Hume, and it was left to Macaulay to effect a dramatic revision of Halifax's reputation.

In his essay on Sir William Temple, in 1838, Macaulay was lukewarm; he was inclined to think that Halifax's 'public life, though far indeed from faultless', had 'as few great stains as that of any politician who took an active part in affairs during [this] troubled and disastrous period', but this was faint praise indeed. Nevertheless, as an historian Macaulay possessed a psychological insight and a nicety of observation with which he is rarely credited, and he noticed that though by the normal canons of political morality Halifax was a turncoat he still exercised a moderating influence. 'He passed from faction to faction. But instead of adopting and inflaming the passions of those whom he joined, he tried to diffuse amongst them something of the spirit of those whom he had just left.'[50]

Ten years later, when he published the *History of England*, he had developed this idea:

> His understanding was keen, sceptical, inexhaustibly fertile in distinctions and objections; his taste refined, his sense of the ludicrous exquisite; his temper placid and forgiving, but fastidious and by no means prone either to malevolence or to enthusiastic admiration. Such a man could not long be constant to any band of political allies. He must not, however, be confounded with the vulgar crowd of renegades. For though, like them he passed from side to side, his transition was always in the direction opposite to theirs. He had nothing in common with those who fly from extreme to extreme, and who regard the party which they have deserted with an animosity far exceeding that of consistent enemies. His place was between the hostile divisions of the community, and he never wandered far beyond the frontier of either. The party to

47. *History of England* (1807 edn.), viii, p. 175.
48. *Constitutional History of England* (Everyman edn.), iii, pp. 98–9.
49. *History of the Revolution* (1834), p. 9.
50. *Essays*, i, pp. 253–4.

which he at any moment belonged was the party which, at that moment, he liked least, because it was the party of which at that moment he had the nearest view. He was therefore always severe upon his violent associates, and was always in friendly relations with his moderate opponents.[51]

This has been quoted at length because it is still the most accurate and perceptive analysis of Halifax's conduct we have, and it is so, perhaps, because Macaulay saw in Halifax his own reflection – the philosopher historian, the politican *manqué*. The following passage could have been a description of Macaulay himself:

All the prejudices, all the exaggerations of both the great parties in the State moved his scorn. He despised the mean arts and unreasonable clamours of demagogues. He despised still more the doctrines of Divine Right and Passive Obedience. He sneered impartially at the bigotry of the Churchman and at the bigotry of the Puritan .... In temper he was what, in our time, is called a Conservative. In theory he was a Republican. Even when his dread of anarchy and his disdain for vulgar delusions led him to side for a time with the defenders of arbitrary power, his intellect was always with Locke and Milton.[52]

Halifax the philosopher-statesman always craved 'the respect at once of courtiers and philosophers'; and indeed, he 'always saw passing events, not in the point of view in which they commonly appear to one who bears a part in them, but in the point of view in which, after the lapse of many years, they appear to the philosophic historian'.[53]

Perhaps Macaulay tipped the balance too heavily in favour of Halifax as a literary or intellectual figure, but his lavish praise for his writings, seconded by the German historian von Ranke, who thought him 'one of the finest pamphleters who has ever lived',[54] did not result in his works being made easily available. They still existed only in eighteenth-century editions, and in 1873 the *Satur-*

51. *History of England*, i, p. 192.
52. ibid., i, p. 191.
53. ibid.
54. Quoted H. C. Foxcroft, 'The Works of George Savile Marquis of Halifax', *English Historical Review*, xi (1896), p. 703. See Macaulay, *History*, i, p. 190, *Essays*, i, p. 254.

day Review complained that as a result scholars and critics were deterred from studying him.[55] When she began to study Halifax in the 1890s Hilda Foxcroft found that the British Museum still ascribed *The Character of a Trimmer* to Sir William Coventry, while on the other hand it credited Halifax with several pamphlets demonstrably written by others.[56] She set this right in 1898, with her monumental *Life and Letters of George Savile Marquis of Halifax*; easily the longest and most ample biography of any seventeenth-century statesman, it also included a full scholarly edition of his works.

Foxcroft was a superb editor,[57] but her talents did not extend to the field of biography. Her *Life* of Halifax is an enormous quarry of fact piled on fact, like the two- and three-decker lives of Victorian statesmen on which it may have been consciously modelled. Today it is more often cited than read. However, the picture of Halifax that emerges from her book is more pragmatical, less philosophical, than Macaulay's: a great patriot, a great liberal statesman, a believer in liberty before his time. It is a coincidence only in the technical sense of the word that it was published in the year of Gladstone's death.

Of course, in many ways Halifax *was* a Gladstonian figure, in the sense in which certain political attitudes and beliefs are timeless; and it is not surprising that he won the admiration of many Victorians. His account of a tussle with James II early in his reign is reminiscent of similar encounters between Gladstone and the Queen, not least in the self-satisfaction he displayed. He told Reresby 'that he had, in two particular and private audiences with the King, told him his mind with that plainness in relation to his service in point of government that he wondered the King (considering his temper) took it with that calmness'.[58] Similarly, Foxcroft's comment on Halifax's liaison with the Duke of Monmouth in 1684 – 'he erred in

55. *Saturday Review*, xxxv, p. 250 (22 Feb 1873).
56. *E.H.R.*, xi, p. 702.
57. Her contribution to this edition is acknowledged below (p. 43). The editor's art reached its apogee with her *Supplement to Burnet's History* (Oxford University Press, 1902).
58. Reresby, *op. cit.*, p. 361.

supposing that a policy so delicately adjusted could be appreciated by the ordinary mind' – could well be applied to Gladstone's manoeuvres over Home Rule two hundred years later.[59]

It is only natural that men should view historical figures through the spectacles of the present, and for a brief period, when the future of the House of Lords was on the anvil, Halifax reappeared as that *rara avis* in English politics, the liberal aristocrat. To Sir Walter Raleigh, writing in 1912, he was 'of the old political families of England, who have borne a hand for generations in the government of the country, [and who] are not easily intoxicated by public duties'.[60] Even today some writers still display unflattering astonishment that a nobleman can write at all, coupled with sycophantic awe when he does make the effort,[61] but it would be fair to say that the high respect in which Halifax is now held is due to the fact that he was a practising politician whose career was directly relevant to his writings. Though Hugh Trevor-Roper takes a rather roseate view of Halifax's political achievements, the spirit of his summing-up is accurate enough:

> His writings were the fruit, not of failure and disgrace, but of a bold and dangerous political career. In consequence they are few; but they are untinged by the bitterness of disappointment. If he saw through the vulgar charms of power, it was not with envy, as unattainable, nor with disgust, as sour; it was with the sane intellectual judgment of one who has known and valued it at its proper estimation.[62]

*

Almost certainly Halifax did not expect to be judged by his writings. *Pièces d'occasion* like *An Anatomy of an Equivalent* were highly polished and carefully printed, but *The Character of a Trimmer* – arguably his most important work – was reprinted twice in his lifetime in editions full of errors and misreadings and under the name of his uncle, Sir William Coventry. His *Thoughts and Reflections*

59. Foxcroft, i, p. 400.

60. *Works of Halifax*, introduction, p. xi.

61. e.g. John Bowle, *Western Political Thought* (Jonathan Cape Ltd, 1947 edn.), p. 369.

62. *Historical Essays* (Macmillan & Co. Ltd, 1957), pp. 254–5.

were probably never intended for publication at all. All this is surprising in a man who thought that 'The government of the world is a great thing; but it is a very coarse one, too, compared with the fineness of speculative knowledge.'[63]

However, if Halifax was slow to set down his ideas in any ordered or systematic form for posterity, he did have what Macaulay termed a 'passion for generalization'.[64] Unlike most pamphleteers, he would argue general propositions before proceeding to particulars, and sometimes – especially in *The Anatomy of an Equivalent* – the reader begins to doubt if he will ever get to the particulars. His avoidance of personal allusion was almost psychopathic, and the dangerous opening pages of *A Letter to a Dissenter* are so skilfully tailored, and carefully obfuscated by use of the passive tense and the third person plural pronoun, that he contrives to avoid referring directly to the Government or the King at all.[65] He was conscious of the eccentricity of this attitude, especially in one who had suffered a great deal himself from pamphlet warfare, and he defended himself as follows: 'No sharpness is to be mingled where healing only is intended; so nothing will be said to expose particular men, how strong soever the temptation may be, or how clear the proofs to make it out.'[66]

But his self-restraint went deeper than this. In his impartiality of judgement, his intellectual curiosity, and his 'passionate desire to press through the study of immediate phenomena to the laws underlying them', Foxcroft saw the first application of the scientific method to political thought.[67] Thinkers like Hobbes and Locke made certain basic assumptions about man and political society, incorporated these assumptions in an intellectual system, then left it to their readers to apply this system to the politics of their time, if they could. Halifax tried to arrange his own scattered and diverse experience of politics in a coherent whole and draw conclusions from it, and he is notable for the judicial calmness with which he is

63. *MTR*, p. 216 below. 64. *Essays*, i, p. 254.

65. pp. 105ff below. Foxcroft (*E.H.R.*, xi, p. 707) points out that this policy was extended to his letters. Note the use of phrases like 'my small friends' (?Shaftesbury) and other evasions in Letters III and XI, pp. 319, 326 below.

66. *LD*, p. 108 below. 67. *E.H.R.*, xi, pp. 725–6.

able to treat some of the most controversial questions of his day; he can even rationalize the Great Rebellion, for instance, as a kind of constitutional calisthenics:

> Till we have another race of mankind, in all constitutions that are bounded there will ever be some matter of strife and contention; and rather than want pretensions men's passions and interests will raise them from the most inconsiderable causes. Our government is like our climate. There are winds which are sometimes loud and unquiet, and yet, with all the trouble they give us, we owe a great part of our health to them; they clear the air, which else would be like a standing pool, and instead of a refreshment would be a disease to us. There may be fresh gales of asserting liberty, without turning into such storms and hurricanes as that the State should run any hazard of being cast away by them. These strugglings, which are natural to all mixed governments, while they are kept from growing into convulsions, do by a mutual agitation of the several parts rather support and strengthen than weaken or maim the constitution; and the whole frame, instead of being torn or disjointed, cometh to be the better and closer knit by being thus exercised.[68]

Naturally, his view of political society was extremely loose, but he took a more optimistic view of human nature – in his middle years at least – than Hobbes or Locke. To him the constitution, and the relations of men to society, were governed by a Law of Nature which he nowhere clearly defines, but was far from being based on self-interest:

> By this Nature is not meant that which fools, libertines and madmen would misquote to justify their excesses; it is innocent and uncorrupted Nature, that which disposeth men to choose virtue without its being prescribed, and which is so far from inspiring ill thoughts into us that we take pains to suppress the good ones it infuseth.[69]

As for fundamentals, the only one he would recognize was the need for supreme power in the state, a power which could not be divided:

> There can be no government without a supreme power; that power is not always in the same hands, it is in different shapes and dresses, but

68. *CT*, p. 63 below.

69. *CT*, p. 51 below.

still, wherever it is lodged it must be unlimited; it hath a jurisdiction over everything else, but it cannot have it above itself. Supreme power can no more be limited than infinity can be measured, because it ceaseth to be the thing; its very being is dissolved when any bounds can be put to it. Where this supreme power is mixed or divided the shape only differeth, the argument is the same.[70]

In this passage from *The Anatomy of an Equivalent* he seems to infer that supreme power rested with King and Parliament together, though he does not precisely say so, and this is the ultimate conclusion of the famous passage in *The Character of a Trimmer* in which he calls upon Charles II to summon Parliament to his assistance.[71] However, he was ready to examine the claims of absolute monarchy, and his contemptuous rejection of this form of government in 1684 is tempered by a more realistic appraisal ten years later; in *A Rough Draft of a New Model at Sea* he was willing to allow the greater efficiency of an absolute monarch, particularly in the conduct of war.[72] (Though this may have been an oblique thrust at William III, the soldier king.)

Similarly, he dismissed republicanism; for if absolute monarchy was 'a thing that leaveth men no liberty', a republic was 'such a one as alloweth them no quiet'.[73] The bias of the English character was towards some form of monarchy, if only 'for the bells and the tinsel, the outward pomp and gilding, and there must be milk for the babes, since the greatest part of mankind are, and ever will be, included in that list' – a cynical judgment, perhaps, but substantially the same as Walter Bagehot's in 1867.[74] But there can be little doubt that his sympathies, like those of many cultivated men in his age, lay with republicanism, and one of the principal reasons why he did not propose it was that the standards of public morality were not high enough.[75]

For in any state Liberty must be balanced by Power. This is a

70. *AE*, p. 135 below. See also *PTR*, p. 196 below.
71. p. 98 below.
72. *CT*, p. 63 below, and *RD*, p. 154.
73. *CT*, p. 54 below.
74. *The English Constitution* (Fontana edn, 1963), p. 86.
75. *CT*, p. 54 below, and *RD*, p. 156.

recurrent theme; in *The Character of a Trimmer*,[76] in *A Rough Draft*,[77] and in the private jottings that form the *Thoughts and Reflections*, where he visualized the struggle as constant and at the same time healthy: 'They are perpetually wrestling, and have had their turns, when they have been thrown, to have their bones broken by it. If they were not both apt to be out of breath, there would be no living.[78] In this unremitting contest the Law was the referee, and in a famous passage he cited the English Constitution as offering the best balance between the two extremes of unrestrained liberty and absolute despotism.[79] That this was not an abstract proposition is shown by his opposition in Council to the proposal to confiscate the charter of the Massachusetts Bay colony in November 1684:

He brought forward every argument he could to prove that an absolute government is not so happy, nor so stable, as one which is tempered by the laws, and which sets limits on the authority of the Prince. He expatiated on the disadvantages of absolute power, and decisively declared that he could not himself bear to live under a king who had the power to take money from his pocket whenever he chose.[80]

But he did not insist that this was the only form of government, or the best for all societies; each nation had the constitution it deserved. In the same way each national constitution, itself adapted to national character, depended on the character of classes or individuals for its smooth operation: a government was no better than the men who operated it. In *The Character of a Trimmer* he made a powerful appeal to Charles II to take control of the Government, and emulate the best rulers of history, who did not need technical legal authority, or physical force, to secure obedience:

Such a magistrate is the life and soul of justice, whereas the law is but the body, and a dead one, too, without his influence to give it warmth and vigour; and by the irresistible power of his virtue he doth so reconcile dominion and allegiance that all disputes between them are silenced and subdued;[81]

76. p. 63 below. 77. p. 157 below.
78. *PTR*, p. 205 below. 79. *CT*, *loc. cit.*
80. French ambassador's despatch, 28 Nov/7 Dec 1684, qu. Charles James Fox, *op. cit.*, App., p. viii. 81. p. 55 below.

and in the *Thoughts and Reflections* he returned to this theme: 'A wise prince may gain such an influence that his countenance would be the last appeal; where it is not so, in some degree his authority is precarious.'[82]

His *Character of King Charles II*, most probably written in the 1690s, can be read as a searching commentary on the right exercise of kingship despite obvious moral lacunae in the king. Charles II's indolence and indifference had been hard to bear, but experience of James II and William III had put him out of sympathy with active, busy rulers, and he had come to realize that in politics there is more than one kind of strength:

> If he loved too much to lie upon his own down bed of ease, his subjects had the pleasure during his reign of lolling and stretching upon theirs. As a sword is sooner broken upon a feather bed than upon a table, so his pliantness broke the blow of a present mischief much better than a more immediate resistance would perhaps have done. Ruin saw this, and therefore removed him first to make way for further overturnings.[83]

Because constitutions could be influenced by force of character they were also subject to circumstance. They were made by man, and could be altered by man:

> A constitution cannot make itself; somebody made it, not at once, but at several times. It is alterable, and by that draweth nearer to perfection; and without suiting itself to differing times and circumstances it could not live. Its life is prolonged by changing seasonably the several parts of it at several times.[84]

In its pragmatism, its rejection of the abstract rigidities of Hobbes and Locke, and the emotional dogma of Divine Right and Non-Resistance, this is a clear echo of the ideas of another great politician, John Pym.[85] It was echoed in its turn by Edmund Burke, when he wrote:

82. *PTR*, p. 196 below.
83. *KCII*, p. 266 below.
84. *PTR*, p. 193 below.
85. See particularly his speech at Manwaring's impeachment in 1628, qu. *The Stuart Constitution*, ed. J. P. Kenyon (Cambridge University Press, 1966), p. 17.

Nothing is more beautiful in the theory of parliaments than that principle of renovation, and union of permanence and change, that are happily mixed in their constitution: that in all our changes we are never either wholly old or wholly new: that there are enough of the old to preserve unbroken the traditionary chain of the maxims and policy of our ancestors and the law and custom of parliament, and enough of the new to invigorate us and bring us to our true character, by being taken fresh from the mass of the people.[86]

It is in the highest degree unlikely that Halifax was directly influenced by Pym, or Burke by Halifax;[87] they are all three in the same tradition of British conservatism, or gradualism, which sees the constitution as made for man, not man for the constitution.

*

However, Halifax had no illusions about the perfection of the British Constitution, and in particular, his approval of Parliament cannot be taken for granted. Only in *The Character of a Trimmer* is Parliament mentioned with any liking or warmth, and it is important to remember that Halifax expected any parliament summoned in 1684 or 1685 to share his hostility to France and the Duke of York, his paramount obsession at that time. Apart from this, his attitude was strangely cool in one who had the reputation of a great parliamentarian, and it is worth remembering that though he sat for Pontefract in the Convention of 1660 he never sought re-election to the House of Commons. (He was raised to the peerage in 1668).[88]

In the 1670s he saw the Commons, and to some extent the Lords, too, succumb to a governmental influence so strong that they were scarcely capable of exercising proper restraint on the executive. In

86. Quoted Charles Parkin, *The Moral Basis of Burke's Political Thought* (Cambridge University Press, 1956), p. 51.

87. I can find no reference to Halifax in the works or correspondence of Edmund Burke. Halifax could have read Pym in Rushworth's *Historical Collections*.

88. Foxcroft's argument (*Character*, p. 17) that there were no general elections after 1661 is unconvincing. The casualty rate in this parliament was high, and by-elections frequent; in any case, there is no evidence that he stood in 1661, or at any other time.

the Exclusion Crisis, at the end of the seventies, he watched the Commons assault the executive with such violence as to tilt the balance of the constitution the other way. In 1685 the balance swung back, with a docile Parliament elected under strong government pressure. In the Convention of 1689, on the other hand, the initiative lay with an irresponsible and destructive House of Commons.

His disillusion was complete when he realized that the Revolution of 1689, far from strengthening Parliament, had actually weakened it. The strain of annual sessions, each of six months, told on the independent Member who enjoyed no supplementary income from the Government; the expansion of the armed forces and the civil administration to meet the needs of the Nine Years' War made more places and pensions available for the needy and dishonest; and the growth of parties in a permanent Parliament produced a new type of professional politician. 'The Parliaments are so altered from their original constitution that between the Court and the Country the House, instead of being united, is like troops of a contrary party facing one another, and watching their advantage.'[89]

He laid the blame principally on the new parties not only because of their hypocrisy – 'the outward blaze only is for religion and liberty; the true lasting fire, like that of the vestals which never went out, is an eagerness to get somewhat for themselves'[90] but also because they suspended that intercourse between politicians of differing views which was vital to consensus politics: 'Party cutteth off one half of the world from the other, so that the mutual improvement of men's understanding by conversing, etc., is lost, and men are half undone when they lose the advantage of knowing what their enemies think of them.'[91]

He could not legislate against parties, but he could legislate against placemen, which is why he supported the Country opposition's Place bills and Triennial bills in the early nineties, and in his last published work urged the electors to throw out Members who had voted against them.[92] *Some Cautions Offered* is an indirect diagnosis

89. *PTR*, p. 206 below.
90. *SCO*, p. 180 below.
91. *PTR*, p. 207 below.
92. *SCO*, p. 187 below.

of the sickness of Parliament, which he explored further in his private notes.[93] Of course, with all their epigrammatic brilliance, the *Thoughts and Reflections* are those of an embittered man, doubly saddened by the death of all his children except two, and the knowledge that his son was childless and likely to remain so. It is noticeable that by far the longest section of the *Miscellaneous Thoughts and Reflections* is that entitled 'Caution and Suspicion'.

In adopting a 'country' policy in the nineties he was really only returning to opposition attitudes in the seventies, and we must remember that that great parliamentarian Edmund Burke was as sceptical of the value of political parties, as pessimistic about parliament, as Halifax. He wrote in 1770: 'The distempers of monarchy were the great subjects of apprehension and redress in the last century; in this, the distempers of parliament.'[94]

In the middle of the twentieth century we are still arguing about the value and efficiency of Parliament, and especially the House of Commons. In some ways Halifax's criticisms are refreshing, in that they suggest that Parliament has always been subject to such attack, and survived; on the other hand, they pose searching questions as to whether the House of Commons has ever been such a valuable and creditable institution as the Whig–Liberal historians of the nineteenth and early twentieth century would like us to believe. The drastic solution of reducing the Commons to a merely legislative body by removing all executive officers from it was rejected by his contemporaries (though quite narrowly), and their decision has been accepted by posterity. But it was made the basis of the American Constitution, which, whatever its deficiencies, has sufficed to govern a great nation.

The really surprising thing is that a man who was so concerned with the establishment of his family, who was so consciously a member of the peerage, and who played such a distinguished role in the House of Lords, should have nothing to say about the function of the aristocracy in the constitution. The theory of a mixed monarchy, with King, Lords and Commons as the three estates,

93. *PTR*, especially the sections on 'Parliaments' and 'Parties', pp. 206–9 below.

94. *Works*, Bohn edn., 1854, i, p. 369.

was common enough in his day,[95] and in another hundred years Burke was to push the theory of aristocracy to the limit, in accordance with the realities of power in the 'classical age of the constitution'. Yet Halifax never mentions the House of Lords, or the aristocracy, or the nobility, anywhere in his works.[96] This lacuna cannot be explained, only recorded.

*

Halifax always had the public reputation of 'a bold and determined atheist', but when Burnet taxed him with it he replied that, 'He was a Christian in submission; he believed as much as he could, and he hoped that God would not lay it to his charge if he could not digest iron as an ostrich did.'

Burnet was sceptical; he noticed that when he was ill he was 'very much touched with a sense of religion', and 'seemed full of good purposes', 'but they went off with his sickness'.[97]

His attitude to the after-life was agnostic: 'The uncertainty of what is to come is such a dark cloud that neither reason nor religion can quite break through it; and the condition of mankind is to be weary of what we do know, and afraid of what we do not.'[98]

However, in his advice to his young daughter he gave religion pride of place,[99] and he himself died in the odour of sanctity. The section of his private memoranda devoted to religion is concerned not so much with matters of faith as of church government, and suggests anti-clericalism rather than atheism: 'If the clergy did not live like temporal men, all the power of princes could not bring them under the temporal jurisdiction', or: 'The several sorts of religion in the world are little more than so many spiritual mono-

95. Corinne C. Weston, *English Constitutional Theory and the House of Lords* (Routledge & Kegan Paul, Ltd, 1965), ch. iii. Cf. Shaftesbury's pronouncements on the function of the nobility, K. H. D. Haley, *op. cit.*, pp. 395–6.

96. Except in *RD* (p. 157 below), where the nobility is coupled with the gentry, and assumed to have a natural propensity for arbitrary power.

97. Burnet, *op. cit.*, i, pp. 492–3.

98. *MTR*, p. 215 below.

99. *AD*, p. 272 below.

polies; if their interests could be reconciled their interests would be so, too'; and so on.[1]

He allowed that religion was necessary to the maintenance of sound government and good order:

> Religion hath such a superiority above all other things, and that indispensable influence upon all mankind, that it is as necessary to our living happily in this world as it is to our being saved in the next; without it man is an abandoned creature, one of the worst beasts Nature hath produced, and fit only for the society of wolves and bears. Therefore in all ages it hath been the foundation of government.

Yet, like all aspects of government, it must adapt itself to changing circumstances, and quarrels over outward forms divided rather than united society:

> The consideration of religion is so twisted with that of government that it is never to be separated, and though the foundations of it are to be unchangeable and eternal, yet the forms and circumstances of discipline are to be suited to the several climates and constitutions, so that they may keep men in a willing acquiescence unto them without discomposing the world by nice disputes which can never be of equal moment with the public peace.[2]

In *The Character of a Trimmer*, where he was addressing a king who was Head of the Church, he could do no less than add that the Church of England was the best qualified of the reformed churches to make these delicate adjustments from time to time. As a result of *A Letter to a Dissenter* he even became for a few brief months one of the principal lay spokesmen of the Church. When the Seven Bishops were indicted for seditious libel in June 1688 they turned immediately for advice to the High Church peers, Nottingham, Rochester and Clarendon – and Halifax.[3] He gave the bishops all the help he could, though in *The Character of a Trimmer* he had taken the divines of the Church to task for their undue preoccupation with affairs of state, their desire to extend ecclesiastical

1. *PTR*, pp. 202–3 below.
2. *CT*, p. 67 below.
3. Foxcroft, *Character*, pp. 246–7; Roger Thomas, 'The Seven Bishops and their Petition', *Journal of Ecclesiastical History*, xii (1961), p. 56.

dominion, and their unforgiving temper towards Papists and Dissenters.[4]

He shared to the full the contemporary prejudice against the Church of Rome; he devoted a whole section of *The Character of a Trimmer* to the Papists, and he returned to the attack in *A Letter to a Dissenter*. But he distinguished the clergy from the laity, and his main complaint was against the intellectual obscurantism of the priests; indeed, he was sensitive enough to appreciate the dreadful sterility of recusant life:

> To live at the best an useless, and by others to be thought a dangerous member of the nation where he is born, is a burden to a generous mind that cannot be taken off by all the pleasure of a lazy, unmanly life, or by the nauseous enjoyment of a dull plenty that produceth no food for the mind.[5]

Only five years after the Popish Plot he was ready to recommend the repeal of the penal laws, and he implored the Protestants not 'to start at every appearance of Popery as if it were just taking possession'.[6] Such calmness and forbearance were rare in 1684.

The Protestant Dissenters were another matter, but he thought that they, too, had been unjustly associated as a body with republicanism and anti-royalism, culminating in the Rye House Plot of 1683; again he put most of the blame on the Dissenting ministers.[7] His solution was to allow the Dissenters the same *de facto* freedom of worship as the Catholics by licensing a limited number of chapels or meeting houses – 'a veil thrown over an innocent and retired conventicle', which would be rather 'a kind omission to inquire strictly than an allowed toleration of that which is against the rule established'.[8]

He was ahead of his time, but only just. By 1687 the Church of England, competing with James II for the alliance of the Dissenters, was obliged to offer as much as Halifax and more. The statesmanship displayed by the Church in this crisis earned his approval,[9] and if the Revolution of 1689 did not bring that reunion of

4. pp. 68 ff. below.
5. *CT*, p. 84 below.
6. ibid., p. 86 below.
7. ibid., p. 69 below.
8. ibid., p. 76 below.
9. *LD*, p. 114 below.

Protestants which many on both sides had hoped for, the Toleration Act of 1689 did at least give the Dissenters the freedom of worship that he had advised in 1684.

Despite setbacks such as Louis XIV's revocation of the Edict of Nantes in 1685, European opinion was moving steadily towards toleration; but England, with its frenzied alarms over Popery, and its grudging suspicion of Dissent, was far from being in the van, and it took courage for a man in Halifax's position to preach against persecution in the mid-eighties. He thought that unless it was pushed to the limits persecution only encouraged dissent, and the English temper was particularly prone to this kind of reaction:

There is in many, and particularly in Englishmen, a mistaken pleasure in resisting the dictates of rigorous authority, a stomach that riseth against a hard imposition – nay, in some even a lust in suffering from a wrong point of honour, which doth not want the applause of the greater part of mankind, who have not learnt to distinguish. Constancy will be thought a virtue even when it is a mistake, and the ill-judging world will be apt to think that opinion most in the right which produceth the greatest number of those who are willing to suffer for it.[10]

The Englishness – some would call it insularity – of Halifax's thought gives it much of its appeal. He is one of the few English political thinkers who have written with English conditions specifically in mind; it was familiarity with the English Constitution at work, not abstract theory, that led him to conclude that all constitutions should be alterable from generation to generation, and his hostility to France, which was consistent throughout life, was inspired as much by theoretical as political considerations. He made a scandalized jotting in his notebook, that Ralph Montagu 'told me some years since that he had rather live here under the King of France than under our government as then'.[11] Passion is something he tried to exclude from his writings, and on the rare occasion when it wells up to the surface it is expressed as love of his country:

Our Trimmer is far from idolatry in other things; in one thing only he cometh somewhat near it; his country is in some degree his idol. He doth not worship the sun, because it is not peculiar to us, it rambleth

10. *CT*, p. 71 below.

11. MS Notebook, Chatsworth, *sub* 'M'.

about the world, and is less kind to us than it is to other countries; but for the earth of England, though perhaps inferior to that of many places abroad, to him there is divinity in it, and he would rather die than see a spire of English grass trampled down by a foreign trespasser.[12]

Anyone who reads his *Advice to a Daughter* will realize that this arch-cynic had another weakness, for his children. Patriotism is a virtue out of fashion today; indulgence to one's children, though much more fashionable, is equally unrewarding.[13] These traits in Halifax bring him nearer to the level of common humanity.

12. *CT*, p. 96 below.
13. As he himself realized. See his comments on 'Families' in *Misc.TR*, p. 238 below.

OUTLINE OF EVENTS

1633 (11 November) Born George Savile, eldest son of Sir William Savile, 3rd baronet, of Thornhill, Yorkshire, by Anne, daughter of Thomas Lord Coventry.
1642 (August) OUTBREAK OF CIVIL WAR.
1643 (February) To Shrewsbury School (?until 1645)
1644 (24 January) Succeeded his father as 4th baronet.
1647 Travel in France and Italy, until 1650 at least (perhaps 1654).
1649 (30 January) EXECUTION OF KING CHARLES I.
1656 (29 December) Married Dorothy, sister of Robert, 2nd Earl of Sunderland.
1660 M.P. for Pontefract in the Convention.
RESTORATION OF KING CHARLES II.
1667 Appointed to the Commission of Public Audit.
1668 (13 January) Created Baron Savile of Eland and Viscount Halifax.
1670 (16 December) Death of first wife.
1672 (17 April) Appointed to the Privy Council.
(November) Married Gertrude, daughter of William Pierrepoint.
1676 (7 January) Dismissed the Privy Council.
1679 (21 April) Re-appointed to the Privy Council.
(16 July) Created Earl of Halifax.
1680 (15 November) DEFEAT OF THE EXCLUSION BILL.
1682 (22 August) Created Marquess of Halifax.
(October) Appointed Lord Privy Seal.
1684 (?December) *Character of a Trimmer* published in MS.
1685 (6 February) ACCESSION OF KING JAMES II.
(February) Appointed Lord President of the Council.
(21 October) Dismissed the Privy Council.
1687 (?late summer) *Letter to a Dissenter* published.
1688 (January) *Advice to a Daughter* published.
(April) *Character of a Trimmer* printed for the first time.
(?late summer) *Anatomy of an Equivalent* published.
(5 November) WILLIAM OF ORANGE LANDS IN ENGLAND.
1689 (22 January) Elected Speaker of the House of Lords.
(14 February) WILLIAM III ACCEPTS THE CROWN.
(February) Appointed Lord Privy Seal.
(19 October) Resigned the Speakership.

1690 (8 February) Resigned the Privy Seal.
1692 (23 June) Dismissed the Privy Council.
1693 *Maxims of State* published.
1694 *Rough Draft of a New Model at Sea* published.
1695 (5 April) Died.
(summer) *Some Cautions Offered* published.

A NOTE ON THIS EDITION

ALL the works of Halifax published individually in his lifetime, plus *Some Cautions Offered*, were re-published in one volume of *Miscellanies* in 1700, and reprinted in 1704 and 1717. (I have consulted the 1717 edition.) The *Character of King Charles II* and the *Thoughts and Reflections* were published for the first time in 1750, in one volume. In 1912 Sir Walter Raleigh published what amounted to a facsimile of these two books, with eighteenth-century punctuation and spelling, and full of minor errors.

The present edition, apart from the letters, is based on that published by the late Miss Hilda Foxcroft in 1898,[1] which was the result of a careful collation of all the manuscript and printed texts. I need not say that she has saved me much labour, and if this book had a dedication it would be to her memory, which is still green amongst seventeenth-century historians. In choice of variant readings I have differed from her only occasionally; in punctuation, capitalization and paragraphing quite often. Apart from this I have silently corrected one glaring false quantity, and here and there inserted a word in square brackets to make the sense more explicit.

His Grace the Duke of Devonshire has been kind enough to give me permission to use and quote from the notebook of Halifax's now in the Chatsworth collections.

My old tutor and friend, Professor J. H. Plumb, has added to the already considerable debt of gratitude I owe him; as always, his criticism has been constructive and helpful. I am also grateful to Mr. Peter Wright, of Penguin Books, for many kindnesses.

J.P.K.

1. Foxcroft, ii, 271 ff.

Facsimile of the title page of
the first edition of
The Character of a Trimmer

THE CHARACTER OF A TRIMMER

HIS

OPINION

OF

I. *The Laws and Government.*
II. *Protestant Religion.*
III. *The Papists.*
IV. *Foreign Affairs.*

Corrected and Amended.

LONDON,
Printed in the Year, 1699.

THE CHARACTER OF A TRIMMER

EDITORIAL INTRODUCTION

This pamphlet was circulated in manuscript in December 1684 and January 1685 or thereabouts. It was printed under the name of Halifax's uncle, Sir William Coventry, in 1688; an attribution that was repeated as late as 1697. However, there can be no doubt whatsoever that it is Halifax's work, though he seems to have regarded it with surprising indifference.[1] The title poses difficulties. It has been shown that 'Trimmers' in 1684 were evangelical or left-wing Anglicans, and it is not at all clear that the pamphlet is in any way related to Sir Roger L'Estrange's attack on Trimmers in *The Observator* for 3 December 1684.[2] If Halifax hoped to appropriate the term for his own use he failed; there is no subsequent evidence of a group of 'Trimmers' in Halifax's sense of the word, and no contemporary described him as a Trimmer. The phrase 'Halifax the Trimmer' is a creation of posterity, and in *The Anatomy of an Equivalent* in 1688 Halifax himself said the term was out of date.[3] William III self-consciously adopted a policy of 'trimming' in 1689 and 1690, in a manner which strongly suggests that he was following Halifax's advice in *The Character of a Trimmer*;[4] but this may simply be evidence of his ignorance of English political conditions. In his *Maxims of State* Halifax criticizes William for this same policy.[5]

1. Foxcroft, ii, pp. 273–9.
2. Donald R. Benson, 'Halifax and the Trimmers', *Huntington Library Quarterly*, xxvii (1963), p. 115. Cf. Foxcroft, ii, pp. 273–4.
3. *AE*, p. 121 below.
4. Foxcroft, ii, pp. 206–7, 252.
5. p. 147 below.

THE CHARACTER OF A TRIMMER

With his opinion concerning religion in relation to the producing quiet amongst ourselves, as also his opinion in relation to things abroad.

THE PREFACE

It must be more than an ordinary provocation that can tempt a man to write in an age over-run with scribblers, as Egypt was with flies and locusts; that worst vermin of small authors hath given the world such a surfeit, that instead of desiring to write, a man would be more inclined to wish, for his own ease, that he could not read. But there are some things which do so raise our passions, that our reason can make no resistance; and when madmen in two extremes shall agree to make common sense treason, and join to fix an ill character upon the only men in the nation who deserve a good one, I am no longer master of my better resolution to let the world alone, and must break loose from my more reasonable thoughts, to expose these false coiners, who would make their copper wares pass upon us for good payment.

Amongst all the engines of dissension, there hath been none more powerful in all times, than the fixing names upon one another of contumely and reproach, and the reason is plain in respect of the People, who though generally they are incapable of making a syllogism or forming an argument, yet they can pronounce a word; and that serveth their turn to throw it with their dull malice at the head of those they do not like. Such things ever begin in jest and end in blood, and the same word which at first maketh the company merry groweth in time to a military signal to cut one another's throats.

These mistakes are to be lamented, though not easily to be cured, being suitable enough to the corrupted nature of mankind; but 'tis hard that men will not only invent ill names, but they will wrest and misinterpret good ones; so afraid some are even of a reconciling sound that they raise another noise to keep it from being heard, lest it should set up and encourage a dangerous sort of men, who prefer peace and agreement before violence and confusion.

Were it not for this, why, after we have played the fool with throwing Whig and Tory at one another, as boys do snowballs, do we grow angry at a new name, which by its true signification might do as much to put us into our wits, as the other hath done to put us out of them?

This innocent word *Trimmer* signifieth no more than this, that if men are together in a boat, and one part of the company would weigh it down on one side, another would make it lean as much to the contrary; it happeneth there is a third opinion of those, who conceive it would do as well, if the boat went even, without endangering the passengers. Now it is hard to imagine by what figure in language, or by what rule in sense, this cometh to be a fault, and it is much more a wonder it should be thought a heresy.

But so it happeneth that the poor Trimmer hath now all the powder spent upon him alone, while the Whig is a forgotten, or at least a neglected enemy; there is no danger now to the state (if some men may be believed) but from the beast called a Trimmer. Take heed of him, he is the instrument that must destroy Church and State; a strange kind of monster, whose deformity is so exposed that, were it a true picture that is made of him, it would be enough to fright children, and make women miscarry at the sight of it.

But it may be worth the examining, whether he is such a beast as he is painted. I am not of that opinion, and am so far from thinking him an infidel either in Church or State, that I am neither afraid to expose the articles of his faith in relation to Government, nor to say that I prefer them before any other political creed that either our angry divines or our refined statesmen would impose upon us.

I have therefore in the following discourse endeavoured to explain the Trimmer's principles and opinions, and then leave it to all discerning and impartial judges, whether he can with justice be so arraigned, and whether those who deliberately pervert a good name do not very justly deserve the worst that can be put upon themselves.

THE TRIMMER'S OPINION ABOUT LAWS AND GOVERNMENT IN GENERAL, WITH SOME REFLECTIONS RELATING TO OUR OWN

Our Trimmer, as he hath a great veneration for laws in general, so he hath a more particular for our own. He looketh upon them as the chains that tie up our unruly passions, which else, like wild beasts let loose, would reduce the world into its first state of barbarism and hostility; all the good things we enjoy we owe to them, and all the ill things we are freed from is by their protection.

God himself thought it not enough to be a creator, without being a lawgiver, and his goodness had been defective towards mankind in making them if he had not prescribed rules to make them happy too.

All laws flow from that of Nature, and where that is not the foundation, they may be legally imposed but they will be lamely obeyed. By this Nature is not meant that which fools and libertines would misquote to justify their excesses; it is innocent and uncorrupted Nature, that which disposeth men to choose virtue without its being prescribed, and which is so far from inspiring ill thoughts into us, that we take pains to suppress the good ones it infuseth.

The civilized world hath ever paid a willing subjection to laws. Even conquerors have done homage to them; as the Romans, who took patterns of good laws even from those they had subdued, and at the same time that they triumphed over an enslaved people, the laws of that very place did not only remain safe, but became victorious. Their new masters, instead of suppressing them, paid them more respect than they had from those who first made them; and by this wise method they arrived to such an admirable constitution of laws, that to this day they reign by them. This excellency of them triumphs still, and the world now payeth an acknowledgment of their obedience to that mighty Empire, though so many ages after it is dissolved. And by a later instance, the Kings of France, who in practice use their laws pretty familiarly, yet think their picture is drawn with most advantage upon their seals, when they are placed in the seat of justice; and though the hieroglyphic is not there of so much use to the people as they would wish, yet it sheweth that no prince is so great as not to think fit for his own credit to give at least an outward, when he refuseth a real worship to the laws.

They are to mankind that [which] the sun is to plants, whilst it cherisheth and preserveth them. Where they have their force and are not clouded or suppressed, everything smileth and flourisheth; but where they are darkened, and are not suffered to shine out, it maketh everything to wither and decay.

They secure men not only against one another but against themselves too; they are a sanctuary to which the Crown hath occasion to resort as often as the People, so that it hath an interest as well as a duty to preserve them.

There would be no end of making a panegyric of laws; let it be enough to add, that without laws the world would become a wilderness, and men little less than beasts. But with all this, the best things may come to be the worst if they are not in good hands; and if it be true that the wisest men generally make the laws, it is as true that the strongest do too often interpret them; and as rivers belong as much to the channel where they run as to the spring from whence they first arise, so the laws depend as much upon the pipes through which they are to pass as upon the fountain from whence they flow. The authority of a king, who is head of the law, as well as the dignity of public justice, is debased when the clear stream of the law is puddled and disturbed by bunglers, or conveyed by unclean instruments to the people.

Our Trimmer would have them appear in their full lustre, and would be grieved to see the day, when instead of their speaking with authority from the seats of justice, they should speak out of a grate, with a lamenting voice like prisoners that desire to be rescued.

He wisheth that the bench may ever have a natural as well as a legal superiority to the bar; he thinketh men's abilities very much misplaced, when the reason of him that pleadeth is visibly too strong for those who are to judge and give sentence. When those from the bar seem to dictate to their superiors upon the bench, their furs will look scurvily about them, and the respect of the world will leave the bare character of a judge to follow the essential knowledge of a lawyer, who may be greater in himself than the other can ever be with all his trappings. An uncontested superiority in any calling will have the better of any discountenance that authority can put upon it, and therefore if ever such an unnatural method should be introduced, it is then that Westminster Hall might be said to stand upon its head, and though justice itself can never be so, yet the administration of it would be rendered ridiculous.[1]

A judge hath such power lodged in him that the King will never be thought to have chosen well where the voice of mankind hath not beforehand recommended the man to his station. When men are made judges of what they do not understand the world censureth such a choice, not out of ill will to the men, but fear for themselves. If the King had the sole power of choosing physicians men would tremble to see bunglers preferred, yet the necessity of taking physic from a doctor is generally not so great as that of receiving justice from a judge. The inferences will be very severe in such cases, for either it will be thought that such men bought what they were not able to deserve, or, which is as bad, that obedience shall be looked upon as a better qualification in a judge than skill or integrity. When such sacred things as the laws are not only touched but guided by profane hands, men will fear that out of the tree of the law, from whence we expect shade and shelter, such workmen will make cudgels to beat us with, or rather, that they will turn the cannon upon our properties, that were entrusted to them for their defence.

To see the laws mangled, disguised, made [to] speak quite another language than their own, to see them thrown from the dignity of protecting mankind to the disgraceful office of destroying them; and notwithstanding their innocence in themselves, to be made the worst instruments that the most refined villainy can make use of, will raise men's anger above the power of laying it down again, and tempt them to follow the evil examples given them of judging without a hearing when so provoked by their desire of revenge.[2]

1. Contemporaries commonly criticized the Bench under Jeffreys LCJ; it is not clear that this criticism was technically justified.

2. This refers to the case of Sir Thomas Armstrong, who fled abroad after the Rye House Plot in 1683, was tried for high treason in his absence and condemned to death. He was kidnapped and brought home in June 1684, when Jeffreys refused him a further hearing and simply sentenced him.

Our Trimmer therefore, as he thinketh the laws are jewels, so he believeth they are nowhere better set, than in the constitution of our English Government, if rightly understood and carefully preserved. It would be too great partiality to say it is perfect or liable to no objection, such things are not of this world; but if it hath more excellencies and fewer faults than any other we know, it is enough to recommend it to our esteem.

The dispute, which is a greater beauty, a Monarchy or a Commonwealth,[3] hath lasted long between their contending lovers, and they have behaved themselves too like lovers (who in good manners must be out of their wits) who have used such figures to exalt their own idols on either side, and such angry aggravations to reproach one another in the contest, that moderate men have in all times smiled upon this eagerness, and thought it differed very little from a downright frenzy. We in England, by a happy use of the controversy, conclude them both in the wrong, and reject them from being our pattern, taking the words in the utmost extent, which is Monarchy, a thing that leaveth men no liberty, and a Commonwealth, such a one as alloweth them no quiet. We think that a wise mean between these barbarous extremes is that which self-preservation ought to dictate to our wishes; and we may say we have attained to this mean in a greater measure than any nation now in being, or perhaps any we have read of, though never so much celebrated for the wisdom or the felicity of their constitutions. We take from one the too great power of doing hurt, and yet leave enough to govern and protect us; we take from the other the confusion of parity, the animosities and the license, and yet reserve a due care of such a liberty as may consist with men's allegiance. But it being hard, if not impossible, to be exactly even, our government hath much the stronger bias towards Monarchy, which by the more general consent and practice of mankind seemeth to have the advantage in dispute against a Commonwealth. The rules of a Commonwealth are too hard for the bulk of mankind to come up to; that form of government requireth such a spirit to carry it on as doth not dwell in great numbers, but is restrained to so very few, especially in this age, that let the methods appear never so reason-

3. sc. Republic.

able in paper, they must fail in practice, which will ever be suited more to men's nature as it is, than as it should be.

Monarchy is liked by the people for the bells and the tinsel, the outward pomp and gilding, and there must be milk for babes, since the greatest part of mankind are, and ever will be, included in that list; and it is approved by wise and thinking men, all circumstances and objections impartially considered. It hath so great an advantage above all other forms, when the administration of that power falleth in good hands, that all other governments look out of countenance when they are set in competition with it. Lycurgus might have saved himself the trouble of making laws, if either he had been immortal, or that he could have secured to posterity a succeeding race of princes like himself; his own example was a better law, than he could with all his skill tell how to make. Such a Prince is a living law, that dictateth to his subjects, whose thoughts in that case never rise above their obedience, the confidence they have in the virtue and knowledge of their master preventing the scruples and apprehensions to which men are naturally inclined in relation to those that govern them. Such a magistrate is the life and soul of justice, whereas the law is but a body, and a dead one too, without his influence to give it warmth and vigour; and by the irresistible power of his virtue, he doth so reconcile dominion and allegiance that all disputes between them are silenced and subdued. And indeed no monarchy can be perfect and absolute, without exception, but where the Prince is superior by his virtue as well as by his character and his power; so that to screw out precedents of unlimited power is a plain diminution to a prince that nature hath made great, and who had better make himself a glorious example to posterity than borrow an authority from dark records raised out of the grave, which besides their non-usage have always in them matter of controversy and debate; and it may be affirmed, that the instances are very rare of Princes having the worst in the dispute with their People if they were eminent either for justice in time of peace, or conduct in time of war, such advantage the crown giveth to those who adorn it by their own personal virtues.

But since for the greater honour of good and wise princes, and the better to set off their character by the comparison, Heaven hath decreed that there must be a mixture, and that such as are perverse or insufficient, or perhaps both, are at least to have their equal turns in the government of the world; and besides that, the will of man is so various and so unbounded a thing, and so fatal too when joined with power misapplied, it is no wonder if those who are to be governed are unwilling to have so dangerous as well as so uncertain a standard of their obedience.

There must be therefore rules and laws, for want of which, or at least the observation of them, it was as capital for a man to say [that] Nero did not play well upon the lute as to commit treason or blaspheme the gods; and even Vespasian himself had like to have lost his life, for sleeping whilst he should have attended and admired that Emperor's impertinence upon the stage. There is a wantonness in great power that men are generally too apt to be corrupted with, and for that reason a wise Prince, to prevent the temptation arising from common frailty, would choose to govern by rules for his own sake, as well as for his people's, since it only secureth him from errors, and doth not lessen the real authority that a good magistrate would care to be possessed of. For if the will of a Prince is contrary either to reason itself, or to the universal opinion of his subjects, the law by a kind restraint rescueth him from a disease that would undo him; if his will on the other side is reasonable and well directed that will immediately becometh a law, and he is arbitrary by an easy and natural consequence, without taking pains, or overturning the world for it.

If Princes consider laws as things imposed on them, they have the appearance of fetters of iron, but to such as would make them their choice as well as their practice they are chains of gold, and in that respect are ornaments, as in others they are a defence to them. And by a comparison not improper for God's vicegerents upon earth, as our Maker never commandeth our obedience to anything that as reasonable creatures we ought not to make our own election,[4] so a good and wise governor, though all laws were abolished, would by the voluntary direction of his own reason, do without constraint the very same things that they would have enjoined.

4. sc. choice.

Our Trimmer thinketh that the King and kingdom ought to be one creature, not to be separated in their political capacity; and when either of them undertake to act apart, it is like the crawling of worms after they are cut in pieces, which cannot be a lasting motion, the whole creature not stirring at a time. If the body have a dead palsy, the head cannot make it move; and God hath not yet delegated such a healing power to Princes as that they can in a moment say to a languishing people, oppressed and in despair, 'Take up your bed and walk'.

The figure of a King is so comprehensive and exalted a thing, that it is a kind of degrading him to lodge that power separately in his own natural person, which can never be safely or naturally great but where the People are so united to him as to be flesh of his flesh, and bone of his bone; for when he is reduced to the single definition of a man, he shrinketh into so low a character, that it is a temptation upon men's allegiance, and an impairing that veneration which is necessary to preserve their duty to him. Whereas a Prince who is so joined to his People that they seem to be his limbs rather than his subjects, clothed with mercy and justice rightly applied in their several places, his throne supported by love as well as by power, and the warm wishes of his devoted subjects, like a never failing incense, still ascending towards him, looketh so like the best image we can frame to ourselves of God Almighty, that men would have much ado not to fall down and worship him, and would be much more tempted to the sin of idolatry, than to that of disobedience.

Our Trimmer is of opinion, that there must be so much dignity inseparably annexed to the royal function as may be sufficient to secure it from insolence and contempt, and there must be condescensions from the throne, like kind showers from heaven, that the Prince may look so much the more like God Almighty's deputy upon earth. For power without love hath a terrifying aspect, and the worship which is paid to it is like that which the Indians give out of fear to wild beasts and devils. He that feareth God only because there is a hell must wish there were no God; and he who feareth the King only because he can punish must wish there were no king. So that without a principle of love there can be no true allegiance, and there must remain perpetual seeds of resistance against a power that is built upon such an unnatural foundation as that of fear and terror. All force is a kind of foul play, and whosoever aimeth at it himself doth by implication allow it to those he playeth with, so that there will be ever matter prepared in the minds of the people when they are so provoked, and the Prince, to secure himself, must live in the midst of his own subjects as if he were in a conquered country, raise arms as if he were immediately to meet or resist an invasion, and all this while sleep as unquietly from the fear of the remedies, as he did before from that of the disease; it being hard for him to forget that more Princes have been destroyed by their guards than by their people, and that even at the time when the rule was *quod principi placuit lex esto*[5] the armies and pretorian bands which were the instruments of that unruly power were frequently the means made use of to destroy them who had it. There will ever be this difference between God and his vicegerents, that God is still above the instruments he useth, and out of the danger of receiving hurt from them; but Princes can never lodge power in any hands, which may not at some time turn it back upon them. For though it is possible enough for a King to have power to satisfy his ambition, yet no kingdom hath money enough to satisfy the avarice of under workmen, who learn from that Prince who will exact more than belongeth to him to expect from him much more than they deserve, and growing angry upon the first disappointment, they are the devils which grow terrible to the conjurers themselves who brought them up, and cannot send them down again. And besides that there can be no lasting radical security but where the governed are satisfied with the governors, it must be a dominion very unpleasant to a Prince of an elevated mind to impose an abject and sordid servility, instead of receiving the willing sacrifice of duty and obedience. The bravest Princes in all times, who were incapable of any other kind of fear, have feared to grieve their own people. Such a fear is a glory, and in this sense it is an infamy not to be a coward, so that the mistaken heroes who are void of this generous kind of fear need no other aggravation to complete their ill characters.

5. What pleases the Prince is law.

When a despotic Prince hath bruised all his subjects with a slavish obedience, all the force he can use cannot subdue his own fears – enemies of his own creation, to which he can never be reconciled, it being impossible to do injustice and not to fear revenge. There is no cure for this fear but the not deserving to be hurt, and therefore a Prince who doth not allow his thoughts to stray beyond the rules of justice hath always the blessing of an inward quiet and assurance, as a natural effect of his good meaning to his people; and though he will not neglect due precautions to secure himself in all events, yet he is incapable of entertaining vain and remote suspicions of those of whom he resolveth never to deserve ill.

It is very hard for a Prince to fear rebellion, who neither doth nor intendeth to do anything to provoke it; therefore too great a diligence in the governors to raise and improve dangers and fears from the People, is no very good symptom, and naturally begetteth an inference that they have thoughts of putting their subjects' allegiance to a trial and therefore not without some reason fear beforehand, that the irregularities they intend may raise men to a resistance.

Our Trimmer thinketh it no advantage to a government to endeavour the suppressing all kind of right which may remain in the body of the People, or to employ small authors in it, whose officiousness or want of money may encourage them to write, though it is not very easy to have abilities equal to such a subject. They forget that in their too high strained arguments for the rights of princes, they very often plead against human nature, which will always give a bias to those reasons which seem to be of her side. It is the People that readeth those books, and it is the People that must judge of them, and therefore no maxims should be laid down for the right of government, to which there can be any reasonable objection. For the world hath an interest, and for that reason is more than ordinary discerning to find out the weak sides of such arguments as are intended to do them hurt; and it is a diminution to a government to promote or countenance such well affected mistakes, which are turned upon it with disadvantage whenever they are detected and exposed; and naturally the too earnest endeavours to take from men the right they have tempt them by the example to claim that which they have not.

In power, as in most other things, the way for Princes to keep it is not to grasp more than their arms can well hold. The nice and unnecessary enquiring into these things, or the licensing some books and suppressing some others without sufficient reason to justify the doing either, is so far from being an advantage to a government that it exposeth it to the censure of being partial, and to the suspicion of having some hidden designs to be carried on by these unusual methods.

When all is said, there is a natural Reason of State, an undefinable thing grounded upon the common good of mankind, which is immortal, and in all changes and revolutions still preserveth its original right of saving a nation, when the letter of the law perhaps would destroy it; and by whatsoever means it moveth, it carrieth a power with it that admitteth of no opposition, being supported by Nature, which inspireth an immediate consent at some critical times into every individual member to that which visibly tendeth to the preservation of the whole. And this being so, a wise Prince, instead of controverting the right of this Reason of State, will by all means endeavour it may be of his side, and then he will be secure.

Our Trimmer cannot conceive that the power of any Prince can be lasting, but where 'tis built upon the foundation of his own unborrowed virtue. He must not only be the first mover and the fountain from whence the great acts of state originally flow, but he must be thought so by his people, that they may preserve their veneration for him; he must be jealous of his power, and not impart so much of it to any about him, as that he may suffer an eclipse by it.

He cannot take too much care to keep himself up, for when a Prince is thought to be led by those with whom he should only advise, and that the commands he giveth are transmitted through him, and are not of his own growth, the world will look upon him as a bird adorned with feathers that are not his own, or consider him rather as an engine than a living creature. Besides, it would be a contradiction for a Prince to fear a commonwealth and at the same time create one himself, by delegating such a power to any number of men near him as is inconsistent with the true figure of a monarch. It is the worst kind of co-ordination the crown can submit to, for it is the exercise of power that draweth the respect along with it, and when that is parted with, the bare character of a King is not sufficient to keep it up.

But though it is a diminution to a Prince to parcel out his power so liberally amongst his favourites, it is worse to divide with any other man, and to bring himself in competition with a single rival. A partner in government is so unnatural a thing, that it is a squint-eyed allegiance that must be paid to such a double bottomed monarchy. The two Czars of Muscovy[6] are an example that the more civilized part of the world will not be prone to follow, and whatever gloss may be put upon this method by those to whom it may be of some use, the Prince will do well to remember and reflect upon the story of certain men who had set up a statue in honour of the sun, yet in a very little time they turned their backs to the sun and their faces to the statue. These mystical unions are better placed in the other world than they are in this, and we shall have much ado to find that in a monarchy God's vicegerency is delegated to more heads than that which is anointed.

Princes may lend some of their light to make another shine, but they must still preserve the superiority of being the brighter planet, and when it happeneth that the reversion is in men's eyes, there is more care necessary to keep up the dignity of possession, that men may not forget who is King, either out of their hopes or fears who shall be. If the sun should part with all his light to any of the stars, the Indians would not know where to find their God, after he had so deposed himself, and would make the light (wherever it went) the object of their worship. All usurpation is alike upon sovereignty, it is no matter from what hand it cometh, and crowned heads are to be the more circumspect, in respect men's thoughts are naturally apt to ramble beyond what is present; they love to work at a distance, and in the greedy expectations which their minds may be filled with of a new master, the old one may be left to look a little out of countenance.[7]

6. Ivan and Peter (later Peter the Great), who reigned jointly until the former's death in 1697.

7. A reference, of course, to James, Duke of York, the heir presumptive.

Our Trimmer owneth a passion for liberty, yet so restrained, that it doth not in the least impair or taint his allegiance. He thinketh it hard for a soul that doth not love liberty ever to raise itself to another world; he taketh it to be the foundation of all virtue, and the only seasoning that giveth a relish to life, and though the laziness of a slavish subjection hath its charms for the more gross and earthly part of mankind, yet to men made of a better sort of clay all that the world can give without liberty hath no taste. It is true, nothing is sold so cheap by unthinking men, but that doth no more lessen the real value of it, than a country fellow's ignorance doth that of a diamond, in selling it for a pot of ale. Liberty is the mistress of mankind, she hath powerful charms which do so dazzle us that we find beauties in her which perhaps are not there, as we do in other mistresses; yet if she was not a beauty, the world would not run mad for her. Therefore since the reasonable desire of it ought not to be restrained, and that even the unreasonable desire of it cannot be entirely suppressed, those who would take it away from a people possessed of it are likely to fail in the attempting, or be very unquiet in the keeping of it.

Our Trimmer admireth our blessed constitution, in which dominion and liberty are so well reconciled. It giveth to the Prince the glorious power of commanding freemen, and to the subjects the satisfaction of seeing the power so lodged as that their liberties are secure. It doth not allow the Crown such a ruining power as that no grass can grow whereever it treadeth, but a cherishing and protecting power; such a one as hath a grim aspect only to the offending subjects, but is the joy and the pride of all the good ones, their own interest being so bound up in it as to engage them to defend and support it; and though in some instances the King is restrained, yet nothing in the government can move without him. Our laws make a true distinction between vassalage and obedience; between a devouring prerogative, and a licentious, ungovernable freedom; and as of all the orders of building, the composite is the best, so ours by a happy mixture and a wise choice of what is best in others, is brought into a form that is our felicity who live under it, and the envy of our neighbours that cannot imitate it. The Crown hath power sufficient to protect our liberties. The People have so much liberty as is necessary to make them useful to the Crown.

Our Government is in a just proportion, no tympany, no unnatural swelling either of power or liberty; and whereas in all overgrown monarchies reason, learning and enquiry are banished and hanged in effigy for mutineers, here they are encouraged and cherished as the surest friends to a government established upon the foundation of law and justice. When all is done, those who look for perfection in this world may look as long as the Jews have done for their Messiah, and therefore our Trimmer is not so unreasonably partial as to free our government from all objections; no doubt there have been fatal instances of its sickness, and more than that, of its mortality for some time, though by a miracle it hath been revived again; but till we have another race of mankind, in all constitutions that are bounded there will ever be some matter of strife and contention; and rather than want pretensions, men's passions and interests will raise them from the most inconsiderable causes.

Our Government is like our climate. There are winds which are sometimes loud and unquiet, and yet with all the trouble they give us, we owe great part of our health unto them; they clear the air, which else would be like a standing pool, and instead of refreshment would be a disease unto us. There may be fresh gales of asserting liberty, without turning into such storms or hurricanes, as that the state should run any hazard of being cast away by them. These strugglings, which are natural to all mixed governments, while they are kept from growing into convulsions do by a mutual agitation from the several parts rather support and strengthen than weaken or maim the constitution; and the whole frame, instead of being torn or disjointed, cometh to be the better and closer knit by being thus exercised. But whatever faults our Government may have, or a discerning critic may find in it when he looketh upon it alone, let any other be set against it, and then it showeth its comparative beauty. Let us look upon the most glittering outside of unbounded authority, and upon a nearer enquiry we shall find nothing but poor and miserable deformity within. Let us imagine a Prince living in his kingdom as if in a great galley, his subjects tugging at the oar, laden with chains, and reduced to real rags, that they may gain him imaginary laurels; let us represent him grazing among his flatterers and receiving their false worship like a child never contradicted and therefore always cozened – or like a lady complimented only to be abused – condemned never to hear truth, and consequently never to do justice, wallowing in the soft bed of wanton and unbridled greatness, not less odious to the instruments themselves than to the objects of his tyranny, blown up into an ambitious dropsy, never to be satisfied by the conquest of other people, or by the oppression of his own. By aiming to be more than a man, he falleth lower than the meanest of them, a mistaken creature, swelled with panegyrics and flattered out of his senses, and not only an encumbrance but a common nuisance to mankind, a hardened and unrelenting soul. Like some creatures that grow fat with poisons, he groweth great by other men's miseries; an ambitious ape of the divine greatness, an unruly giant that would storm even Heaven itself, but that his scaling ladders are not long enough; in short, a wild and devouring creature in rich trappings, and with all his pride no more than a whip in God Almighty's hand, to be thrown into the fire when the world hath been sufficiently scourged with it. This picture, laid in right colours, would not incite men to wish for such a government, but rather to acknowledge the happiness of our own, under which we enjoy all the privilege reasonable men can desire, and avoid all the miseries many others are subject to; so that our Trimmer would fain keep it with all its faults, and doth as little forgive those who give the occasion of breaking it, as he doth those that take it.

Our Trimmer is a friend to Parliaments, notwithstanding all their faults and excesses, which of late have given such matter of objection to them. He thinketh that though they may at some times be troublesome to authority, yet they add the greatest strength to it under a wise administration. He believeth no government is perfect except a kind of omnipotence reside in it, to be exerted upon great occasions. Now this cannot be obtained by force alone upon the people, let it be never so great, there must be their consent too, or else a nation moveth only by being driven, a sluggish and constrained motion, void of that life and vigour which is necessary to produce great things; whereas the virtual consent of the whole being included in their representatives, and the King giving the sanction to the united sense of the people, every act done by such an authority seemeth to be an effect of their choice as well as a part of their duty; and they do, with an eagerness of which men are incapable whilst under a force, execute whatsoever is so enjoined as their own will, better explained by Parliament, rather than from the terror of incurring the penalty of the law for omitting it. And by means of this political omnipotence whatever sap or juice there is in a nation may be to the last drop produced, whilst it riseth naturally from the root; whereas all power exercised without consent is like the giving wounds and gashes, and tapping a tree at unseasonable times, for the present occasion, which in a very little time must needs destroy it.

Our Trimmer believeth that, by the advantage of our situation, there can hardly any such sudden disease come upon us, but that the King may have time enough left to consult with his physicians in Parliament. Pretences indeed may be made, but a real necessity so pressing that no delay is to be admitted is hardly to be imagined, and it will be neither easy to give an instance of any such thing for the time past, or reasonable to presume it will ever happen for the time to come. But if that strange thing should fall out, our Trimmer is not so strait-laced as to let a nation die, or be stifled, rather than it should be helped by any but the proper officers. The cases themselves will bring the remedies along with them, and he is not afraid to allow that in order to its preservation there is a hidden power in government, which would be lost if it was defined, a certain mystery, by virtue of which a nation may at some critical times be secured from ruin. But then it must be kept as a mystery; it is rendered useless when touched by unskilful hands, and no government ever had or deserved to have that power, which was so unwary as to anticipate their claim to it. Our Trimmer cannot help thinking it had been better, if the Triennial Act[8] had been observed first, because it is the law, and he would not have the Crown, by such an example, teach the nation to break it. All irregularity is catching, it

8. Of 1664, according to which Charles II should have called another Parliament by March 1684, at least six months before this pamphlet was written.

hath a contagion in it, especially in an age so much more inclined to follow ill patterns than good ones.

He would have had a Parliament, because it is an essential part of the constitution, even without the law, it being the only provision in extraordinary cases, in which there would be otherwise no remedy; and there can be no greater solecism in government than a failure of justice.

He would have had one, because nothing else can unite and heal us; all other means are mere shifts and projects, houses of cards, to be blown down with the least breath, and that cannot resist the difficulties which are ever presumed in things of this kind. And he would have had one because it might have done the King good, and could not possibly have done him hurt without his own consent, which in that case is not to be supposed; therefore for him to fear it is so strange and so little to be comprehended, that the reasons can never be presumed to grow in our soil, or to thrive in it when transplanted from any other country; and no doubt there are such irresistible arguments for calling a Parliament, that though it might be denied to the unmannerly, mutinous petitions of men that are malicious and disaffected, it will be granted to the soft and obsequious murmurs of his Majesty's best subjects, and there will be such a rhetoric in their silent grief, that it will at last prevail against the artifices of those who, either out of guilt or interest, are afraid to throw themselves upon their country, knowing how scurvily they have used it. That day of judgment will come, though we know neither the day nor the hour, and our Trimmer would live so as to be prepared for it, with full assurance in the meantime that the lamenting voice of a nation cannot long be resisted, and that a Prince who could so easily forgive his people when they had been in the wrong[9] cannot fail to hear them when they are in the right.

9. The Act of Indemnity and Oblivion, 1660, was a remarkably merciful gesture; it pardoned all offences committed during the Interregnum, except regicide.

THE TRIMMER'S OPINION CONCERNING RELIGION IN RELATION TO THE PRODUCING QUIET AMONGST OURSELVES

Religion hath such a superiority above all other things, and that indispensable influence upon all mankind, that it is as necessary to our living happy in this world as it is to our being saved in the next; without it man is an abandoned creature, one of the worst beasts Nature hath produced, and fit only for the society of wolves and bears. Therefore in all ages it hath been the foundation of government, and though false gods have been imposed upon the credulous part of the world, yet they were gods still in their opinion, and the awe and reverence men had to them and their oracles kept them within bounds towards one another, which the laws with all their authority could never have effected. Without the help of religion the laws would not be able to subdue the perverseness of men's wills, which are wild beasts, and require a double chain to keep them down. For this reason it is said, that it is not a sufficient ground to make war upon a neighbouring state because they are of another religion, let it be never so differing; yet if they worship nor acknowledge no deity at all, they may be invaded as public enemies of mankind, because they reject the only thing that can bind them to live well with one another. The consideration of religion is so twisted with that of government that it is never to be separated, and though the foundations of it ought to be unchangeable and eternal, yet the terms and circumstances of discipline are to be suited to the several climates and constitutions, so that they may keep men in a willing acquiescence unto them, without discomposing the world by nice disputes which can never be of equal moment with the public peace.

Our religion here in England seemeth to be distinguished by a peculiar effect of God Almighty's goodness, in permitting it to be introduced – or more properly, restored – by a more regular method than the circumstances of most other Reformed Churches would allow them to do, in relation to the government; and the dignity with which it hath supported itself since, and the great men our Church hath produced, ought to recommend it to the esteem of all Protestants at least. Our Trimmer is very partial to it, for these reasons and many more, and desireth that it may preserve its due jurisdiction and authority, so far he is from wishing it oppressed by the unreasonable and malicious cavils of those who take pains to raise objections against it.

The questions will then be, how and by what methods this Church shall best support itself (the present circumstances considered) in relation to Dissenters of all sorts? I will first lay this for a ground, that as there can be no true religion without charity, so there can be no human prudence without bearing and condescension. This principle doth not extend to oblige the Church always to yield to those who are disposed to contest with her, the expediency of doing it is to be considered and determined according to the occasion; and this leads me to lay open the thoughts of our Trimmer in reference first to the Protestant and then to the Popish Recusants.

What hath lately happened among us maketh an apology necessary for saying anything that looketh like favour towards a sort of men who have brought themselves under such a disadvantage. The late conspiracy[10] hath such broad symptoms of the disaffection of the whole party that upon the first reflections, while our thoughts are warm, it would almost persuade us to put them out of the protection of our good nature, and to think that the Christian indulgence which our compassion for other men's sufferings cannot easily deny seemeth not only to be forfeited by the ill appearances that are against them, but even becometh a crime when it is so misapplied. Yet for all this, upon second and cooler thoughts, moderate men will not be so ready to involve a whole party in the guilt of a few, and to admit inferences and presumptions to be evidence in a case where the sentence must be so heavy, as it ought to be against all those who have a fixed resolution against the government established. Besides, men who act by a principle grounded upon moral virtue can never let it be clearly extinguished by the most repeated provocations; if a right thing agreeable to Nature and good sense taketh root in the heart of a man that is

10. The Rye House Plot (1683) to assassinate Charles II and his brother, in which many left-wing Dissenters were implicated.

impartial and unbiased, no outward circumstances can ever destroy it. It is true, the degrees of a man's zeal for the prosecution of it may be differing; the faults of other men, the consideration of the public, and the seasonable prudence by which wise men will ever be directed, may give great allays; they may lessen and for a time perhaps suppress the exercise of that which in general proposition may be reasonable, but still whatever is so will inevitably grow and spring up again, having a foundation in Nature which is never to be destroyed.

Our Trimmer therefore endeavoureth to separate the detestation of those who had either a hand or a thought in the late plot from the principle of prudential as well as Christian charity towards mankind, and for that reason would fain use the means of reclaiming such of the Dissenters as are not incurable, and even of bearing to a degree those that are, as far as may consist with the public interest and security. He is far from justifying an affected separation from the communion of the Church, and even in those that mean well and are misled, he looketh upon it as a disease that hath seized upon their minds, very troublesome to themselves as well as dangerous by the consequence it may produce. He doth not go about to excuse their making it an indispensable duty to meet in numbers to say their prayers; such meetings may prove mischievous to the state – at least the laws, which are the best judges, have determined that there is a danger in them. He hath good nature enough to lament that the perverseness of a part should have drawn rigorous laws upon the whole body of the Dissenters, but when they are once made no private opinion must stand in opposition to them. If they are in themselves reasonable, they are in that respect to be regarded, even without being enjoined; and if by the change of time and circumstances they should become less reasonable than when they were first made even then they are to be obeyed too, because they are laws, till they are mended or repealed by the same authority that enacted them.

He hath too much deference to the constitution of our government to wish for more prerogative Declarations in favour of scrupulous men,[11] or to dispense with penal laws in such manner, or to

11. The Declaration of Indulgence in 1672 suspended all the penal laws against Protestant Dissenters and popish recusants. It was withdrawn the following year.

such an end, that suspecting men might with some reason pretend that so hated a thing as persecution could never make way for itself with any hopes of success, otherwise than by preparing the deluded world by a false prospect of liberty and indulgence. The inward springs and wheels by which the engine moved are now so fully laid open and exposed that it is not supposable that such a baffled experiment should ever be tried again; the effect it had at the time, and the spirit it raised, will not easily be forgotten, and it may be presumed the remembrance of it may secure us from any more attempts of that nature for the future; we must no more break a law to give men ease, than we are to rifle an house with a devout intention of giving the plunder to the poor; in this case our compassion would be as ill directed as our charity in the other. In short, the veneration due to the laws is never to be thrown off, let the pretences be never so specious.

Yet with all this he cannot bring himself to think that an extraordinary diligence to take the uttermost penalty of laws upon a poor offending neighbour is of itself such an all-sufficient virtue, that without anything else to recommend men it should entitle them to all kind of preferments and rewards; he would not detract from the merits of those who execute the laws, yet he cannot think such a piece of service as this can entirely change the man, and either make him a better divine or a more knowing magistrate than he was before, especially if it be done with a partial and unequal hand in reverence to greater and more dangerous offenders.

Our Trimmer would have those mistaken men ready to throw themselves into the arms of the Church, and he would have those arms as ready to receive them that shall come to us; he would have no supercilious look to fright those strayed sheep from coming into the fold again, no ill-natured maxims of eternal suspicion, or a belief that those who have once been in the wrong can never be in the right again, but a visible preparation of mind to receive with joy all the proselytes that shall come to us, and a much greater earnestness to reclaim than punish them. It is to be confessed that when there is a great deal to forgive, it is a hard task enough for the charity of a Church so provoked, but that must not cut off all hopes of being reconciled; yet if there must be some anger left still, let it break out into a Christian revenge, and by being kinder to the children of disobedience than they deserve, let the injured Church triumph by throwing shame and confusion of face upon them. There should not always be storms and thunder, a clear sky would sometimes make the Church look more like Heaven, and would do more towards the reclaiming those wanderers than a perpetual terror which seemeth to have no intermission. For there is in many, and particularly in Englishmen, a mistaken pleasure in resisting the dictates of rigorous authority, a stomach that riseth against a hard imposition – nay, in some even a lust in suffering from a wrong point of honour, which doth not want the applause of the greater part of mankind, who have not learnt to distinguish. Constancy will be thought a virtue even when it is a mistake, and the ill-judging world will be apt to think that opinion most in the right which produceth the greatest number of those who are willing to suffer for it. All this is prevented, and falleth to the ground, by using well-timed indulgence, and the stubborn adversary who valueth himself upon his resistance whilst he is oppressed yieldeth insensibly to kinder methods, when they are applied to him, and the same man naturally melteth into conformity, who perhaps would never have been beaten into it. We may be taught by the compassion that attendeth the most criminal men when they are condemned, that their faults are much more natural things than [our] punishments, and that even the most necessary acts of severity do some kind of violence to our nature, whose indulgence will not be confined within the strait bounds of inexorable justice; so that this should be an argument for gentleness, besides that it is the likeliest way to make these men ashamed of their separation, whilst the pressing them too hard tendeth rather to make them proud of it.

Our Trimmer would have the clergy supported in their lawful rights, and in all the power and dignity that belongeth to them, and yet he thinketh that possibly there may be in some of them a too great eagerness to extend the ecclesiastical jurisdiction, which though it may be well intended, yet the straining of it too high hath an appearance of ambition that raiseth men's objections to it, and is so far unlike the apostolic zeal, which was quite otherwise employed, that the world draweth inferences from it which do the Church no service.

He is troubled to see men of all sides sick of a calenture[12] of a mistaken devotion, and it seemeth to him that the devout fire of mutual charity with which the primitive Christians were inflamed is long since extinguished, and instead of it a devouring fire of anger and persecution breaketh out in the world. We wrangle now one with another about religion till the blood cometh, whilst the Ten Commandments have no more authority with us than if they were so many obsolete laws, or proclamations out of date. He thinketh that a nation will hardly be mended by principles of religion where morality is made a heresy; and therefore as he believeth devotion misplaced when it geteth into a conventicle, he concludeth that loyalty is so too when it is lodged in a drunken club. Those virtues deserve a better seat of empire, and they are degraded when such men undertake their defence as have too great need of an apology for themselves.

Our Trimmer wisheth that some knowledge may go along with the zeal on the right side, and that those who are in possession of the pulpit would quote at least so often the authority of the scriptures as they do that of the state. There are many who borrow too often arguments from the government to use against their adversaries, and neglect those that are more proper and would be more powerful; a divine groweth less, and putteth a diminution on his own character,[13] when he quoteth any law but that of God Almighty to get the better of those who contest with him; and as it is a sign of a decayed constitution when Nature with good diet cannot expel noxious humours without calling foreign drugs to her assistance, so it looketh like want of health in a church, when instead of depending upon the power of that truth which it holdeth, and the good examples of them that teach it, to support itself and to suppress errors, it should have a perpetual recourse to the secular authority, and even upon the slightest occasions.

12. A feverish madness. 13. sc. calling, or profession.

Our Trimmer hath his objections to the too busy diligence and to the overdoing of some of the dissenting clergy, and he doth as little approve of those of our Church who wear God Almighty's liveries as some old warders in the Tower do the King's, who do nothing that belongeth to their place but receive their wages for it. He thinketh that the liberty of the late times gave men so much light, and diffused it so universally amongst the people, that they are not now to be dealt with as they might have been in ages of less inquiry; and therefore though in some well chosen and dearly loved auditories good resolute nonsense backed with authority may prevail, yet generally men are become so good judges of what they hear that the clergy ought to be very wary before they go about to impose upon their understandings, which are grown less humble than they were in former times, when the men in black had made learning such a sin in the laity that for fear of offending they made a conscience of being able to read. But now the world is grown saucy, and expecteth reasons, and good ones too, before they give up their own opinions to other men's dictates, though never so magisterially delivered to them.

Our Trimmer is far from approving the hypocrisy which seemeth to be the reigning vice amongst some of the Dissenting clergy, he thinketh it the most provoking sin men can be guilty of in relation to Heaven; and yet (which may seem strange) that very sin which shall destroy the soul of the man who preacheth may help to save those of the company that hear him, and even those who are cheated by the false ostentation of his strictness of life, may by that pattern be encouraged to the real practice of those Christian virtues which he doth so deceitfully profess. So that the detestation of this fault may possibly be carried on too far by our own orthodox divines, if they think it cannot be enough expressed without bending the stick another way – a dangerous method, and a worse extreme for men of that character, who by going to the outmost line of Christian liberty will certainly encourage others to go beyond it. No man doth less approve the ill-bred methods of some of the Dissenters in rebuking authority, who behave themselves as if they thought ill manners necessary to salvation; yet he cannot but distinguish and desire a mean between the sauciness of some of the

Scotch Apostles,[14] and the indecent courtship of some silken divines, who, one would think, do practice to bow at the altar only to learn to make the better legs at court.[15]

Our Trimmer approveth the principles of our Church, that dominion is not founded in grace, and that our obedience is to be given to a popish king in other things at the same time that our compliance with him in his religion is to be denied; yet he cannot but think it a very extraordinary thing if a Protestant church should by a voluntary election choose a papist for their guardian, and receive directions for the supporting their religion from one who must believe it a mortal sin not to endeavour to destroy it. Such a refined piece of breeding would not seem to be very well placed in the clergy, who will hardly find precedents to justify such an extravagant piece of courtship, and which is so unlike the primitive methods which ought to be our pattern. He hath no such unreasonable tenderness for any sorts of men as to expect their faults should not be impartially laid open as often as they give occasion for it, and yet he cannot but smile to see that the same man who setteth up all the sails of his rhetoric to fall upon the Dissenters, when Popery is to be handled he doth it so gingerly that he looketh like an ass mumbling of thistles, so afraid he is of letting himself loose where he may be in danger of letting his duty get the better of his discretion.

Our Trimmer is far from relishing the impertinent wanderings of those who pour out long prayers upon the congregation, and all from their own stock, which God knoweth for the most part is a barren soil, which produceth weeds instead of flowers, and by this means they expose religion itself, rather than promote men's devotions. On the other side, there may be too great restraint put upon men whom God and Nature hath distinguished from their fellow labourers by blessing them with a happier talent, and by giving them not only good sense but a powerful utterance too,

14. Slightly obscure. It may be a precise reference to the Covenanters, who were still engaged in a guerilla war with the Government at Edinburgh; on, the other hand it may be merely a general reference to Presbyterianism, popularly regarded as a Scots disease.

15. 'To make a leg' was to make an exaggerated bow with one foot thrust forward and the forehead brought down as near to it as possible.

hath enabled them to gush out upon the attentive auditory with a mighty stream of devout and unaffected eloquence. When a man so qualified, endued with learning too, and above all, adorned with a good life, breaketh out into a warm and well delivered prayer before his sermon, it hath the appearance of a divine rapture; he raiseth and leadeth the hearts of the assembly in another manner than the most studied or best composed form of set words can ever do; and the 'Pray-wees', who serve up all their sermons with the same garnishing, would look like so many statues or men of straw in the pulpit compared with those who speak with such a powerful zeal, that men are tempted at the moment to believe Heaven itself hath dictated their words to them.

Our Trimmer is not so unreasonably indulgent to the Dissenters as to excuse the irregularities of their complaints, and to approve their threatening styles, which are so ill-suited to their circumstances as well as to their duty; he would have them to show their grief and not their anger to the government, and by such a submission to authority as becometh them. If they cannot acquiesce in what is imposed, let them deserve a legislative remedy to their sufferings, there being no other way to give them perfect redress; and either to seek it or pretend to give it by any other method would not only be vain but criminal too in those that go about it. Yet with all this there may in the meantime be a prudential latitude left as to the manner of prosecuting the laws now in force against them; the government is in some degree answerable for such an administration of them as may be free from the censure of impartial judges, and in order to that, it would be necessary that one of these methods be pursued; either to let loose the laws to their utmost extent, without any moderation or restraint, in which at least the equality of the Government would be without objection, the penalties being exacted without remission from the Dissenters of all kinds. Or, if that will not be done (and indeed there is no reason it should) there is a necessity of some connivance to the Protestant Dissenters to excuse that which in humanity must be allowed to the Papists, even without any leaning towards them, which must not be supposed in those who are or shall be in the administration of public business; and it will follow that, according to our circumstances, the distribution of such connivance must be made in such a manner that the greatest part of it may fall on the Protestant side, or else the objections will be so strong, and the inferences so clear, that the friends as well as the enemies of the crown will be sure to take hold of them.

It will not be sufficient to say that the Papists may be connived at because they are good subjects and that the Protestant Dissenters must suffer because they are ill ones; these general maxims will not convince discerning men, neither will any late instances make them forget what passed at other times in the world. Both sides have had their turns in being good and ill subjects, and therefore it is easy to imagine what suspicions would arise in the present conjuncture if such a partial argument as this should be imposed upon us. The truth is, this matter speaks so much of itself, that it is not only unnecessary but it may be unmannerly to say any more of it.

Our Trimmer therefore could wish, that since – notwithstanding the laws which deny churches to say mass in – not only the exercise but also the ostentation of Popery is as well or better performed in the chapels of so many foreign ministers, where the English openly resort in spite of proclamations and Orders of Council, which are grown to be as harmless things to them as the Pope's bulls and excommunications are to heretics who are out of his reach; I say, he could wish that by a seasonable as well as an equal piece of justice there might be so much consideration had of the Protestant Dissenters, as that there might be at some times, and at some places, a veil thrown over an innocent and retired conventicle; and that such an indulgence might be practised with less prejudice to the Church, or diminution to the laws, it might be done so as to look rather like a kind omission to inquire more strictly than an allowed toleration of that which is against the rule established.

Such a skilful hand as this is very necessary in our circumstances, and the Government, by making no sort of men entirely desperate, doth not only secure itself from the danger of any wild and villainous attempts, but layeth such a foundation for healing and uniting laws whenever a Parliament shall meet, that the seeds of differences and animosities between the several contending sides may (Heaven consenting) be for ever destroyed.

THE TRIMMER'S OPINION CONCERNING THE PAPISTS

To speak of Popery leadeth me into such a sea of matter that it is not easy to forbear launching into it, being invited by such a fruitful theme, and by a variety never to be exhausted; but to confine it to the present subject, I will only say a short word of the religion itself, of its influences here at this time, and of our Trimmer's opinion in relation to our manner of living with it.

If a man would speak maliciously of this religion, one may say it is like those diseases where as long as one drop of the infection remaineth there is still danger of having the whole mass of blood corrupted by it. In Sweden there was an absolute cure, and nothing of Popery heard of, till Queen Christina (whether moved by arguments of this or the other world would not be good manners to inquire), thought fit to change her religion and country, and to live at Rome, where she might find better judges of her virtues and less ungentle censures of those princely liberties to which she was sometimes disposed,[16] than when she lived at Stockholm, where the good breeding is as much inferior to that of Rome in general as the civility of the religion, the cardinals having rescued the Church from those clownish methods the Fishermen had first introduced, and mended that pattern so effectually that a man of that age, if he should now come into the world, would not possibly know it.

In Denmark, the Reformation was entire; in some states of Germany, as well as in Geneva, the cure was universal but in the rest of the world where the Protestant religion took place the Popish humour was too tough to be totally expelled, and so it was in England, though the change was made with all the advantage imaginable to the Reformation, it being countenanced and introduced by legal authority, and by that means might have been perhaps as perfect as in any other place, if the short reign of Edward VI and the succession of a popish Queen had not given such advantage to that religion that it hath subsisted ever since under all the hardships that have been put upon it. It hath been a

16. Lesbianism is intended.

strong, compact body, and made the more so by these sufferings; it was not strong enough to prevail, but it was still able, with the help of foreign support, to carry on an interest which gave the crown trouble, and to make a considerable (not to say dangerous) figure in the nation. So much as this could not have been done without some hopes, nor these hopes kept up without some reasonable grounds; in Queen Elizabeth's time the Spanish zeal for their religion, and the revenge for 88, gave warmth to the Papists here, and above all, the right of the Queen of Scots to succeed was while she lived sufficient to give them a better prospect of their affairs; in King James's time their hopes were supported by the treaty of the Spanish Match, and his gentleness towards them, which they were ready to interpret more in their own favour than was either reasonable or became them, so little tenderness they have, even where it is most due, if the interest of their religion cometh in competition with it.

As for the late King,[17] though he gave the most glorious evidence that ever man did of his being a Protestant, yet by the more than ordinary influence the Queen was thought to have over him, and it so happening that the greater part of his anger was directed against the Puritans, there was such an advantage given to men disposed to suspect, that they were ready to interpret it a leaning towards Popery, without which handle it was morally impossible that the ill-affected part of the nation could ever have seduced the rest into a rebellion.

That which helped to confirm many well-meaning men in their misapprehensions of the King was the long and unusual intermission of Parliaments, so that every year that passed without one made up a new argument to increase their suspicion, and made them presume that the Papists had a principal hand in keeping them off. This raised such heats in men's minds, to think that men who were obnoxious to the laws, instead of being punished should have credit enough to secure themselves, even at the price of destroying the fundamental constitution, that it broke out into a flame which before it could be quenched had almost reduced the nation to ashes.

Amongst the miserable effects of that unnatural war, none hath

17. Charles I.

been more fatal to us than the forcing our Princes to breathe in another air and to receive the early impressions of a foreign education. The barbarity of the English towards the King and the Royal Family might very well tempt him to think the better of everything he found abroad, and might naturally produce more gentleness, at least, towards a religion by which he was hospitably received at the same time that he was thrown off and persecuted by the Protestants (though his own subjects, too, to aggravate the offence). The Queen Mother (as generally ladies do with age) grew more devout and earnest in her religion, and besides the temporal rewards of getting larger subsidies from the French clergy she had motives of another kind to persuade her to show her zeal; and since by the Roman dispensatory a soul converted to the Church is a sovereign remedy, and layeth up a mighty stock of merit, she was solicitous to secure herself in all events, and therefore first set upon the Duke of Gloucester, who depended so much upon her good will that she might for that reason have been induced to believe the conquest would not be difficult. But it so fell out that he, either from his own constancy or that he had those near him by whom he was otherways advised, chose rather to run away from her importunity than by staying to bear the continual weight of it. It is believed she had better success with another of her sons, who, if he was not quite brought off from our religion, at least such beginnings were made as made them very easy to be finished; his being of a generous and aspiring nature, and in that respect less patient in the drudgery of arguing, might probably help to recommend a Church to him that exempts the laity from the vexation of inquiring; perhaps he might (though by mistake) look upon that religion as more favourable to the enlarged power of Kings, a consideration which might have its weight with a young Prince in his warm blood, and that was brought up in arms.[18]

I cannot hinder myself from a small digression, to consider with admiration[19] that the old Lady of Rome, with all her wrinkles, should yet have charms able to subdue great Princes; so far from handsome, and yet so imperious; so painted, and yet so pretending;

18. Compare the parallel passage in his KCII, p. 249 below.

19. sc. amazement.

after having abused, deposed and murdered so many of her lovers, she still findeth others glad and proud of their new chains; a thing so strange to indifferent[20] judges, that those who will allow no other miracles in the Church of Rome must needs grant that this is one not to be contested. She sitteth in her shop, and selleth at dear rates her rattles and her hobby-horses, whilst the deluded world still continueth to furnish her with customers.

But whither am I carried with this contemplation? It is high time to return to my text, and to consider the wonderful manner of the King's coming home again, led by the hand of Heaven, and called by the voice of his own people, who received him, if possible, with joys equal to the blessing of peace and union which his restoration brought along with it. By this there was an end put to the hopes some might have abroad, of making use of his less happy circumstances to throw him into foreign interests and opinions which had been wholly inconsistent with our religion, our laws and all other things that are dear to us. Yet for all this some of those tinctures and impressions might so far remain as, though they were very innocent in him, yet they might have ill effects here, by softening the animosity which seemeth necessary to the Defender of the Protestant Faith, in opposition to such a powerful and irreconcilable enemy.

You may be sure, that among all the sorts of men who applied themselves to the King at his first coming home for his protection, the Papists were not the last, nor, as they fain would have flattered themselves, the least welcome, having their past sufferings as well as their present professions to recommend them; and there was something that looked like a particular consideration of them, since it so happened that the indulgence promised to Dissenters at Breda was carried on in such a manner that the Papists were to divide with them.[21] And though the Parliament, notwithstanding its resignation to the Crown in all other things, rejected with scorn and

20. sc. impartial.

21. The Declaration Charles issued from Breda in 1660 gave, amongst other things, 'a liberty for tender consciences'. This was usually thought to apply only to Protestants, though the wording is ambiguous. In any case it was abortive.

anger a Declaration[22] framed for this purpose, yet the birth and steps of it gave such an alarm that men's suspicions, once raised, were not easily laid asleep again.

To omit other things, the breach of the Triple League, and the Dutch War[23] with its appurtenances, carried jealousies to the highest pitch imaginable, and fed the hopes of one party and the fears of the other to such a degree, that some critical revolutions were generally expected when the ill success of that war, and the sacrifice France thought fit to make of the Papists here to their own interest abroad, gave them another check; and the Act of enjoining the Test to all in offices[24] was thought to be no ill bargain to the nation, though bought at the price of £1,200,000, and the money applied to the continuance of the war against the Dutch, than which nothing could be more unpopular or less approved. Notwithstanding these discouragements, Popery is a plant that may be mowed down, but the root will still remain, and in spite of the laws it will sprout up and grow again; especially if it should happen that there should ever be men in power who in weeding out our garden will take care to cherish and keep it alive; and though the law for excluding them from places of trust was tolerably kept as to the outward form, yet there were many circumstances which, being improved by the quick-sighted malice of ill-affected men, did help to keep up the world in their suspicions, and to blow up jealousies to such a height both in and out of Parliament, that the remembrance of them is very unpleasant, and the example so extravagant that it is to be hoped nothing in our age like it will be re-attempted.[25]

But to come closer to the case in question: in this condition we stand with the Papists. What shall now be done, according to our Trimmer's opinion, in order to the better bearing this grievance, since as I have said before, there is no hopes of being entirely freed from it; Papists we must have among us, and if their religion keepeth them from bringing honey to the hive, let the Government try at least by gentle means to take away the sting from them. The first

22. The Declaration of Indulgence, 1672. See note to p. 69 above.

23. The Third Dutch War, 1672–4.

24. The Test Act of 1673.

25. A reference to the crisis of the 'Popish Plot', 1678–81.

foundation to be laid is, that a distinct consideration is to be had of the Popish clergy, who have such an eternal interest against all accommodation that it is a hopeless thing to propose anything to them less than all; their stomachs having been set for it ever since the Reformation, they have pinned themselves to a principle that admits no mean: they believe Protestants will be damned, and therefore by an extraordinary effect of Christian charity they would destroy one half of England that the other might be saved. Then for this world they must be in possession for God Almighty, to receive his rents for him, not to account till the Day of Judgment, which is a good kind of tenure, and ye cannot well blame the good men, that they stir up the laity to run any hazard in order to the getting them restored. What is it to the priest if the deluded zealot undoeth himself in the attempt? He singeth masses as jollily, and with as good a voice, at Rome or St. Omers as ever he did; he is a single man, and can have no wants but such as may be easily supplied, yet that he may not seem altogether insensible or ungrateful to those that are his martyrs he is ready to assure their executors, and if they please will procure a grant *sub annulo Piscatoris*, that the good man by being hanged hath got a good bargain, and saved the singeing of some hundred years, which he would else have had in purgatory. There is no cure for this order of men, no expedient to be proposed; so that though the utmost severity of the laws against them may in some sort be mitigated, yet no treaty can be made with men who in this case have left themselves no free will, but are so muffled by zeal, tied by vows, and kept up by such unchangeable maxims of the priesthood, that they are to be left as desperate patients, and looked upon as men that will continue in an eternal state of hostility till the nation is entirely subdued to them.

It is, then, only the lay Papists that are capable of being treated with, and we are to examine of what temper they are, and what arguments are the most likely to prevail upon them, and how far it is advisable for the Government to be indulgent to them. The lay Papists generally keep their religion, rather because they will not break company with those of their party than out of settled zeal that hath any root in them; most of them do by the mediation of the priests marry amongst one another, to keep up an ignorant position by hearing only one side; others by a mistake look upon it as the better escutcheon, the more ancient religion of the two; and as some men of a good pedigree will despise meaner men, though never so much superior to them by nature, so these undervalue Reformation as an upstart, and think there is more honour in supporting an old error than in embracing what seemeth to them to be a new truth. The laws have made them men of pleasure, by excluding them from public business, and it happeneth well that they are so, since they will the more easily be persuaded by arguments of ease and conveniency to them. They have not put off the man in general, nor the Englishman in particular; those who in the late storm against them went into other countries, though they had all the advantage that might recommend them to a good reception, yet in a little time they chose to steal over again, and live here with hazard rather than abroad with security. There is a smell in our native earth better than all the perfumes in the East; there is something in a mother, though never so angry, that the children will naturally trust sooner than the most studied civilities of strangers, let them be never so hospitable; therefore it is not advisable, nor at all agreeing with the rules of governing prudence, to provoke men by hardships to forget that nature which else is sure to be of our side.

When these men by fair usage are put again into their right senses they will have quite differing reflections from those which rigour and persecution had raised in them. A lay Papist will first consider his abbey lands,[26] which notwithstanding whatever hath been or can be alleged, must sink considerably in the value the moment that Popery prevails. And it being a disputable matter whether zeal might not in a little time get the better of the law in that case, a considering man will admit that as an argument to persuade him to be content with things as they are, rather than run this or the other hazard by a change, in which perhaps he may have no other advantage, than that his now humble confessor may be raised to a bishopric, and from thence look down superciliously upon his patron, or which is worse, run to take possession for God

26. It was ironic that many Catholic families did in fact hold monastic estates confiscated by Henry VIII.

Almighty of his abbey, in such a manner as the usurping landlord (as he will then be called) shall hardly be admitted to be so much as a tenant to his own lands, lest his title should prejudge that of the Church, which will then be the landlord. He will think what disadvantage it is to be looked upon as a separate creature, depending upon a foreign interest and authority, and for that reason exposed to the jealousy and suspicion of his countrymen. He will reflect what an encumbrance it is to have his house a pasture for hungry priests to graze in, which have such a never-failing influence upon the foolish, which is the greatest part of every man's family, that a man's dominion even over his own children is mangled and divided if not totally undermined by them. Then to be subject to what arbitrary taxes the popish convocation shall impose upon him for the carrying on the common interest of that religion, under penalty of being marked out for half an heretic by the rest of the party; to have no share in business, no opportunity of showing his own value to the world; to live at the best an useless, and by others to be thought a dangerous member of the nation where he is born, is a burden to a generous mind that cannot be taken off by all the pleasure of a lazy unmanly life, or by the nauseous enjoyment of a dull plenty that produceth no food for the mind, which will ever be considered in the first place by a man that hath a soul. When he shall think that if his religion, after wading through a sea of blood, come at last to prevail, it would infinitely lessen if not entirely destroy the glory, riches, strength and liberty of his own country, and what a sacrifice this is to make to Rome, where they are wise enough to wonder there should be such fools in the world as to venture, struggle and contend, nay even die martyrs, for that which, should it succeed, would prove a judgment instead of a blessing to them, he will conclude that the advantages of throwing some of their children back again to God Almighty when they have too many of them are not equal to the inconveniences they may either feel or fear by continuing their separation from the religion established.

Temporal things will have their weight in the world, and though zeal may prevail for a time, and get the better in a skirmish, yet the war endeth generally on the side of flesh and blood, and will do so till mankind is another thing than it is at present; and therefore a wise Papist, in cold blood considering these and many other circumstances, will believe it worth his pains to see if he can unmuffle himself from the mask of Infallibility, and will think it reasonable to set his imprisoned senses at liberty, and that he hath a right to see with his own eyes, hear with his own ears, and judge by his own reason. The consequence of which might probably be, that weighing things in a right scale and seeing them in their true colours, he would distinguish between the merit of suffering for a good cause and the foolish ostentation of drawing inconveniences upon himself; and therefore will not be unwilling to be convinced that our Protestant creed may make him happy in the other world, and the easier in this. A few of such wise proselytes would by their example draw so many after them that the party would insensibly melt away, and in a little time, without any angry word, we should come to an union that all good men would have reason to rejoice at.

But we are not to presume upon these conversions without preparing men for them by kind and reconciling arguments; nothing is so against our nature, as to believe those can be in the right who are too hard upon us; there is a deformity in everything that doth us hurt, it will look scurvily in our eye while the smart continueth, and a man must have an extraordinary measure of grace to think well of a religion that reduceth him and his family to misery. In this respect our Trimmer would consent to the mitigation of such laws as were made (as it is said King Henry VIII got Queen Elizabeth) in a heat against Rome. It may be said that even states as well as private men are subject to passion; a just indignation of a villainous attempt produceth at the same time such remedies as perhaps are not without some mixture of revenge, and therefore though time cannot repeal a law, it may by a natural effect soften the execution of it; there is less danger to rouse a lion when at rest, than to awake laws that were intended to have their times of sleeping, nay more than that, in some cases their natural periods of life, too, dying of themselves without the solemnity of being revoked any otherwise than by the common consent of mankind, who cease to execute when the reasons in great measure fail [those] that first created and justified the rigour of such unusual penalties.

Our Trimmer is not eager to pick out the sore places in history against this or any other party; quite contrary, is very solicitous to find out anything that may be healing, and tend to an agreement; but to prescribe the means of this gentleness so as to make it effectual, must come from the only place that can furnish remedies for this cure, *viz.* a Parliament. In the meantime, it is to be wished there might be such a mutual calmness of mind as that the Protestants might not be so jealous as still to smell the match that was to blow up the King and both Houses in the Gunpowder Treason, or to start at every appearance of Popery as if it were just taking possession. On the other side, let not the Papists suffer themselves to be led by any hopes, though never so flattering, to a confidence or ostentation which must provoke men to be less kind to them; let them use modesty on their side, and the Protestants indulgence on theirs. By this means there would be an overlooking of all venial faults, a tacit connivance at all things that do not carry scandal with them, and would amount to a kind of natural dispensation with the severer laws, since there would be no more accusers to be found when the occasions of anger and animosity are once removed. Let the Papists in the meantime remember that there is a respect due from all lesser numbers to greater, a deference to be paid by an opinion that is exploded to one that is established; such a thought well digested will have an influence upon their behaviour, and produce such a temper as must win the most eager adversaries out of their ill humour to them, and give them a title to all the favour that may be consistent with the public peace and security.

THE TRIMMER'S OPINION IN RELATION TO THINGS ABROAD

The world is so composed that it is hard, if not impossible, for a nation not to be a great deal involved in the fate of their neighbours, and though by the felicity of our situation we are more independent than any other people, yet we have in all ages been concerned for our own sakes in the revolutions abroad. There was a time when England was the over-balancing power of Christendom, and that either by inheritance or conquest the better part of France received laws from us. After that, we being reduced into our own limits, France and Spain became the rivals for the universal monarchy, and our third power, though in itself less than either of the other, happened to be superior to any of them, by that choice we had of throwing the scales on that side to which we gave our friendship, and I do not know whether this figure did not make us as great as our former conquest. To be a perpetual umpire of two great contending powers, who gave us all their courtship and offered all their incense at our altar, whilst the fate of either Prince seemed to depend upon the oracles we delivered, for a King of England to sit on his throne, as in the supreme court of justice to which the two great monarchs appeal, pleading their cause and expecting their sentence, declaring which side was in the right, or at least, if we pleased, which side should have the better of it, was a piece of greatness which was peculiar to us, and no wonder if we endeavoured to preserve it, as we did for a considerable time, it being our safety as well as glory to maintain it.

But by a fatality upon our councils, or by the refined policy of this latter age, we have thought fit to use industry to destroy this mighty power which we have so long enjoyed; and that equality between the two monarchs, which we might for ever have preserved, hath been chiefly broken by us, whose interest it was above all others to maintain it. When one of them, like the overflowing of the sea, had gained more upon the other than our convenience, or indeed our safety, would allow, instead of mending the banks, or making new ones, we ourselves with our own hands helped to cut them, to invite and make way for a farther inundation. France and Spain have had their several turns in making use of our mistakes, and we have been formerly as deaf to the instances of the then weaker part of the world to help them against the House of Austria, as we can now be to the earnestness of Spain, that we would assist them against the power of France. Gondomar was as saucy, and as powerful too in King James's court, as any French ambassador can have been at any time since; men talked as wrong then on the Spanish side, and made their court by it as well as any can have done since by talking as much for the French; so that from that time, instead of weighing in a wise balance the power of either crown, it looketh as if we had learnt only to weigh the pensions, and take the heaviest.

It would be tedious as well as unwelcome to recapitulate all our wrong steps, so that I will go no farther than the King's Restoration, at which time the balance was on the side of France, and that by the means of Cromwell, who for a separate interest of his own had sacrificed that of the nation, by joining with the stronger side to suppress the power of Spain, which he ought to have supported. Such a method was natural enough to an usurper, and showed he was not the lawful Father of the People by his having so little care of them; and the example coming from that hand one would think should, for that reason, be less likely to be followed. But to go on, home cometh the King, followed with courtships from all nations abroad, of which some did it not only to make them forget how familiarly they had used him when he was in other circumstances, but to bespeak the friendship of a Prince who, besides his other greatness was yet more considerable by being re-established by the love of his people.

France had an interest either to dispose us to so much goodwill, or at least to put us into such a condition that we might give no opposition to their designs; and Flanders[27] being a perpetual object in their eye, a lasting beauty for which they have an incurable passion, and she not being kind enough to consent to them, they meditated to commit a rape upon her, which they thought would not be easy to do while England and Holland were agreed to rescue her whenever they should hear her cry out for help to them. To this end they put in practice seasonable and artificial whispers, to widen things between us and the States; Amboyna[28] and the Fishery must be talked of here, the freedom of the seas, and the preservation of trade must be insinuated there; and there being combustible matter on both sides in a little time it took fire, which gave those that kindled it sufficient cause to smile and hug themselves, to see

27. The Spanish Netherlands, roughly comprising Belgium with part of northern France.

28. The Dutch massacre of English merchants at Amboyna in the Moluccas in 1623 was never forgotten. 'The Fishery' was the North Sea Fishery.

us both fall into the net they had laid for us. And it is observable and of good example to us, if we will take it, that their design being to set us together at cuffs to weaken us, they kept themselves indifferent lookers-on till our victories began to break the balance, and then the King of France, like a wise prince, was resolved to support the beaten side, and would no more let the power of the sea, than we ought to suffer the monarchy of Europe, to fall into one hand. In pursuance to this he took part with the Dutch, and in a little time made himself umpire of the peace between us. Some time after, upon pretence of his Queen's title to part of Flanders, by right of devolution, he falleth into it with a mighty force, for which the Spaniard was so little prepared that he made a very swift progress, and had such a torrent of undisputed victory that England and Holland, though the wounds they had given one another were yet green, being struck with the apprehension of so near a danger to them, thought it necessary for their own defence to make up a sudden League, into which Sweden was taken, to interpose for a peace between the two crowns.[29]

This had so good an effect that France was stopped in its career, and the Peace of Aix la chapelle was a little after concluded. It was a forced put, and though France wisely dissembled their inward dissatisfaction, yet from that very moment they resolved to untie the triple knot, whatever it cost them; for his Christian Majesty, after his conquering meals, ever riseth with a stomach, and he liked the pattern so well, that it gave him a longing desire to have the whole piece. Amongst the other means used for the attaining this end, the sending over the Duchess of Orleans[30] was not the least powerful; she was a very welcome guest here, and her own charms and dexterity, joined with all other advantages that might help her persuasions, gave her such an ascendant that she should hardly fail of success. One of the preliminaries of her treaty, though a trivial thing in itself, yet was considerable in the consequence, as very small circumstances often are in relation to the government of the world. About that time a general humour in opposition to

29. The Triple Alliance, or 'Triple League', 1668.

30. Charles II's youngest sister, Henriette-Anne, who had been raised a Catholic.

France had made us throw off their fashion, and put on vests, that we might look more like a distinct people, and not be under the servility of imitation, which ever payeth a greater deference to the original than is consistent with the equality all independent nations should pretend to. France did not like this small beginning of ill humours, at least of emulation, and wisely considering that it is a natural introduction first to make the world their apes, that they may be afterwards their slaves, it was thought that one of the instructions Madame brought along with her was to laugh us out of these vests, which she performed so effectually that in a moment, like so many footmen who had quitted their master's livery, we all took it again, and returned to our old service; so that the very time of doing it gave a very critical advantage to France, since it looked like an evidence of our returning to their interest as well as to their fashion, and would give such a distrust of us to our new allies that it might facilitate the dissolution of this knot, which tied them so within their bounds that they were very impatient till they were freed from the restraint.

But the Lady had a more extended commission than this, and without doubt laid the foundation of a new strict alliance, quite contrary to the other in which we had been so lately engaged; and of this there were such early appearances that the world began to look upon us as falling into apostasy from the common interest. Notwithstanding this, France did not neglect at the same time to give good words to the Dutch, and even to feed them with hopes of supporting them against us, when on a sudden that never to be forgotten declaration of war against them cometh out, only to vindicate his own glory, and to revenge the injuries done to his brother in England, by which he became our second in this duel; so humble can this Prince be, when at the same time he doth us more honour than we deserve, he layeth a greater share of the blame upon our shoulders than did naturally belong to us.

The particulars of that war, our part in it while we stayed in it, and when we were out of breath, our leaving the French to make an end of it, are things too well known to make it necessary, and too unwelcome in themselves to incite me to repeat them; only the wisdom of France is in this to be observed, that when we had made a separate peace, which left them single to oppose the united force of the Confederates, they were so far from being angry that they would not so much as show the least coldness, hoping to get as much by our mediation for a peace as they would have expected from our assistance in the war, our circumstances at that time considered. This seasonable piece of indulgence in not reproaching us, but rather allowing those necessities of state which we gave for our excuse, was such an engaging method that it went a great way to keep us still in their chains, when to the eye of the world we had absolutely broke loose from them. And by what passed afterwards at Nimeguen,[31] though the King's neutrality gave him the outward figure of a mediator, it appeared that his interposition was extremely suspected of partiality by the Confederates, who upon that ground did both at and before the conclusion of that treaty treat his ministers there with a great deal of neglect. In this Peace as well as in that of the Pyrenees and Aix la Chapelle, the King of France at the moment of making it, had the thought of breaking it; for a very little time after[32] he broached his pretensions upon Alost, which were things that if they had been offered by a less formidable hand would have been smiled at; but ill arguments, being seconded by good armies, carry such a power with them that naked sense is a very unequal adversary. It was thought that these airy claims were chiefly raised with the prospect of getting Luxemburg for the equivalent; and this opinion was confirmed by the blocking it up afterwards, pretending to the county of Chimay, that it might be entirely surrounded by the French dominions; and it was so pressed that it might have fallen in a little time, if the King of France had not sent orders to his troops to retire, and his Christian generosity, which was assigned for the reason of it, made the world smile, since it is seen how differently his devout zeal worketh in Hungary.[33] That specious reason was in many respects ill-

31. The Congress to make peace between France and the Confederates (Holland, Spain and the Empire), 1677–8.

32. 1683.

33. Louis XIV gave way at the insistence of the Pope, because the Turks were besieging Vienna; and this is undoubtedly the true reason, despite Halifax's faith in the coercive value of Parliament. But Louis's understanding with the Ottoman Sultan gave some cause for cynicism. (See p. 93 below.)

timed, and France itself gave it so faintly that at the very time it looked out of countenance. The true ground of his retiring is worth our observation; for at the instance of the Confederates offices were done, and memorials given, but all ineffectual till the word 'Parliament' was put into them; that powerful word had such an effect, that even at that distance it raised the siege, which may convince us of what efficacy the King of England's words are when he will give them their full weight, and threaten with his Parliament. It is then that he appeareth that great figure we ought to represent him in our minds, the nation his body, he the head, and joined with that harmony that every word he pronounceth is the word of a kingdom. Such words, as appeareth by this example, are as effectual as fleets and armies, because they can create them, and without this his words sound abroad like a faint whisper, that is either not heard, or (which is worse) not minded. But though France had made this step of forced compliance, it did not mean to leave off the pursuit of their pretensions and therefore immediately proposed the arbitration to the King; but it appeared that notwithstanding his merit towards the Confederates in saving Luxemburg, the remembrances of what had passed before had left such an ill taste in their mouths that they could not relish our being put into a condition to dispose of their interests, and therefore declined it by insisting upon a general treaty, to which France hath ever since continued to be averse. Our great earnestness also to persuade the Confederates to consent to it was so unusual and so suspicious a method, that it might naturally make them believe that France spake to them by our mouth, and for that reason, if there had been no other, might hinder the accepting it; and so little care hath been taken to cure this or other jealousies the Confederates may have entertained, that quite contrary, their ministers here every day take fresh alarms from what they observe in small as well as in greater circumstances; and they being apt both to take and improve apprehensions of this kind, draw such inferences from them as make them entirely despair of us. Thus we now stand, far from being innocent spectators of our neighbours' ruin, and by a fatal mistake forgetting what a certain forerunner it is to our own.

And now it is time our Trimmer should tell something of his

opinion upon this present state of things abroad. He first professeth to have no bias either for or against France, and that his thoughts are wholly directed by the interest of his own country. He alloweth, and hath read, that Spain used the same methods when it was in its height as France doth now, and therefore it is not partiality that moveth him, but the just fear which all reasonable men must be possessed with, of an overgrowing power. Ambition is a devouring beast; when it hath swallowed one province, instead of being cloyed, it hath so much the greater stomach to another, and being fed becometh still the more hungry; so that for the Confederates to expect a security from anything but their own united strength is a most miserable fallacy; and if they cannot resist the encroachments of France by their arms, it is in vain for them to dream of any other means of preservation. It would have the better grace, besides the saving so much blood and ruin, to give up all at once, make a present of themselves to appease this haughty monarch, rather than be whispered, flattered or cozened out of their liberty.

Nothing is so soft as the first applications of a greater prince to engage a weaker, but that smiling countenance is but a vizard, it is not the true face; for as soon as their turn is served the courtship flies to some other prince or state, where the same part is to be acted over again; leaveth the old mistaken friend to neglect and contempt, and like an insolent lover to a cast-off mistress, reproaches her with that infamy of which he himself was the author. Sweden, Bavaria, the Palatinate, &c. may by their fresh examples teach other princes what they are reasonably to expect, and what snakes are hid under the flowers the Court of France so liberally throweth upon them whilst they can be useful. The various methods and deep intrigues, with the differing notes in several countries, do not only give suspicion but assurance that everything is put in practice by which universal monarchy may be obtained. Who can reconcile the withdrawing of his troops from Luxemburg, in consideration of the war in Hungary which was not then declared, and presently after encouraging the Turk to take Vienna, and consequently to destroy the Empire? Or who can think that the persecution of the poor Protestants of France will be accepted by

God as an atonement for hazarding the loss of the whole Christian Faith? Can he be thought in earnest, when he seemed to be afraid of the Spaniards, and for that reason must have Luxemburg, and that he cannot be safe from Germany, unless he is in possession of Strasburg? All injustice and violence must in itself be grievous, but the aggravation of supporting them by false arguments and insulting reasons has something in it yet more provoking than the injuries themselves; and the world hath ground enough to apprehend from such a method of arguing, that even their senses are to be subdued as well as their liberties.

Then the variety of arguments used by France in several countries is very observable. In England and Denmark nothing is insisted on but the greatness and authority of the Crown; on the other side, the great men in Poland are commended who differ in opinion with the king, and they argue like friends to the privilege of the Diet against the separate power of the crown. In Sweden they are troubled that the King should have changed something there of late, by his single authority, from the ancient and settled constitutions. At Ratisbon,[34] the most Christian Majesty taketh the liberties of all the Electors and free states into his protection, and telleth them the Emperor is a dangerous man, an aspiring hero that would infallibly devour them if he was not at hand to resist him on their behalf. But above all, in Holland he hath the most obliging tenderness for the Commonwealth, and is in such disquiets lest it should be invaded by the Prince of Orange, that they can do no less in gratitude than undo themselves when he bids them, to show how sensible they are of his excessive good nature. Yet in spite of all these contradictions, there are in the world such refined statesmen as will upon their credit affirm the following paradoxes to be real truth: first, that France alone is sincere and keepeth its faith, and consequently that it is the only friend we can rely upon; that the King of France, of all men living, hath the least mind to be a conqueror; that he is a sleepy, tame creature, void of all ambition, a poor kind of a man, that hath no farther thoughts than to be quiet; that he is charmed by his friendship to us; that it is impossible he should ever do us hurt, and therefore though

34. The seat of the Imperial Diet.

Flanders was lost it would not in the least concern us; that he would fain help the Crown of England to be absolute, which would be to take pains to put it into a condition to oppose him, as it is, and must be, our interest as long as he continueth in such an over-balancing power and greatness.

Such a creed as this, if once received, might prepare our belief for greater things, and as he that taught men to eat a dagger began first with a penknife, so if we can be prevailed with to digest the smaller mistakes, we may at last make our stomachs strong enough for that of transubstantiation.

Our Trimmer cannot easily be converted out of his senses by these state sophisters, and yet he hath no such peevish obstinacy as to reject all correspondence with France because we ought to be apprehensive of the too great power of it; he would not have the King's friendship to the Confederates extended to the involving him in any unreasonable or dangerous engagements, neither would he have him lay aside the consideration of his better establishment at home out of his excessive zeal to secure his allies abroad, but sure there might be a mean between these two opposite extremes, and it may be wished that our friendship with France should at least be so bounded that it may consist with the humour as well as the interest of England. There is no woman but hath her fears of contracting too near an intimacy with a much greater beauty, because it exposeth her too often to a comparison that is not advantageous to her, and sure it may become a prince to be as jealous of his dignity as a lady can be of her good looks, and to be as much out of countenance to be thought an humble companion to so much a greater power. To be always seen in an ill light, to be so darkened by the brightness of a greater star, is somewhat mortifying; and when England might ride Admiral at the head of the Confederates, to look like the kitchen yacht[35] to the Grand Louis is but a scurvy figure for us to make in the map of Christendom. It would rise upon our Trimmer's stomach if ever (which God forbid) the power of calling and intermitting Parliaments here should be transferred to the Crown of France, and that all the opportunities of our own

35. There was a *Kitchen* yacht in the Royal Navy, but the term may be used here figuratively, of a naval provision ship, or bum boat.

settlements at home should give way to their projects abroad, and that our interest should be so far sacrificed to our compliance, that all the omnipotence of France can never make us full amends for it. In the meantime, he shrinketh at the dismal prospect he can by no means drive away from his thoughts, that when France hath gathered all the fruit arising from our mistakes, and that we can bear no more for them, they will cut down the tree and throw it into the fire. All this while, some superfine statesmen, to comfort us, would fain persuade the world that this or that accident may save us, and for all that is or ought to be dear to us would have us to rely wholly upon chance, not considering that Fortune is Wisdom's creature, and that God Almighty loves to be on the wisest as well as the strongest side. Therefore this is such a miserable shift, such a shameful evasion, that they would be laughed to death for it, if the ruining consequence of this mistake did not more dispose men to rage, and a detestation of it.

Our Trimmer is far from idolatry in other things, in one thing only he cometh near it; his country is in some degree his idol. He doth not worship the sun, because it is not peculiar to us, it rambleth about the world, and is less kind to us than it is to other countries; but for the earth of England, though perhaps inferior to that of many places abroad, to him there is divinity in it, and he would rather die than see a spire of English grass trampled down by a foreign trespasser. He thinketh there are a great many of his mind, for all plants are apt to taste of the soil in which they grow, and we that grow here have a root that produceth in us a stock of English juice, which is not to be changed by grafting or foreign infusion; and I do not know whether anything less will prevail than the modern experiment by which the blood of one creature is transmitted into another; according to which, before the French blood can be let into our bodies every drop of our own must be drawn out of them.[36]

Our Trimmer cannot but lament, that by a sacrifice too great for one nation to make to another we should be like a rich mine made useless only for want of being wrought, and that the life and vigour which should move us against our enemies is miserably applied to

36. There *were* some experiments in blood transfusion at the time; Pepys mentions one (*Diary*, 21, 30 November 1667).

tear our own bowels; that being made by our happy situation not only safer, but if we please greater too, than other countries which far exceed us in extent; that having courage by nature, learning by industry and riches by trade we should corrupt all these advantages so as to make them insignificant, and by a fatality which seemeth peculiar to us, misplace our active rage against one another, whilst we are turned into statues on that side where lieth our greatest danger; to be unconcerned not only at our neighbour's ruin but our own, and let our island lie like a great hulk in the sea, without rudder or sail, all the men cast away in her, or as if we were all children in a great cradle, and rocked asleep to a foreign tune.

I say, when our Trimmer representeth to his mind our roses blasted and discoloured, whilst the lilies triumph and grow insolent upon the comparison; when he considereth our own once flourishing laurels now withered and dying, and nothing left us but a remembrance of a better part in history than we shall make in the next age, which will be no more to us than an escutcheon hung upon our door when we are dead; when he foreseeth from hence growing infamy from abroad, confusion at home, and all this without the possibility of a cure in respect of the voluntary fetters good men put upon themselves by their allegiance – without a good measure of preventing grace, he would be tempted to go out of the world like a Roman philosopher rather than endure the burden of life under such a discouraging prospect. But mistakes, as all other things, have their periods, and many times the nearest way to cure is not to oppose them, but stay till they are crushed with their own weight. For Nature will not allow anything to continue long that is violent; violence is a wound, and a wound must be curable in a little time or else it is mortal; but a nation comes near being immortal, therefore the wound will one time or another be cured, though perhaps by such rough methods, if too long forborn, as may even make the best remedies we can prepare to be at the same time a melancholy contemplation to us.

There is but one thing (God Almighty's Providence excepted) to support a man from sinking under these afflicting thoughts, and that is the hopes we draw singly from the King himself, without the mixture of any other consideration. Though the nation was lavish of their kindness to him at his first coming, yet there remaineth still a stock of warmth in men's hearts for him. Besides, the good influences of his happy planet are not yet all spent, and though the stars of men past their youth are generally declining, and have less force, like the eyes of decaying beauties, yet by a blessing peculiar to himself, we may yet hope to be saved even by his autumnal fortune. He hath something about him that will draw down a healing miracle for his and our deliverance. A Prince which seemeth fitted for such an offending age, in which men's crimes have been so general that the not forgiving his people had been the destroying of them, whose gentleness giveth him a natural dominion that hath no bounds, with such a noble mixture of greatness and condescension, an engaging look that disarmeth all men of their ill humours and their resentments; something in him that wanteth a name, and can be no more defined than it can be resisted; a gift of Heaven, of its last finishing, where it will be peculiarly kind; the only prince in the world that dares be familiar, or that hath right to triumph over those forms which were first invented to give awe to those who could not judge, and to hide defects from those that could; a prince that hath exhausted himself by his liberality, and endangered himself by his mercy, who out-shineth by his own light and natural virtues all the varnish of studied acquisitions. His faults are like shades to a good picture, or like alloy to gold, to make it the more useful; he may have some, but for any man to see them through so many reconciling virtues is a sacrilegious piece of ill nature, of which no generous mind can be guilty. A Prince that deserveth to be loved for his own sake, even without the help of a comparison; our love, our duty and our danger all join to cement our obedience to him. In short, whatever he can do, it is no more possible for us to be angry with him than with the bank that secureth us from the raging sea, the kind shade that hideth us from the scorching sun, the welcome hand that reacheth us a reprieve, or with the guardian angel that rescueth our souls from the devouring jaws of wretched eternity.

CONCLUSION

To conclude, our Trimmer is so fully satisfied of the truth of those principles by which he is directed in reference to the public that he will neither be bawled, threatened, laughed nor drunk out of them; and instead of being converted by the arguments of his adversaries to their opinions, he is very much confirmed in his own by them. He professeth solemnly that were it in his power to choose he would rather have his ambition bounded by the commands of a great and wise master than let it range with a popular licence, though crowned with success; yet he cannot commit such a sin against the glorious thing called liberty, nor let his soul stoop so much below itself, as to be content without repining to have his reason wholly subdued, or the privilege of acting like a sensible creature torn from him by the imperious dictates of unlimited authority, in what hand soever it happens to be placed. What is there in this that is so criminal as to deserve the penalty of that most singular apophthegm, *A Trimmer is worse than a rebel?* What do angry men ail to rail so against moderation? Doth it not look as if they were going to some very scurvy extreme, that is too strong to be digested by the more considering part of mankind?

These arbitrary methods, besides the injustice of them, are (God be thanked) very unskilful too, for they fright the birds, by talking so loud, from coming into the nets that are laid for them; and when men agree to rifle a house they seldom giving warning, or blow a trumpet, but there are some small statesmen who are so full charged with their own expectations that they cannot contain, and kind Heaven, by sending such a seasonable curse upon their undertakings, hath made their ignorance an antidote against their malice. Some of these cannot treat peaceably; yielding will not satisfy them, they will have men by storm; there are others that must have plots, to make their service more necessary and have an interest to keep them alive, since they are to live upon them, and persuade the King to retrench his own greatness so as to shrink into the head of a party, which is the betraying him into such an unprincely mistake, and to such a wilful diminution of himself, that they are the last enemies he ought to allow himself to forgive. Such men, if they could, would prevail with the sun to shine only upon them and their friends, and to leave all the rest of the world in the dark. This is a very unusual monopoly, and may come within the equity of the law which maketh it treason to imprison the King, when such unfitting bounds are put to his favour, and he confined to the narrow limits of a particular set of men that would enclose him. These honest and only loyal gentlemen, if they may be allowed to bear witness for themselves, make a King their engine, and degrade him into a property at the very time that their flattery would make him believe they paid divine worship to him.

Besides these there is a flying squadron on both sides, that are afraid the world should agree, small dabblers in conjuring, that raise angry apparitions to keep men from being reconciled, like wasps that fly up and down, buzz and sting to keep men unquiet. But these insects are commonly short-lived creatures, and no doubt in a little time mankind will be rid of them. They were giants at least who fought once against Heaven, but for such pigmies as these to contend against it is such a provoking folly that the insolent bunglers ought to be laughed and hissed out of the world for it; they should consider there is a soul in that great body of the people, which may for a time be drowsy and inactive, but when the Leviathan is roused it moveth like an angry creature, and will neither be convinced nor resisted. The people can never agree to show their united powers till they are extremely tempted and provoked to it, so that to apply cupping-glasses to a great beast naturally disposed to sleep, and to force the tame thing whether it will or no to be valiant, must be learnt out of some other book than Machiavelli, who would never have prescribed such a preposterous method. It is to be remembered that if Princes have law and authority on their sides, the People on theirs may have Nature which is a formidable adversary; duty, justice, religion, nay, even human prudence too, biddeth the people suffer anything rather than resist; but our corrupted nature, where ever it feels the smart, will run to the nearest remedy. Men's passions in this case are to be considered as much as their duty, let it be never so strongly enforced, for if their passions are provoked, they being as much a part of us as our limbs, they lead men into a short way of arguing that admitteth no distinction, and from the foundation of self-defence they will draw inferences that will have miserable effects upon the quiet of a government.

Our Trimmer therefore dreads a general discontent, because he thinketh it differeth from a rebellion only as a spotted fever doth from the plague, the same species under a lower degree of malignity. It worketh several ways; sometimes like a slow poison that hath its effects at a great distance from the time it was given, sometimes like dry flax prepared to catch at the first fire, or like seed in the ground ready to sprout upon the first shower; in every shape it is fatal, and our Trimmer thinketh no pains or precaution can be too great to prevent it.

In short, he thinketh himself in the right, grounding his opinion upon that truth which equally hateth to be under the oppressions of wrangling sophistry on the one hand or the short dictates of mistaken authority on the other.

Our Trimmer adoreth the goddess Truth, though in all ages she hath been scurvily used, as well as those that worshipped her; it is of late become such a ruining virtue that mankind seemeth to be agreed to commend and avoid it. Yet the want of practice which repealeth the other laws hath no influence upon the Law of Truth, because it hath a root in Heaven, and an intrinsic value in itself that can never be impaired. She showeth her greatness in this, that her enemies even when they are successful are ashamed to own it; nothing but powerful Truth hath the prerogative of triumphing, not only after victories but in spite of them, and to put Conquest herself out of countenance; she may be kept under and suppressed, but her dignity still remaineth with her, even when she is in chains. Falsehood with all her impudence hath not enough to speak ill of her before her face; such majesty she carrieth about her that her most prosperous enemies are fain to whisper their treason. All the power upon earth can never extinguish her; she hath lived in all ages; and let the mistaken zeal of prevailing authority christen any opposition to it with what name they please, she maketh it not only an ugly and unmannerly, but a dangerous thing to persist. She hath lived very retired indeed, nay sometimes so buried that only some few of the discerning part of mankind could have a glimpse of her; with all that she hath eternity in her, she knoweth not how to die, and from the darkest clouds that shade and cover her she breaketh from time to time with triumph for her friends and terror to her enemies.

Our Trimmer, therefore, inspired by this divine virtue, thinketh fit to conclude with these assertions: That our climate is a Trimmer, between that part of the world where men are roasted, and the other where they are frozen; That our Church is a Trimmer between the frenzy of platonic visions and the lethargic ignorance of popish dreams; That our laws are Trimmers, between the excess of unbounded power and the extravagance of liberty not enough restrained; That true virtue hath ever been thought a Trimmer, and to have its dwelling in the middle between the two extremes; that even God Almighty himself is divided between his two great attributes, his mercy and his justice.

In such company, our Trimmer is not ashamed of his name, and willingly leaveth to the bold champions of either extreme the honour of contending with no less adversaries than Nature, Religion, Liberty, Prudence, Humanity and Commonsense.

A LETTER TO A DISSENTER

EDITORIAL INTRODUCTION

This was provoked by James II's Declaration of Indulgence, April 4th, 1687, which suspended all the penal laws against Catholic recusants and Protestant Dissenters, and by the Addresses from various congregations and groups of Nonconformists thanking him for his action, some of them pledging political support. It was published clandestinely and its precise date is uncertain, but the first of many answers to it was published in September, and it was clearly written after July 6th, when James dissolved his first Parliament and announced his intention of summoning another.

A LETTER TO A DISSENTER

Upon Occasion of His Majesties late Gracious Declaration of Indulgence

SIR,

Since addresses are in fashion, give me leave to make one to you. This is neither the effect of fear, interest or resentment; therefore you may be sure it is sincere; and for that reason it may expect to be kindly received. Whether it will have power enough to convince dependeth upon the reasons, of which you are to judge, and upon your preparation of mind to be persuaded by truth, whenever it appeareth to you. It ought not to be the less welcome for coming from a friendly hand, one whose kindness to you is not lessened by difference of opinion, and who will not let his thoughts for the public be so tied or confined to this or that sub-division of Protestants as to stifle the charity which, besides all other arguments, is at this time become necessary to preserve us.

I am neither surprised nor provoked to see that in the condition you were put into by the laws, and the ill circumstances you lay under by having the Exclusion and Rebellion laid to your charge, you were desirous to make yourselves less uneasy and obnoxious to authority. Men who are sore run to the nearest remedy with too much haste to consider all the consequences; grains of allowance are to be given, where Nature giveth such strong influences. When to men under sufferings it offereth ease, the present pain will hardly allow time to examine the remedies; and the strongest reason can hardly gain a fair audience from our mind, whilst so possessed, till the smart is a little allayed.

I do not know whether the warmth that naturally belongeth to new friendships, may not make it a harder task for me to persuade you. It is like telling lovers, in the beginning of their joys, that they will in a little time have an end. Such an unwelcome style doth not easily find credit. But I will suppose you are not so far gone in your new passion, but that you will hear still; and therefore I am under the less discouragement when I offer to your consideration two things. The first is, the cause you have to suspect your new friends. The second, the duty incumbent upon you, in Christianity and prudence, not to hazard the public safety, neither by desire of ease, nor of revenge.

To the first: Consider that notwithstanding the smooth language which is now put on to engage you, these new friends did not make you their choice, but their refuge. They have ever made their first courtships to the Church of England, and when they were rejected there, they made their application to you in the second place. The instances of this might be given in all times. I do not repeat them, because whatsoever is unnecessary must be tedious, the truth of this assertion being so plain as not to admit a dispute. You cannot therefore reasonably flatter yourselves that there is any inclination to you. They never pretended to allow you any quarter, but to usher in liberty for themselves under that shelter. I refer you to Mr. Coleman's Letters, and to the Journals of Parliament,[1] where you may be convinced if you can be so mistaken as to doubt; nay, at this very hour they can hardly forbear, in the height of their courtship, to let fall hard words of you. So little is Nature to be restrained; it will start out sometimes, disdaining to submit to the usurpation of art and interest.

This alliance between Liberty and Infallibility is bringing together the two most contrary things that are in the world. The Church of Rome doth not only dislike the allowing liberty, but by its principles it cannot do it. Wine is not more expressly forbid to the Mahometans, than giving heretics liberty to the Papists; they are no more able to make good their vows to you, than men married before, and their wife alive, can confirm their contract with another. The continuance of their kindness would be a habit of sin, of which they are to repent, and their absolution is to be had upon no other terms than their promise to destroy you. You are therefore to be hugged now, only that you may be the better squeezed at another time. There must be something extraordinary when the Church of Rome setteth up bills, and offereth plaisters for tender consciences. By all that hath hitherto appeared, her skill in chirurgery lieth chiefly

1. Edward Coleman's letters furnished 'proof' of the Popish Plot in 1678; other 'evidence' was printed in the Commons' Journals.

in a quick hand to cut off limbs, but she is the worst at healing of any that ever pretended to it.

To come so quick from another extreme is such an unnatural motion that you ought to be upon your guard; the other day you were sons of Belial, now you are angels of light. This is a violent change, and it will be fit for you to pause upon it, before you believe it; if your features are not altered neither is their opinion of you, whatever may be pretended. Do you believe less than you did, that there is idolatry in the Church of Rome? Sure you do not. See then how they treat both in words and writing those who entertain that opinion. Conclude from hence how inconsistent their favour is with this single article, except they give you a dispensation for this too, and by a *non obstante* secure you that they will not think the worse of you.

Think a little how dangerous it is to build upon a foundation of paradoxes. Popery now is the only friend to liberty, and the known enemy to persecution; the men of Taunton and Tiverton[2] are above all other eminent for loyalty. The Quakers, from being declared by the Papists not to be Christians, are now made favourites and taken into their particular protection; they are on a sudden grown the most accomplished men of the kingdom in good breeding, and give thanks with the best grace, in double refined language. So that I should not wonder though a man of that persuasion, in spite of his hat, should be Master of the Ceremonies.[3] Not to say harsher words, these are such very new things that it is impossible not to suspend our belief, till by a little more experience we may be informed whether they are realities or apparitions. We have been under shameful mistakes if these opinions are true; but for the present we are apt to be incredulous, except we could be convinced that the priests' words in this case too are able to make such a sudden and effectual change, and that their power is not limited to the sacrament, but that it extendeth to alter the nature of all other things, as often as they are so disposed.

Let me now speak of the instruments of your friendship, and then

2. Somerset was the centre of Nonconformist support for Monmouth's Rebellion in 1685.

3. Probably a reference to William Penn, James's friend and confidant.

leave you to judge whether they do not afford matter of suspicion. No sharpness is to be mingled where healing only is intended, so nothing will be said to expose particular men, how strong soever the temptation may be, or how clear the proofs to make it out; a word or two in general, for your better caution, shall suffice. Suppose then, for argument's sake, that the mediators of this new alliance should be such as have been formerly employed in treaties of the same kind and there detected to have acted by order, and to have been empowered to give encouragements and rewards. Would not this be an argument to suspect them?

If they should plainly be under engagements to one side, their arguments to the other ought to be received accordingly; their fair pretences are to be looked upon as part of their commission, which may not improbably give them a dispensation in the case of truth, when it may bring a prejudice upon the service of those by whom they are employed.

If there should be men who, having formerly had means and authority to persuade by secular arguments, have in pursuance of that power sprinkled money amongst the Dissenting ministers; and if those very men should now have the same authority, practice the same methods, and disburse where they cannot otherwise persuade, it seemeth to me to be rather an evidence than a presumption of the deceit.[4]

If there should be ministers amongst you who, by having fallen under temptations of this kind, are in some sort engaged to continue their frailty by the awe they are in lest it should be exposed, the persuasions of these unfortunate men must sure have the less force, and their arguments, though never so specious, are to be suspected when they come from men who have mortgaged themselves to severe creditors, that expect a rigorous observation of the contract, let it be never so unwarrantable.

If these, or any others, should at this time preach up anger and vengeance against the Church of England, may it not without injustice be suspected that a thing so plainly out of season springeth rather from corruption than mistake; and that those who act this

4. An obscure reference, perhaps to the distribution of money amongst the Dissenting clergy by Charles II in 1672.

choleric part do not believe themselves, but only pursue higher directions, and endeavour to make good that part of their contract which obligeth them, upon a forfeiture, to make use of their inflaming eloquence? They might apprehend their wages would be retrenched if they should be moderate; and therefore whilst violence is their interest, those who have not the same arguments have no reason to follow such a partial example.

If there should be men who, by the load of their crimes against the government, have been bowed down to comply with it against their conscience; who by incurring the want of a pardon have drawn upon themselves a necessity of an entire resignation; such men are to be lamented, but not to be believed.[5] Nay, they themselves, when they have discharged their unwelcome task, will be inwardly glad that their forced endeavours do not succeed, and are pleased when men resist their insinuations, which are far from being voluntary or sincere, but are squeezed out of them by the weight of their being so obnoxious.

If in the height of this great dearness, by comparing things, it should happen that at this instant there is a much surer friendship with those who are so far from allowing liberty that they allow no living to a Protestant under them, let the scene lie in what part of the world it will, the argument will come home, and sure it will afford sufficient ground to suspect. Apparent contradictions must strike us; neither nature nor reason can digest them. Self-flattery, and the desire to deceive ourselves to gratify present appetite, with all their power, which is great, cannot get the better of such broad conviction as some things carry along with them. Will you call these vain and empty suspicions? Have you been at all times so void of fears and jealousies as to justify your being so unreasonably valiant in having none upon this occasion? Such an extraordinary courage at this unseasonable time, to say no more, is too dangerous a virtue to be commended.

If then, for these and a thousand other reasons, there is cause to suspect, sure your new friends are not to dictate to you, or advise

5. This refers to prominent Dissenting ministers who had been convicted of complicity in the Rye House Plot or Monmouth's Rebellion, and bound over.

you. For instance, the addresses that fly abroad every week, and murder us with *Another to the same*; the first draughts are made by those who are not very proper to be secretaries to the Protestant Religion, and it is your part only to write them out fairer again. Strange! that you who have been formerly so much against set forms, should now be content the priests should indite for you. The nature of thanks is an unavoidable consequence of being pleased or obliged; they grow in the heart, and from thence show themselves either in looks, speech, writing or action. No man was ever thankful because he was bid to be so, but because he had, or thought he had, some reason for it. If then there is cause in this case to pay such extravagant acknowledgments, they will flow naturally, without taking such pains to procure them; and it is unkindly done to tire all the post-horses with carrying circular letters to solicit that which would be done without any trouble or constraint. If it is really in itself such a favour, what needeth so much pressing men to be thankful, and with such eager circumstances that where persuasions cannot delude threatenings are employed to fright them into a compliance. Thanks must be voluntary, not only unconstrained but unsolicited, else they are either trifles or snares; they either signify nothing, or a great deal more than is intended by those that give them. If an inference should be made that whosoever thanketh the King for his Declaration is by that engaged to justify it in point of law, it is a greater stride than, I presume, all those care to make who are persuaded to address. If it shall be supposed that all the thankers will be repealers of the Test, whenever a Parliament shall meet, such an expectation is better prevented before than disappointed afterwards; and the surest way to avoid the lying under such a scandal is not to do anything that may give a colour to the mistake. These bespoken thanks are little less improper than love letters that were solicited by the lady to whom they are to be directed; so, that besides the little ground there is to give them, the manner of getting them doth extremely lessen their value. It might be wished that you would have suppressed your impatience, and have been content for the sake of religion to enjoy it within yourselves without the liberty of a public exercise, till a Parliament had allowed it. But since that could not be, and that the artifices of some amongst you have made use of the well-meant zeal of the generality to draw them into this mistake, I am so far from blaming you with that sharpness which perhaps the matter in strictness would bear, that I am ready to err on the side of the more gentle construction.

There is a great difference between enjoying quietly the advantages of an act irregularly done by others, and the going about to support it against the laws in being. The law is so sacred that no trespass against it is to be defended; yet frailties may in some measure be excused, when they cannot be justified. The desire of enjoying a liberty from which men have been so long restrained may be a temptation that their reason is not at all times able to resist. If in such a case some objections are leapt over, indifferent men will be more inclined to lament the occasion than to fall too hard upon the fault, whilst it is covered with the apology of a good intention; but where, to rescue yourselves from the severity of one law, you give a blow to all the laws by which your religion and liberty are to be protected, and instead of silently receiving the benefit of this indulgence, you set up for advocates to support it, you become voluntary aggressors, and look like counsel retained by the Prerogative against your old friend Magna Carta, who hath done nothing to deserve her falling thus under your displeasure.

If the case then should be that the price expected from you for this liberty is giving up your right in the laws, sure you will think twice before you go any further in such a losing bargain. After giving thanks for the breach of one law, you lose the right of complaining of the breach of all the rest; you will not very well know how to defend yourselves when you are pressed, and having given up the question when it was for your advantage, you cannot recall it when it shall be to your prejudice. If you will set up at one time a power to help you, which at another time, by parity of reason, shall be made use of to destroy you, you will neither be pitied nor relieved against a mischief you drew upon yourselves, by being so unreasonably thankful. It is like calling in auxiliaries to help, who are strong enough to subdue you. In such a case your complaints will come too late to be heard, and your sufferings will raise mirth instead of compassion.

If you think, for your excuse, to expound your thanks so as to restrain them to this particular case, others, for their ends, will extend them further. And in these differing interpretations, that which is backed by authority will be the most likely to prevail; especially when by the advantage you have given them they have in truth the better of the argument, and that the inferences from your own concessions are very strong and express against you. This is so far from being a groundless supposition, that there was a late instance of it, the last session of Parliament, in the House of Lords,[6] where the first thanks, though things of course, were interpreted to be the approbation of the King's whole speech, and a restraint from the further examination of any part of it, though never so much disliked; and it was with difficulty obtained not to be excluded from the liberty of objecting to this mighty prerogative of dispensing, merely by this innocent and usual piece of good manners, by which no such thing could possibly be intended.

This showeth that some bounds are to be put to your good breeding, and that the constitution of England is too valuable a thing to be ventured upon a compliment. Now that you have for some time enjoyed the benefit of the end, it is time for you to look into the danger of the means. The same reason that made you desirous to get liberty must make you solicitous to preserve it, so that the next thought will naturally be, not to engage yourself beyond retreat, and to agree so far with the principles of all religion as not to rely upon a death-bed repentance.

There are certain periods of time, which being once past, make all cautions ineffectual, and all remedies desperate. Our understandings are apt to be hurried on by the first heats, which, if not restrained in time, do not give us leave to look back till it is too late. Consider this in the case of your anger against the Church of England, and take warning by their mistake in the same kind, when after the late King's Restoration they preserved so long the bitter

6. In November 1685 James II asked Parliament to approve his commissioning of Catholic army officers in despite of the Test Act. Halifax sarcastically suggested that the Lords thank his Majesty 'for speaking plainly'. The government spokesman seized upon this opportunity to move a formal vote of thanks, and it was some days before the matter could be raised again. Halifax was so upset that he not only raised the matter here, but again in 1692 (Foxcroft *Character*, pp. 316–17) at remarkable length.

taste of your rough usage to them in other times, that it made them forget their interest, and sacrifice it to their revenge.

Either you will blame this proceeding in them, and for that reason not follow it, or if you allow it, you have no reason to be offended with them; so that you must either dismiss your anger or lose your excuse – except you should argue more partially than will be supposed of men of your morality and understanding.

If you had now to do with those rigid prelates who made it a matter of conscience to give you the least indulgence, but kept you at an uncharitable distance, and even to your most reasonable scruples continued stiff and inexorable, the argument might be fairer on your side; but since the common danger hath so laid open that mistake that all the former haughtiness towards you is for ever extinguished, and that it hath turned the spirit of persecution into a spirit of peace, charity, and condescension, shall this happy change only affect the Church of England? And are you so in love with separation as not to be moved by this example? It ought to be followed, were there no other reason than that it is virtue; but when besides that it is become necessary to your preservation, it is impossible to fail the having its effect upon you.

If it should be said that the Church of England is never humble but when she is out of power, and therefore loseth the right of being believed when she pretendeth to it, the answer is first, it would be an uncharitable objection, and very much mistimed; an unseasonable triumph, not only ungenerous but unsafe; so that in these respects it cannot be urged without scandal, even though it could be said with truth. Secondly, this is not so in fact, and the argument must fall, being built upon a false foundation; for whatever may be told you at this very hour, and in the heat and glare of your present sunshine, the Church of England can in a moment bring clouds again, and turn the royal thunder upon your heads, blow you off the stage with a breath, if she would give but a smile or a kind word; the least glimpse of her compliance would throw you back into the state of suffering, and draw upon you all the arrears of severity which have accrued during the time of this kindness to you. And yet the Church of England, with all her faults, will not allow herself to be rescued by such unjustifiable means, but chooseth to bear the weight of power rather than lie under the burden of being criminal.

It cannot be said that she is unprovoked; books and letters come out every day, to call for answers, yet she will not be stirred. From the supposed authors, and the style, one would swear they were undertakers, and had made a contract to fall out with the Church of England. There are lashes in every address, challenges to draw the pen in every pamphlet – in short, the fairest occasions in the world given to quarrel; but she wisely distinguisheth between the body of Dissenters, whom she will suppose to act as they do with no ill intent, and these small skirmishers, picked and sent out to picqueer,[7] and to begin a fray[8] amongst the Protestants, for the entertainment as well as the advantage of the Church of Rome.

This conduct is so good, that it will be scandalous not to applaud it. It is not equal dealing to blame our adversaries for doing ill, and not commend them when they do well. To hate them because they persecuted, and not to be reconciled to them when they are ready to suffer rather than receive all the advantages that can be gained by a criminal compliance, is a principle no sort of Christians can own, since it would give an objection to them never to be answered.

Think a little who they were that promoted your former persecutions, and then consider how it will look to be angry with the instruments, and at the same time to make a league with the authors of your sufferings.

Have you enough considered what will be expected from you? Are you ready to stand in every borough by virtue of a *congé d'elire*,[9] and instead of election, be satisfied if you are returned?

Will you in Parliament justify the Dispensing Power, with all its consequences, and repeal the Test, by which you will make way for the repeal of all the laws that were made to preserve your religion, and to enact others that shall destroy it?

Are you disposed to change the liberty of debate into the merit of

7. To skirmish. 8. affray.

9. The writ giving Deans and Chapters leave to elect a named candidate to a Bishopric – that is, nominating him.

obedience, and to be made instruments to repeal or enact laws, when the Roman Consistory are Lords of the Articles?[10]

Are you so linked with your new friends as to reject any indulgence a Parliament shall offer you, if it shall not be so comprehensive as to include the Papists in it?

Consider that the implied conditions of your new treaty are no less than that you are to do everything you are desired, without examining, and that for this pretended liberty of conscience, your real freedom is to be sacrificed. Your former faults hang like chains still about you, you are let loose only upon bail; the first act of non-compliance sendeth you to jail again.

You may see that the Papists themselves do not rely upon the legality of this power which you are to justify, since the being so very earnest to get it established by a law, and the doing such very hard things in order, as they think, to obtain it, is a clear evidence that they do not think that the single power of the Crown is in this case a good foundation; especially when this is done under a Prince so very tender of all the rights of sovereignty, that he would think it a diminution to his prerogative, where he conceiveth it strong enough to go alone, to call in the legislative help to strengthen and support it.

You have formerly blamed the Church of England, and not without reason, for going so far as they did in their compliance; and yet as soon as they stopped, you see they are not only deserted but prosecuted. Conclude then from this example, that you must either break off your friendship, or resolve to have no bounds in it. If they do not succeed in their design, they will leave you first; if they do, you must either leave them when it will be too late for your safety, or else after the queasiness of starting at a surplice, you must be forced to swallow transubstantiation.

Remember that the other day those of the Church of England were Trimmers for enduring you, and now by a sudden turn you are become the favourites. Do not deceive yourselves, it is not the nature of lasting plants thus to shoot up in a night; you may look gay and green for a little time, but you want a root to give you a

10. The government committee which controlled the agenda of the Scots Parliament.

continuance. It is not so long since as to be forgotten, that the maxim was, It is impossible for a Dissenter not to be a rebel. Consider at this time in France even the new converts are so far from being employed that they are disarmed; their sudden change maketh them still to be distrusted, notwithstanding that they are reconciled. What are you to expect then from your dear friends, to whom, whenever they shall think fit to throw you off again, you have in other times given such arguments for their excuse?

Besides all this, you act very unskilfully against your visible interest if you throw away the advantages of which you can hardly fail in the next probable revolution. Things tend naturally to what you would have, if you would let them alone, and not by an unseasonable activity lose the influences of your good star, which promiseth you everything that is prosperous.

The Church of England convinced of its error in being severe to you; the Parliament, whenever it meeteth, sure to be gentle to you; the next heir bred in the country which you have so often quoted for a pattern of indulgence; a general agreement of all thinking men that we must no more cut ourselves off from the Protestants abroad, but rather enlarge the foundations upon which we are to build our defences against the common enemy; so that in truth all things seem to conspire to give you ease and satisfaction, if by too much haste to anticipate your good fortune you do not destroy it.

The Protestants have but one article of human strength to oppose the power which is now against them, and that is, not to lose the advantage of their numbers by being so unwary as to let themselves be divided.

We all agree in our duty to our Prince; our objections to his belief do not hinder us from seeing his virtues; and our not complying with his religion hath no effect upon our allegiance. We are not to be laughed out of our Passive Obedience, and the Doctrine of Non-Resistance; though even those who perhaps owe the best part of their security to that principle are apt to make a jest of it.

So that if we give no advantage by the fatal mistake of misapplying our anger, by the natural course of things this danger will pass away like a shower of hail; fair weather will succeed, as lowering as the sky now looketh, and all by the plain and easy receipt:[11] *Let us be still, quiet, and undivided, firm at the same time to our Religion, our Loyalty, and our Laws*; and so long as we continue this method, it is next to impossible that the odds of 200 to one should lose the bet; except the Church of *Rome*, which hath been so long barren of miracles, should now in her declining age be brought to bed of one that would outdo the best she can brag of in her legend.

To conclude, the short question will be, whether you will join with those who must in the end run the same fate with you? If Protestants of all sorts in their behaviour to one another have been to blame, they are upon the more equal terms, and for that very reason it is fitter for them now to be reconciled. Our disunion is not only a reproach but a danger to us; those who believe in modern miracles have more right, or at least more excuse, to neglect all secular cautions, but for us it is as justifiable to have no religion as wilfully to throw away the human means of preserving it.

I am,

Dear Sir,
Your most Affectionate humble Servant,
T.W.

11. Recipe.

THE ANATOMY OF AN EQUIVALENT

EDITORIAL INTRODUCTION

The only clue to the dating of this pamphlet is a casual reference to it as 'new' in October 1688. This induces Miss Foxcroft to associate it with James II's Proclamation of 21 September, in which the Equivalent was first publicly offered. However, the Equivalent – a statutory guarantee of the rights and privileges of the Church of England in return for the repeal of the Test Act – was first suggested, apparently by William Penn, in November or December 1687, and it was the subject of intermittent discussion in political circles thereafter. Moreover, only a week after James's Proclamation William's impending invasion was announced, and it seems unlikely that in these circumstances Halifax would have written a long and closely argued pamphlet on an issue which was likely to prove a dead letter. It could have been published any time in 1688.

THE ANATOMY OF AN EQUIVALENT

1. THE world hath of late years never been without some extraordinary word to furnish the coffee-houses and fill the pamphlets. Sometimes it is a new one invented, and sometimes an old one revived. They are usually fitted to some present purpose, with intentions as differing as the various designs several parties may have, either to delude the people or to expose their adversaries. They are not of long continuance, but after they have passed a little while, and that they are grown nauseous by being so often repeated, they give place to something that is newer. Thus after Whig, Tory and Trimmer have had their time, now they are dead and forgotten, being supplanted by the word *Equivalent*, which reigneth in their stead.

The birth of it is in short this: after many repeated essays to dispose men to the repeal of Oaths and Tests made for the security of the Protestant Religion, the general aversion to comply in it was found to be so great that it was thought advisable to try another manner of attempting it, and to see whether by putting the same thing into another mould, and softening an harsh proposition by a plausible term, they might not have better success.

To this end, instead of an absolute quitting of these laws without any condition, which was the first proposal, now it is put into gentler language, and runneth thus: If you will take away the *Oaths* and *Tests*, you shall have as good a thing for them. This, put into the fashionable word, is now called an *Equivalent*.

2. So much to the word itself. I will now endeavour in short to examine and explain, in order to the having it fully understood:

First, what is the nature of a true equivalent; and

In the next place, what things are not to be admitted under that denomination.

I shall treat these as general propositions, and though I cannot undertake how far they may be convincing, I may safely do it that they are impartial; of which there can be no greater evidence than that I make neither inference nor application, but leave that part entirely to the reader, according as his own thoughts shall direct and dispose him.

3. I will first take notice, that this word, by the application which hath been made of it in some modern instances, lieth under some disadvantage, not to say some scandal. It is transmitted hither from France; and if, as in most other things that we take from them we carry them beyond the pattern, it should prove so in this, we should get into a more partial style than the principles of English justice will I hope ever allow us to be guilty of.

The French King's *Equivalents* in Flanders are very extraordinary bargains; his manner of proposing and obtaining them is very differing from the usual methods of equal dealing. In a later instance Denmark, by the encouragement as well as by the example of France, hath proposed things to the Duke of Holstein which are called *Equivalents*, but that they are so the world is not yet sufficiently convinced, and probably the parties concerned do not think them to be so, and consequently do not appear to be at all disposed to accept them. Princes enjoin and prescribe such things when they have strength and power to supply the want of arguments; and according to practice in these cases, the weaker are never thought to have an ill bargain, if they have anything left them. So that the first qualification of an equivalent must be, that the appraisers be indifferent, else it is only a sound,[1] there can be nothing real in it. For where the same party that proposeth a bargain claimeth a right to set the value – or which is worse, hath power too to make it good – the other may be forced to submit to the conditions, but he can by no means ever be persuaded to treat upon them.

4. The next thing to be considered is, that to make an *Equivalent* in reality an equal thing in the proposer, it must be a better thing than that which is required by him; just as good is subject to the hazard of not being quite so good. It is not easy to have such an even hand as to make the value exactly equal; besides, according to the maxim in law, *melior conditio possidentis*, the offer is not fair except the thing offered is better in value than the thing demanded. There

1. A feint.

must be allowance for removing what is fixed, and there must be something that may be a justification for changing. The value of things very often dependeth more upon other circumstances than upon what is merely intrinsic to them; therefore the calculation must be made upon that foot, perhaps in most cases; and particularly the want which one of the parties may have of the thing he requireth, maketh it more valuable to him than it is in itself. If the party proposing doth not want the thing he would have in exchange, his requiring it is impertinent; if he doth, his want of it must go into the appraisement and by consequence every proposer of an *Equivalent* must offer a better thing, or else he must not take it unkindly to be refused, except the other party hath an equal want of the same thing, which is very improbable, since naturally he that wanteth most will speak first.

5. Another thing necessary to the making a fair bargain is that, let the parties who treat[2] be never so unequal in themselves, yet as to the particular thing proposed there must be an exact equality, as far as it relateth to the full liberty of taking or refusing, concurring or objecting, without any consequence of revenge, or so much as dissatisfaction. For it is impossible to treat where it is an affront to differ; in that case there is no mean between the two extremes, either an open quarrel or an entire submission. The way of bargaining must be equal, else the bargain itself cannot be so. For example, the proposer is not only to use equal terms as to the matter, but fair ones in the manner too. There must be no intimations of anger in case of refusal, much less any open threatening. Such a style is so ill suited to the usual way of treating that it looketh more like a breach of the peace than the making a bargain. It would be yet more improper and less agreeing with the nature of an *Equivalent* if, whilst two men are chaffering about the price, one of them should actually take the thing in question at his own rate, and afterwards desire to have his possession confirmed by a formal agreement. Such a proceeding would not only destroy that particular contract, but make it impossible to have any other with the party that could be guilty of such a practice.

2. Negotiate. ('Treaty', in a similar way, usually means 'negotiation'.)

6. Violence preceding destroyeth all contract, and even though the party that offereth it should have a right to the thing he so taketh, yet it is to be obtained by legal means, else it may be forfeited by his irregularity in the pursuit of it. The Law is such an enemy to violence, and so little to be reconciled to it, that in the case of a rape the punishment is not taken off though the party injured afterwards consenteth. The justice of the Law hath its eye upon the first act, and the maxim of *volenti non fit injuria* doth not in this case help the offender, it being a plea subsequent to the crime, which maketh it to be rejected as a thing wrong dated and out of time.

In taking away goods or money it is the same thing. The party robbed, by giving them afterwards to the taker, doth not exempt him from the punishment of the violence; quite contrary, the man from whom they were taken is punishable, if he doth not prosecute. If the case should be, that a man thus taking away a thing without price claimeth a right to take it, then whether it is well or ill founded is not the question; but sure, the party from whom it is so taken, whilst he is treating to sell or exchange it, can never make a bargain with so arbitrary a chapman, there being no room left after that to talk of the value.

7. To make an equal bargain there must be a liberty of differing, not only in everything that is really essential, but in everything that is thought so by either party, and most especially by him who is in possession of the thing demanded. His opinion must be a rule to him, and even his mistake in the value, though it may not convince the man he has to deal with, yet he will be justified for not accepting what is offered till that mistake is fairly rectified and overruled.[3]

When a security is desired to be changed, that side which desireth it must not pretend to impose upon the other so as to dictate to them, and tell them without debate that they are safe in what is proposed, since of that the counsel on the other side must certainly be the most competent judges. The hand it cometh from is a great circumstance, either to invite or discourage in all matters

3. Ruled out or crossed out.

of contract; the qualifications of the party offering must suit with the proposition itself, else let it be never so fair there is ground for suspicion.

8. When men are of a temper that they think they have wrong done them if they have not always the better side of a bargain; if they happen to be such as by experience have been found to have an ill memory for their word; if the character they bear doth not recommend their justice wherever their interest is concerned – in these cases thinking men will avoid dealing, not only to prevent surprise, but to cut off the occasions of difficulty or dispute.

It is yet more discouraging when there are either a precedent practice, or standing maxims of gross partiality, in assuming a privilege of exemption from the usual methods of equal dealing.

To illustrate this by an instance. Suppose that in any case the Church of Rome should have an interest to promote a bargain, let her way of dealing be a little examined, which will direct those with whom she treateth how far they are to rely upon what she proposeth to them. We may begin with the quality in the world the least consisting with equal dealing, viz., an incurable partiality to herself which, that it may arrive to its full perfection, is crowned with infallibility. At the first setting out, she maketh herself incapable of dealing upon terms of equality by the power she claimeth of binding and loosing, which hath been so often applied to treaties as well as to sins.

If the definition of justice is to deal equally, she cannot be guilty of it without betraying her prerogative, and according to her principles she giveth up the superiority derived to her by Apostolical Succession if she degradeth herself so as to be judged by the rules of common right, especially if the bargain should be with heretics, who in her opinion have forfeited the claim they might otherwise have had to it.

9. Besides, her taste hath been so spoiled by unreasonable bargains, that she can never bring down her palate to anything that is fair or equal. She hath not only judged it an *Equivalent*, but a great bargain

for the other side, to give them absolutions and indulgence for the real payment of great sums, for which she hath drawn bills to have them repayed with interest in Purgatory.

This spiritual bank hath carried on such a trade upon these advantageous terms that it can never submit to the small profits an ordinary bargain would produce.

The several Popes have in exchange for the Peter Pence, and all their other rents and fines out of England, sent sanctified roses, relics and other such wonder-working trifles. And by virtue of their character of Holy Fathers have used Princes like children, by sending them such rattles to play with, which they made them buy at extravagant rates – besides which they were to be thankful too, into the bargain.

A chip of the Cross, a piece of St Laurence's grid-iron, a hair of St Peter, have been thought *Equivalents* for much more substantial things. The Popes, being Masters of the Jewel House, have set the rates upon them, and they have passed, though the whole shop would not take up the value of a bodkin in Lombard Street upon the credit of them.[4]

They are unconscionable purchasers, for they get all the money from the living by praying for them when they are dead. And it is observable that the Northern part of Christendom, which best understandeth trade, were the first that refused to make any more bargains with them, so that it looketh as if the chief quarrel to the heretics was not as they were ill Christians but as they were unkind merchants, in so discourteously rejecting the commodities of the growth of Rome.

To conclude this head, there is no bartering with infallibility, it being so much above equality that it cannot bear the indignity of a true *Equivalent*.

10. In all bargains there is a necessity of looking back, and reflecting how far a present proposal is reconcilable with a former practice – for example, if at any time a thing is offered quite differing from the

4. One of the functions of the Master of the King's Jewel House was to value finished articles in gold or silver. To 'take up' is to borrow on credit. For 'bodkin' we would say 'pin'.

arguments used by the proposer, and inconsistent with the maxims held out by him at other times. Or in a public case, if the same men who promote and press a thing with the utmost violence do in a little time after with as much violence press the contrary, and profess a detestation of the very thing for which they had before employed all their interest and authority. Or if in the case of a law already made, there should be a privilege claimed to exempt those from the obligation of observing it, who yet should afterwards desire and press to have a new law made in exchange for the old one, by which they would not be bound; and that they should propose a security by a thing of the very same nature as that which they did not allow to be any before. These incoherences must naturally have the effect of raising suspicion, or rather they are a certain proof, that in such circumstances it is irrational for men to expect an effectual *Equivalent*.

11. If whatsoever is more than ordinary is suspicious, everything that is unnatural is more so. It is not only unnecessary but unnatural too, to persuade with violence what it is folly to refuse; to push men with eagerness into a good bargain for themselves is a style very much unsuitable to the nature of the thing. But it goeth further and is yet more absurd, to grow angry with men for not receiving a proposal that is for their advantage; men ought to be content with the generosity of offering good bargains, and should give their compassion to those who do not understand them; but by carrying their good nature so far as to be choleric in such a case they would follow the example of the Church of Rome, where the definition of charity is very extraordinary. In her language the writ *de heretico comburendo* is a love letter, and burning men for differing with them in opinion, howsoever miscalled cruelty, is, as they understand it, the perfection of flaming charity.

When anger in these cases lasteth long, it is most probable that it is for our own sakes. Good nature for others is one of those diseases that is cured by time, and especially where it is offered and rejected; but for ourselves it never faileth, and cannot be extinguished but with our life. It is fair if men can believe that their friends love them next to themselves, to love them better is too much; the expression is so unnatural that it is cloying, and men must have no sense who in this case have no suspicion.

12. Another circumstance necessary to a fair bargain is that there must be openness and freedom allowed as the effect of that equality which is the foundation of contracting. There must be full liberty of objecting, and making doubts and scruples. If they are such as can be answered, the party convinced is so much the more confirmed and encouraged to deal, instead of being hindered by them; but if instead of an answer to satisfy, there is nothing but anger for a reply, it is impossible not to conclude that there is never a good one to give; so that, the objection remaining without being fully confuted, there is an absolute bar put to any further treaty.

There can be no dealing where one side assumeth a privilege to impose, so as to make an offer and not bear the examination of it this is giving judgment, not making a bargain. Where it is called unmannerly to object, or criminal to refuse, the surest way is for men to stay where they are rather than treat upon such disadvantage.

If it should happen to be in any country where the governing power should allow men liberty of conscience in the choice of their religion, it would be strange to deny them liberty of speech in making a bargain. Such a contradiction would be so discouraging, that they must be unreasonably sanguine who in that case can entertain the hopes of a fair *Equivalent.*

13. An equal bargain must not be a mystery nor a secret; the purchaser or proposer is to tell directly and plainly what it is he intendeth to give in exchange for that which he requireth. It must be viewed and considered by the other party, that he may judge of the value; for without knowing what it is he cannot determine whether he shall take or leave it. An assertion in general, that it shall be as good or a better thing, is not in this a sufficient excuse for the mistake of dealing upon such uncertain terms. In all things that are dark and not enough explained, suspicion naturally followeth; a secret generally implieth a defect or a deceit, and if a false light is an objection, no light at all is yet a greater. To pretend to give a

better thing, and to refuse to show it, is very near saying it is not so good a one; at least so it will be taken in common construction. A mystery is yet a more discouraging thing to a Protestant, especially if the proposition should come from a Papist; it being one of his great objections to that Church, that there are so many of them invisible and impossible, which are so violently thrust upon their understandings that they are overlaid with them. They think that rational creatures are to be convinced only by reason, and that reason must be visible and freely exposed; else they will think themselves used with contempt instead of equality, and will never allow such a suspected secrecy to be a fit preface to a real *Equivalent*.

14. In matters of contract, not only the present value but the contingencies and consequences, as far as they can be fairly supposed, are to be considered. For example, if there should be a possibility that one of the parties may be ruined by accepting, and the other only disappointed by his refusing, the consequences are so extremely unequal that it is not imaginable a man should take that for an *Equivalent* which hath such a fatal possibility at the heels of it.

If it should happen in a public case, that such a proposal should come from the minor part of an assembly or nation to the greater, it is very just that the hazard of such a possibility should more or less likely fall upon the lesser part, rather than upon the greater, for whose sake and advantage things are and must be calculated in all public constitutions. Suppose in any mixed Government the chief magistrate should propose upon a condition, in the Senate, Diet, or other supreme Assembly, either to enact or abrogate one or more laws, by which a possibility might be let in of destroying their religion and property, which in other language signifieth no less than soul and body; where could be the *Equivalent* in the case, not only for the real loss, but even for the fear of losing them? Men can fall no lower than to lose all, and if losing all destroyeth them, the venturing all must fright them.

In an instance when men are secure that how far soever they may be over-run by violence yet they can never be undone by law, except they give their assistance to make it possible; though it should neither be likely nor intended, still the consequence which may happen is too big for any present thing to make amends for it. Whilst the word *possible* remaineth, it must forbid the bargain. Wherever it falleth out, therefore, that in an example of a public nature the changing, enacting, or repealing a law may naturally tend to the misplacing the legislative power in the hands of those who have a separate interest from the body of a People, there can be no treating till it is demonstrably made out that such a consequence shall be absolutely impossible. For if that shall be denied by those who make the proposal, if it is because they cannot do it, the motion at first was very unfair. If they can and will not, it would be yet less reasonable to expect that such partial dealers would ever give an *Equivalent* fit to be accepted.

15. It is necessary in all dealing to be assured in the first place that the party proposing is in a condition to make good his offer; that he is neither under any former obligations or pretended claims which may render him incapable of performing it; else he is so far in the condition of a minor, that whatever he disposeth by sale or exchange may be afterwards resumed, and the contract becometh void, being originally defective for want of a sufficient legal power in him that made it.

In the case of a strict settlement, where the party is only tenant for life,[5] there is no possibility of treating with one under such fetters; no purchase or exchange of lands or anything else can be good, where there is such an incapacity of making out a title, the interest vested in him being so limited, that he can do little more than pronounce the words of a contract, he can by no means perform the effect of it.

In more public instances, the impossibility is yet more express; as suppose in any kingdom where the people have so much liberty left them as that they may make contracts with the Crown, there should be some peculiar rights claimed to be so fixed to the royal function that no king for the time being could have power to part

5. The strict settlement, on the marriage of the heir, settled the estate on *his* heir, when he should be born. If the heir was born before his grandfather died, his father and grandfather were never more than tenants of estates which they apparently owned.

with them, being so fundamentally tied to the office that they can never be separated. Such rights can upon no occasion be received in exchange for anything the Crown may desire from the people: that can never be taken in payment which cannot lawfully be given, so that if they should part with that which is required upon those terms it must be a gift, it cannot be a bargain.

There is not in the whole dictionary a more intractable word than *inherent*, and less to be reconciled to the word *Equivalent*.

The party that will contract in spite of such a claim is content to take what is impossible to grant, and if he complaineth of his disappointment, he neither can have remedy, nor deserveth it.

If a right so claimed happeneth to be of so comprehensive a nature as that by a clear inference it may extend to everything else, as well as to the particular matter in question, as often as the supreme magistrate shall be so disposed, there can in that case be no treating with a prerogative that swalloweth all the right the people can pretend to; and if they have no right to anything of which they are possessed it is a jest, and not a bargain, to observe any formality in parting with it.

A claim may be so stated that, by the power and advantage of interpreting, it shall have such a murdering eye, that if it looketh upon a law, like a basilisk it shall strike it dead. Where is the possibility of treating, where such a right is assumed? Nay, let it be supposed that such a claim is not well founded in law, and that upon a free disquisition it could not be made out; yet even in this case, none that are well advised will conclude a bargain till it is fully stated and cleared, or indeed, so much as engage in a treaty, till by way of preliminary all possibility shall be removed of any trouble or dispute.

16. There is a collateral circumstance in making a contract, which yet deserveth to be considered as much as anything that belongeth to it; and that is the character and figure of the parties contracting—if they treat only by themselves, and if by others, the qualifications of the instruments they employ.

The proposer especially must not be so low as to want credit, nor so raised as to carry him above the reach of ordinary dealing;

in the first there is scandal, in the other, danger. There is no rule without some exception, but generally speaking the means should be suited to the end, and since all men who treat pretend an equal bargain, it is desirable that there may be equality in the persons as well as in the thing.

The manner of doing things hath such an influence upon the matter, that men may guess at the end by the instruments that are used to obtain it, who are a very good direction how far to rely upon or suspect the sincerity of that which is proposed. An absurdity in the way of carrying on a treaty in any one circumstance, if it is very gross, is enough to persuade a thinking man to break off, and take warning from such an ill appearance. Some things are so glaring that it is impossible not to see, and consequently not to suspect them; as suppose in a private case, there should be a treaty of marriage between two honourable families, and the proposing side should think fit to send a woman that had been carted,[6] to persuade the young lady to an approbation and consent; the unfitness of the messenger must naturally dispose the other party to distrust the message, and to resist the temptation of the best match that could be offered, when conveyed by that hand and ushered in by such a discouraging preliminary.

In a public instance the suspicion arising from unfit mediators still groweth more reasonable, in proportion as the consequence is much greater of being deceived. If a Jew should be employed to solicit all sorts of Christians to unite and agree, the contrariety of his profession would not allow men to stay till they heard his arguments; they would conclude from his religion that either the man himself was mad, or that he thought those to be so whom he had the impudence to endeavour to persuade.

Or suppose an Adamite[7] should be very solicitous and active, in all places, and with all sorts of persons, to settle the Church of England in particular, and a fair liberty of conscience for all Dis-

6. Paraded in a cart, the standard punishment for prostitutes.

7. The Adamites were a mediaeval sect who adopted the nakedness of Adam. By this time it had become a term of abuse for various 'enthusiastic' Protestant sects, and here Halifax may be sneering at the Quakers, who were accused of Adamite tendencies.

senters. Though nothing in the world has more to be said for it than naked truth, yet if such a man should run up and down without clothes, let his arguments be never so good, or his commission never so authentic, his figure would be such a contradiction to his business, that how serious soever that might be in itself, his interposition would make a jest of it.

Though it should not go so far as this, yet if men have contrarieties in their way of living not to be reconciled; as if they should pretend infinite zeal for liberty, and at that time be in great favour and employed by those who will not endure it; if they are affectedly singular, and conform to the generality of the world in no one thing but in playing the knave; if demonstration is a familiar word with them, most especially where the thing is impossible; if they quote authority to supply their want of sense, and justify the value of their arguments not by reason but by their being paid for them – in which, by the way, those who pay them have probably a very melancholy *Equivalent*; if they brandish a Prince's word like a sword in a crowd, to make way for their own impertinence, and in dispute, as criminals formerly fled to the statue of the Prince for sanctuary, if they should now, when baffled, creep under the protection of a king's name, where out of respect they are no farther to be pursued – in these cases, though the prospositions should be really good, they will be corrupted by passing through such conduits, and it would be a sufficient mistake to enter into a treaty; but it would be little less than madness from such hands to expect an *Equivalent*.

17. Having touched upon these particulars as necessary in order to the stating the nature of an equal bargain, and the circumstances belonging to it, let it now be examined in two or three instances, what things are not to be admitted by way of contract, to pass under the name of an *Equivalent*.

First, though it will be allowed that in the general corruption of mankind, which will not admit justice alone to be a sufficient tie to make good a contract, that a punishment added for the breach of it is a fitting or rather a necessary circumstance, yet it does not follow that in all cases a great penalty upon the party offending is an absolute and an entire security. It must be considered in every particular case how far the circumstances may rationally lead a man to rely more or less upon it.

In a private instance, the penalty inflicted upon the breach of contract must be, first, such a one as the party injured can enforce, and secondly, such a one as he will enforce, when it is in his power.

If the offending party is in a capacity of hindering the other from bringing the vengeance of the law upon him; if he hath strength or privilege sufficient to overrule the letter of the contract; in that case a penalty is but a word, there is no consequence belonging to it. Secondly, the forfeiture or punishment must be such as the man aggrieved will take. For example, if upon a bargain one of the parties shall stipulate to subject himself, in case of his failure, to have his ears cut or his nose slit by the other, with security given that he shall not be prosecuted for executing this part of the agreement, the penalty is no doubt heavy enough to discourage a man from breaking his contract; but on the other side it is of such a kind that the other, how much soever he may be provoked, will not in cold blood care to inflict it. Such an extravagant clause would seem to be made only for show and sound, and no man would think himself safer by a thing which one way or other is sure to prove ineffectual.

In a public case, suppose in a government so constituted that a law may be made in the nature of a bargain, it is in itself no more than a dead letter, the life is given to it by the execution of what it containeth; so that let it in itself be never so perfect, it dependeth upon those who are entrusted with seeing it observed.

If it is in any country, where the chief magistrate chooseth the judges and the judges interpret the laws, a penalty in any one particular law can have no effect but what is precarious. It may have a loud voice to threaten, but it has not an hand to give a blow; for as long as the governing power is in possession of this prerogative, let who will choose the meat, if they choose the cooks, it is they that will give the taste to it. So that it is clear that the rigour of a penalty will not in all cases fix a bargain, neither is it universally a true position that the increase of punishment for the breach of a new law is an *Equivalent* for the consent to part with an old one.

18. In most bargains there is a reference to the time to come, which is therefore to be considered as well as that which cometh within the compass of the present valuation.

Where the party contracting hath not a full power to dispose what belongeth to him or them in reversion, who shall succeed after him in his right, he cannot make any part of what is so limited to be the condition of the contract. Further, he cannot enjoin the heir or successor to forbear the exercise of any right that is inherent to him, as he is a man; neither can he restrain him, without his own consent, from doing any act which in itself is lawful, and liable to no objection. For example, a father cannot stipulate with any other man that in consideration of such a thing done, or to be done, his son shall never marry; because marriage is an institution established by the laws of God and Man, and therefore nobody can be so restrained by any power from doing such an act, when he thinketh fit, being warranted by an authority that is not to be controlled.

19. Now, as there are rights inherent in men's persons in their single capacities, there are rights as much fixed to the body politic, which is a creature that never dieth. For instance, there can be no government without a Supreme Power; that power is not always in the same hands, it is in different shapes and dresses, but still, wherever it is lodged, it must be unlimited; it hath a jurisdiction over everything else, but it cannot have it above itself. Supreme Power can no more be limited than infinity can be measured, because it ceaseth to be the thing; its very being is dissolved when any bounds can be put to it.

Where this Supreme Power is mixed, or divided, the shape only differeth, the argument is still the same.

The present State of Venice cannot restrain those who succeed them in the same power from having an entire and unlimited sovereignty; they may indeed make present laws which shall retrench their present power, if they are so disposed, and those laws, if not repealed by the same authority that enacted them, are to be observed by the succeeding Senate till they think fit to abrogate them, and no longer. For if the Supreme Power shall still reside in the Senate, perhaps composed of other men, or of other minds (which will be sufficient) the necessary consequence is, that one Senate must have as much right to alter such a law as another could have to make it.

20. Suppose the Supreme Power in any state should make a law to enjoin all subsequent law makers to take an oath never to alter it, it would produce these following absurdities.

First, all Supreme Power being instituted to promote the safety and benefit, and to prevent the prejudice and danger which may fall upon those who live under the protection of it, the consequence of such an oath would be, that all men who are so trusted shall take God to witness, that such a law once made, being judged at the time to be advantageous for the public, though afterwards by the vicissitude of times, or the variety of accidents or interests, it should plainly appear to them to be destructive, they will suffer it to have its course, and will never repeal it.

Secondly, if there could in any nation be found a set of men who, having a part in the supreme legislative power, should as much as in them lieth betray their country by such a criminal engagement, so directly opposite to the nature of their power, and to the trust reposed in them; if these men have their power only for life, when they are dead such an oath can operate no farther; and though that would be too long a lease for the life of such a monster as an oath so composed, yet it must then certainly give up the ghost. It could bind none but the first makers of it, another generation would never be tied up by it.

Thirdly, in those countries where the supreme assemblies are not constant standing courts, but called together upon occasions, and composed of such as the people choose for that time only, with a trust and character that remaineth no longer with them than till that assembly is regularly dissolved; such an oath taken by the members of a senate, diet, or other assembly so chosen, can have very little effect, because at the next meeting there may be quite another set of men who will be under no obligation of that kind. The eternity intended to that law by those that made it, will be cut off by new men who shall succeed them in their power, if they have a differing taste, or another interest.

21. To put it yet farther, suppose a clause in such a law, that it shall be criminal in the last degree for any man chosen in a subsequent assembly to propose the repealing of it; and since nothing can be enacted which is not first proposed, by this means it seemeth as if a law might be created which should never die. But let this be examined.

First, such a clause would be so destructive to the being of such a Constitution, as that it would be as reasonable to say that a king had right to give or sell his kingdom to a foreign prince, as that any number of men who are entrusted with the Supreme Power, or any part of it, should have a right to impose such shackles upon the liberty of those who are to succeed them in the same trust. The ground of that trust is, that every man who is chosen into such an assembly is to do all that in him lieth for the good of those who chose him. The English of such a clause would be, that he is not to do his best for those that chose him, because though he should be convinced that it might be very fatal to continue that law, and therefore very necessary to repeal it, yet he must not repeal it, because it is made a crime, and attended with a penalty.

But secondly, to show the emptiness as well as injustice of such a clause, it is clear that although such an invasion of right should be imposed, it will never be obeyed. There will only be deformity in the monster, it will neither sting nor bite. Such law givers would only have the honour of attempting a contradiction which can never have any success; for, as such a law in itself would be a madness, so the penalty would be a jest; which may be thus made out.

22. A law that carrieth in itself reason enough to support it is so far from wanting the protection of such a clause, or from needing to take such an extraordinary receipt for long life, that the admitting it must certainly be the likeliest and the shortest way to destroy it. Such a clause in a law must imply an opinion that the greatest part of mankind is against it, since it is impossible such an exorbitance should be done for its own sake; the end of it must be to force men by a penalty to that which they could not be persuaded to whilst their reason is left at liberty. This position being granted, which I think can hardly be denied, put the case that a law should be made

with this imaginary clause of immortality, after which another assembly is chosen, and if the majority of the electors shall be against this law, the greater part of the elected must be so too, if the choice is fair and regular; which must be presumed, since the supposition of the contrary is not to come within this argument. When these men shall meet, the majority will be visible beforehand of those who are against such a law, so that there will be no hazard to any single man in proposing the repeal of it, when he cannot be punished but by the majority, and he hath such a kind of assurance as cometh near a demonstration, that the greater number will be of his mind, and consequently, that for their own sakes they will secure him from any danger.

For these reasons, wherever in order to the making a bargain a proposition is advanced to make a new law, which is to tie up those who neither can nor will be bound by it, it may be a good jest, but it will never be a good *Equivalent.*

23. In the last place, let it be examined how far a promise ought to be taken for a security in a bargain.

There is great variety of methods for the security of those that deal, according to their dispositions and interests; some are binding, others inducing circumstances, and are to be so distinguished.

First, ready payment is without exception, so of that there can be no dispute. In default of that, the good opinion men may have of one another is a great ingredient to supply the want of immediate performances. Where the trust is grounded upon inclination only the generosity is not always returned, but where it springeth from a long experience it is a better foundation, and yet that is not always secure. In ordinary dealing one promise may be an *Equivalent* to another, but it is not so for a thing actually granted or conveyed; especially if the thing required in exchange for it is of great value, either in itself or in its consequences. A bare promise as a single security in such a case is not an equal proposal; if it is offered by way of addition, it generally giveth cause to doubt the title is crazy, where so slender a thing is brought in to be a supplement.

24. The earnest of making good a promise, must be such a behaviour

preceding as may encourage the party to whom it is made to depend upon it. Where instead of that there hath been want of kindness and, which is worse, an invasion of right, a promise hath no persuading force; and till the objection to such a proceeding is forgotten (which can only be the work of time), and the skin is a little grown over the tender part, the wound must not be touched. There must be some intermission at least to abate the smart of unkind usage, or else a promise in the eye of the party injured is so far from strengthening a security that it raiseth more doubts, and giveth more justifiable cause to suspect it.

A word is not like a bone that, being broken and well set again, is said to be sometimes stronger in that very part; it is far from being so in a word given and not made good. Every single act either weakeneth or improveth our credit with other men; and as an habit of being just to our word will confirm, so an habit of too freely dispensing with it must necessarily destroy it. A promise hath its effect to persuade a man to lay some weight upon it, where the promiser hath not only the power, but may reasonably be supposed to have the will of performing it; and further, that there be no visible interest of the party promising to excuse himself from it, or to evade it.

All obligations are comparative, and where they seem to be opposite, or between the greater and the lesser, which of them ought to have precedence in all respects every man is apt to be his own judge.

25. If it should fall out that the promiser, with full intent at the time to perform, might by the interposition of new arguments, or differing advice, think himself obliged to turn the matter of conscience on the other side, and should look upon it to be much a greater fault to keep his word than to break it; such a belief will untie the strictest promise that can be made, and though the party thus absolving himself should do it without the mixture or temptation of private interest, being moved to it merely by his conscience, as then informed; yet how far soever that might diminish the fault in him, it would in no degree lessen the inconveniences to the party who is disappointed, by the breach of an engagement upon which he relied.

26. A promise is to be understood in the plain and natural sense of the words, and to be sure not in his who made it, if it was given as part of a bargain. That would be like giving a man power to raise the value of his money in the payment of his debt, by which, though he paid but half or less, he might pretend according to the letter to have made good the contract.

The power of interpreting a promise entirely taketh away the virtue of it. A merchant who should once assume that privilege would save himself the trouble of making any more bargains.

It is still worse if this jurisdiction over a man's promise should be lodged in hands that have power to support such an extraordinary claim; and if in other cases forbearing to deal upon those terms is advisable, in this it becometh absolutely necessary.

27. There must in all respects be a full liberty to claim a promise, to make it reasonable to take it in any part of payment; else it would be like agreeing for a rent, and at the same time making it criminal to demand it.

A superiority of dignity or power in the party promising maketh it a more tender thing for the other party to treat upon that security. The first maketh it a nice thing to claim, the latter maketh it a difficult thing to obtain.

In some cases, a promise is in the nature of a covenant, and then between equal parties the breach of it will bear a suit; but where the greatness of the promiser is very much raised above the level of equality, there is no forfeiture to be taken. It is so far from the party grieved his being able to sue or recover damages, that he will not be allowed to explain or expostulate, and instead of his being relieved against the breach of promise, he will run the hazard of being punished for breach of good manners. Such a difficulty is putting all or part of the payment in the fire, where men must burn their fingers before they can come at it.

That cannot properly be called good payment which the party to whom it is due may not receive with ease and safety. It was a King's brother of England who refused to lend the Pope money, for this reason. That he would never take the bond of one upon whom he could not distrain.

The argument is still stronger against the validity of a promise, when the contract is made between a prince and a subject. The very offering a king's word in mortgage is rather a threatening in case of refusal than an inducing argument to accept it; it is unfair at first, and by that giveth greater cause to be cautious, especially if a thing of that value and dignity as a king's word ought to be should be put into the hands of state-brokers to strike up a bargain with it.

28. When God Almighty maketh covenants with mankind, his promise is a sufficient security, notwithstanding his superiority and his power; because first, he can neither err nor do injustice. It is the only exception to his omnipotence, that by the perfection of his being he is incapacitated to do wrong. Secondly, at the instant of his promise, by the extent of his foresight, which cannot fail, there is no room left for the possibility of anything to intervene which might change his mind. Lastly, he is above the receiving either benefit or inconvenience, and therefore can have no interest or temptation to vary from his word, when once he hath granted it.

Now though Princes are God's vicegerents, yet, their commission not being so large as that these qualifications are devolved to them, it is quite another case and since the offering a security implieth it to be examined by the party to whom it is proposed, it must not be taken ill that objections are made to it, even though the Prince himself should be the immediate proposer.

Let a familiar case be put. Suppose a Prince, tempted by a passion too strong for him to resist, should descend so as to promise marriage to one of his subjects, and as men are naturally in great haste upon such occasions, should press to take possession before the necessary forms could be complied with; would the poor lady's scruples be called criminal for not taking the security of the royal word? Or would her allegiance be tainted by her resisting the sacred person of her sovereign, because he was impatient of delay? Courtesy in this case might persuade her to accept it, if she was so disposed, but sure the just exercise of power can never claim it.[5]

5. Almost certainly this is a reflection on James II's first wife, Anne Hyde, who was pregnant when he married her in 1661.

29. There is one case where it is more particularly a duty to use very great caution in accepting the security of a promise, and that is when men are authorised and trusted by others to act for them. This putteth them under much greater restraints than those who are at liberty to treat for themselves. It is lawful, though it is not prudent, for any man to make an ill bargain for himself, but it is neither the one nor the other where the party contracting treateth on behalf of another, by whom he is intrusted. Men who will unwarily accept an ill security if it is for themselves, forfeit their own discretion, and undergo the penalty, but they are not responsible to anybody else. They lie under the mortification and the loss of committing the error, by which though they may expose their judgment to some censure, yet their morality suffers no reproach by it.

But those who are deputed by others to treat for them upon terms of best advantage, though the confidence placed in them should prevent the putting any limits to their power in their commission, yet the condition implied if not expressed, is that the persons so trusted shall neither make an ill bargain nor accept a slight security.

The obligation is yet more binding when the trust is of a public nature. The aggravation of disappointing a body of men that rely upon them carrieth the fault as high as it can go, and perhaps no crime of any kind can outdo such a deliberate breach of trust, or would more justly make men forfeit the protection of human society.

30. I will add one thing more upon this head, which is, that it is not always a true proposition, that it is safe to rely upon a promise if at the time of making it it is the interest of the promiser to make it good. This, though many times it is a good inducement, yet it hath these exceptions to it. First, if the proposer hath at other times gone plainly against his visible interest, the argument will turn the other way, and his former mistakes are so many warnings to others not to come within the danger of any more. Let the inducements to those mistakes be never so great and generous, that does not alter the nature, they are mistakes still.

Interest is an uncertain thing, it goeth and cometh, and varieth according to times and circumstances; as good build upon a quicksand, as upon a presumption that interest shall not alter. Where are the men so distinguished from the rest of mankind, that it is impossible for them to mistake their interest? Who are they that have such an exemption from human frailty, as that it can never happen to them not to their interest for want of understanding, or not to leap over it by excess of zeal.

Above all, Princes are the most liable to mistake; not out of any defect in their nature, which might put them under such an unfortunate distinction – quite contrary, the blood they derive from wise and great ancestors doth rather distinguish them on the better side, besides that their great character and office of governing giveth a noble exercise to their reason which can very hardly fail to raise and improve it. But there is one circumstance annexed to their glorious calling which in this respect is sufficient to outweigh all those advantages; it is that mankind, divided in most things else, agree in this, to conspire in their endeavours to deceive and mislead them, which maketh it above the power of human understanding to be exactly guarded as never to admit a surprise, and the highest applause that could ever yet be given to the greatest men that ever wore a crown is that they were no oftener deceived.

Thus I have ventured to lay down my thoughts of the nature of a bargain, and the due circumstances belonging to an *Equivalent*, and will now conclude with this short word: 'Where distrusting may be the cause of provoking anger, and trusting may be the cause of bringing ruin, the choice is too easy to need the being explained.'

MAXIMS OF STATE

EDITORIAL INTRODUCTION

These maxims circulated in manuscript in 1692, perhaps earlier, and were published as a broadsheet in 1693, with the catchpenny title 'Maxims found amongst the papers of the great Almansor'. They received their present title, and were acknowledged as Halifax's, when they were reprinted in the *Miscellanies* of 1700.

MAXIMS OF STATE

1. THAT a Prince who falleth out with laws breaketh with his best friends.

2. That the exalting his own authority above his laws is like letting in his enemy to surprise his guards; the laws are the only guards he can be sure will never run away from him.

3. A Prince that will say he can do no good except he may do everything teacheth the People to say they are slaves if they must not do whatever they have a mind to.

4. That Power and Liberty are like heat and moisture; where they are well mixed, everything prospers; where they are single, they are destructive.

5. That Arbitrary Power is like most other things that are very hard, they are also very apt to break.

6. That the profit of places should be measured as they are more or less conducing to the public service; and if business is more necessary than splendour, the instrument of it ought in proportion to be better paid. That the contrary method is as impertinent as it would be to let the carving of a ship cost more than all the rest of it.

7. That where the least useful part of the People have the most credit with the Prince men will conclude that the way to get everything is to be good for nothing.

8. That an extravagant gift to one man raiseth the market to everybody else; so that in consequence the unlimited bounty of an unthinking Prince maketh him a beggar, let him have never so much money.

9. That if ordinary beggars are whipped, the daily beggars in fine clothes (out of a proportionable respect to their quality) ought to be hanged.

10. That pride is as loud a beggar as want, and a great deal more saucy.

11. That a Prince who will give more to importunity than merit had as good set out a proclamation to all his loving subjects, forbidding them to do well upon the penalty of being undone by it.

12. That a wise Prince will not oblige his courtiers, who are birds of prey, so as to disoblige his People, who are beasts of burden.

13. That it is safer for a Prince to judge of men by what they do to one another, than what they do to him.

14. That it is a gross mistake to think that a knave between man and man can be honest to a king, whom of all other men generally make the least scruple to deceive.[1]

15. That a Prince who can ever trust the man that hath once deceived him loseth the right of being faithfully dealt with by any other person.

16. That it is not possible for a Prince to find out such an honest knave as will let nobody else cheat him.

17. That if a Prince doth not show an aversion to knaves, there will be an inference that will be very natural, let it be never so unmannerly.

18. That a Prince who followeth his own opinion too soon is in danger of repenting it too late.

19. That it is less dangerous for a Prince to mind too much what the People say than too little.

20. That a Prince is to take care that the greater part of the People may not be angry at the same time; for though the first beginning of their ill humour should be against one another, yet if not stopped, it will naturally end in anger against him.

21. That if Princes would reflect how much they are in the power of their ministers, they would be more circumspect in the choice of them.

22. That a wise Prince will support good servants against men's anger, and not support ill ones against their complaint.

23. That Parties in a state generally, like freebooters, hang out false colours; the pretence is the public good, the real business is to catch prizes. Like the Tartars, wherever they succeed, instead of improving their victory they presently fall upon the baggage.

24. That a Prince may play so long between two parties, that they may in time join together, and be in earnest with him.

1. This and the next three maxims may refer to Sunderland, James II's first minister, who reappeared at Court in 1692.

25. That there is more dignity in open violence, than in the unskilful cunning of a Prince who goeth about to impose upon the People.

26. That the People will ever suspect the remedies for the diseases of the state where they are wholly excluded from seeing how they are prepared.

27. That changing hands without changing measures is as if a drunkard in a dropsy should change his doctors and not his diet.

28. That a Prince is to watch that his reason may not be so subdued by his nature, as not to be so much a man of peace as to be a jest in an army, nor so much a man of war as to be out of his element in his Council.

29. That a man who cannot mind his own business is not to be trusted with the King's.

30. That quality alone should only serve to make a show in the embroidered part of the government; but that ignorance, though never so well born, should never be admitted to spoil the public business.

31. That he who thinks his place below him will certainly be below his place.

32. That when a Prince's example ceaseth to have the force of a law, it is a sure sign that his power is wasting, and that there is but little distance between men's neglecting to imitate and their refusing to obey.

33. That a People may let a King fall, yet still remain a People; but if a King let his People slip from him, he is no longer King.

A ROUGH DRAFT OF A NEW MODEL AT SEA

EDITORIAL INTRODUCTION

I am inclined to agree with Miss Foxcroft that this pamphlet was probably written in 1666 or 1667, not only because of Halifax's referring to himself as a 'man without doors' (p. 161 below), that is, outside Parliament, but because of the whole tone of the concluding paragraph. Also, the dispute between gentlemen captains and those who had risen from the ranks ('tarpaulins'), was particularly hot during the 1660s, and not during the 1690s, when more pressing problems of general naval strategy were paramount. Halifax may have published it in order to establish his views on the comparative virtues of absolute and limited monarchy, in a passage (p. 154 below) added for the occasion, or he may have intended it as an oblique attack on the Whig Junto leader Admiral Hon. Edward Russel.

A ROUGH DRAFT OF A NEW MODEL AT SEA

I WILL make no other introduction to the following discourse, than that as the importance of our being strong at sea was ever very great, so in our present circumstances it is grown to be much greater; because, as formerly our force of shipping contributed greatly to our trade and safety, so now it is become indispensably necessary to our very being.

It may be said now to England, Martha, Martha, thou art busy about many things, but one thing is necessary. To the question, What shall we do to be saved in this world? there is no other answer but this, Look to your moat.

The first article of an Englishman's political creed must be, that he believeth in the sea, &c.; without that there needeth no General Council to pronounce him incapable of salvation here.

We are in an island, confined to it by God Almighty not as a penalty but a grace, and one of the greatest that can be given to mankind. Happy confinement, that hath made us free, rich, and quiet; a fair portion in this world, and very well worth the preserving; a figure that ever hath been envied, and could never be imitated, by our neighbours. Our situation hath made greatness abroad by land conquests unnatural things to us. It is true, we have made excursions, and glorious ones too, which make our names great in history, but they did not last.

Admit the English to be giants in courage, yet they must not hope to succeed in making war against Heaven, which seemeth to have enjoined them to acquiesce in being happy within their own circle. It is no paradox to say that England hath its root in the sea, and a deep one too, from whence it sendeth its branches into both the Indies. We may say further in our present case, that if allegiance is due to protection, ours to the sea is due from that rule, since by that, and by that alone, we are to be protected; and if we have of late suffered usurpation of other methods, contrary to the homage we owe to that which must preserve us, it is time now to restore the sea to its right; and as there is no repentance effectual without amendment, so there is not a moment to be lost in the going about it.

It is not pretended to launch into such a voluminous treatise as to set down everything to which so comprehensive a subject might lead me; for as the sea hath little less variety in it than the land, so the naval force of England extendeth itself into a great many branches, each of which are important enough to require a discourse apart, and peculiarly applied to it. But there must be preference to some considerations above others, when the weight of them is so visibly superior that it cannot be contested. It is there, first, that the foundations are to be laid of our naval economy. Amongst these, there is one article which in its own nature must be allowed to be the corner-stone of the building: the choice of officers, with the discipline and encouragement belonging to them. Upon this head only, I shall then take the liberty to venture my opinion into the world, with a real submission to those who may offer anything better for the advantage of the public.

The first question then will be, Out of what sort of men the Officers of the Fleet are to be chosen? And this immediately leadeth us to the present controversy between the Gentlemen and the Tarpaulins.

The usual objections on both sides are too general to be relied upon. Partiality and common prejudices direct most men's opinions, without entering into the particular reasons which ought to be the ground of it. There is so much ease in acquiescing in generals, that the ignorance of those who cannot distinguish, and the largeness of those who will not, maketh men very apt to decline the trouble of stricter enquiries, which they think too great a price for being in the right, let it be never so valuable.

This maketh them judge in the lump, and either let their opinions swim along with the stream of the world, or give them up wholly to be directed by success. The effect of this is, that they change their minds upon every present uneasiness, wanting a steady foundation upon which their judgment should be formed. This is a perching upon the twigs of things, and not going to the root. But sure the matter in question deserveth to be examined in another manner, since so much dependeth upon it.

To state the thing impartially, it must be owned that it seemeth to lie fairest for the Tarpaulin. It giveth an impression that must have so much weight as to make a man's opinion lean very much on that side, it carrieth so much authority with it, it seemeth to be so unquestionable, that those are fittest to command at sea who have not only made it their calling but their element; that there must naturally be a prejudice to anything that can be said against it. There must therefore be some reason extraordinary to support the argument on the other side, or else the Gentlemen could never enter the lists against such a violent objection, which seemeth not to be resisted. I will introduce my argument with an assertion, which as I take to be true almost in all Cases, so it is necessary to be explained and enforced in this. The assertion is, that there is hardly a single proposition to be made which is not deceitful, and the tying our reason too close to it may in many cases be destructive. Circumstances must come in, and are to be made a part of the matter of which we are to judge; positive decisions are always dangerous, more especially in politics. A man who will be master of an argument must do like a skilful general, who sendeth scouts on all sides, to see whether there may not be an enemy. So he must look round to see what objections can be made, and not go on in a straight line, which is the ready way to lead him into a mistake.

Before, then, that we conclude what sort of men are fittest to command at sea, a principle is to be laid down, that there is a differing consideration to be had of such a subject-matter, as is in itself distinct and independent, and of such an one as being a limb of a body, or a wheel of a frame, there is a necessity of suiting it to the rest, and preserving the harmony of the whole. A man must not in that case restrain himself to the separate consideration of that single part, but must take care it may fall in and agree with the shape of the whole creature of which it is a member. According to this proposition, which I take to be indisputable, it will not I hope appear an affectation, or an extravagant fit of unseasonable politics, if, before I enter into the particular state of the present question, I say something of the Government of England, and make that the ground-work of what sort of men are most proper to be made use of to command at sea.

The forms of government to which England must be subjected are either Absolute Monarchy, a Commonwealth, or a Mixed Monarchy, as it is now; with those natural alterations that the exigency of affairs may from time to time suggest. As to Absolute Monarchy, I will not allow myself to be transported into such invectives as are generally made against it; neither am I ready to enter into the aggravating style of calling everything slavery that restraineth men in any part of their freedom; one may discern in this, as in most other things, the good and bad of it. We see by too near an instance, what France doth by it; it doth not only struggle with the rest of Christendom, but is in a fair way of giving law to it.

This is owing in great measure to a despotic and undivided power; the uncontrollable authority of the directive councils maketh everything move without disorder or opposition, which must give an advantage that is plain enough of itself, without being proved by the melancholy experience we have of it at this time.

I see and admire this; yet I consider at the same time that all things of this kind are comparative: that as on one side without government men cannot enjoy what belongeth to them in particular, nor can a nation be secure, or preserve itself in general; so on the other side, the end of government being that mankind should live in some competent state of freedom, it is very unnatural to have the end destroyed by the means that were originally made use of to attain it. In this respect something is to be ventured, rather than submit to such a precarious state of life as would make it a burden to a reasonable creature; and therefore, after I have owned the advantages in some kind of an unlimited government, yet, while they are attended with so many other discouraging circumstances I cannot think but that they may be bought too dear; and if it should be so, that it is not possible for a state to be great and glorious unless the subjects are wretchedly miserable, I am not ashamed to own my low-spirited frailty, in preferring such a model of government as may agree with the reasonable enjoyment of a free people before such a one by which empire is to be extended at such an unnatural price. Besides, whatever men's opinions may be one way or another in the general question, there is an argument in our case that shutteth the door to any answer to it: viz., we cannot subsist under a despotic power, our very being would be destroyed by it. For we are to consider, we are a very little spot in the map of the world, and make a great figure only by trade, which is the creature of liberty; one destroyed, the other falleth to the ground by a natural consequence that will not admit a dispute. If we would be measured by our acres, we are poor inconsiderable people; we are exalted above our natural bounds by our good laws and our excellent constitution. By this we are not only happy at home, but considerable abroad. Our situation, our humour, our trade, do all concur to strengthen this argument. So that all other reasons must give place to such a one as maketh it out, that there is no mean between a free nation and no nation.

We are no more a people, nor England can no longer keep its name, from the moment that our liberties are extinguished; the vital strength that should support us being withdrawn, we should then be no more than the carcass of a nation, with no other security than that of contempt; and to subsist upon no other tenure than that we should be below the giving temptation to our stronger neighbours to devour us. In my judgment, therefore, there is such a short decision to be made upon this subject, that in relation to England, an Absolute Monarchy is as unreasonable a thing to be wished, as I hope it will be impossible to be obtained.

It must be considered in the next place, whether England is likely to be turned into a Commonwealth. It is hard at any time to determine what will be the shape of the next revolution, much more at this time would it be inexcusably arrogant to undertake it. Who can foresee whether it will be from without, or from within, or from both? Whether with or without the concurrence of the People? Whether regularly produced, or violently imposed? I shall not therefore magisterially declare it impossible that a Commonwealth should be settled here; but I may give my humble opinion, that according to all appearances it is very improbable.

I will first lay it down for a principle, that it is not a sound way of arguing to say that if it can be made out that the form of a

Commonwealth will best suit with the interest of the nation, it must for that reason of necessity prevail.

I will not deny but that *interest will not lie* is a right maxim, wherever it is sure to be understood; else one had as good affirm that no man in particular, nor mankind in general, can ever be mistaken. A nation is a great while before they can see, and generally they must feel first before their sight is quite cleared. This maketh it so long before they can see their interest, that for the most part it is too late for them to pursue it. If men must be supposed always to follow their true interest, it must be meant of a new manufactory of mankind by God Almighty; there must be some new clay, the old stuff never yet made any such infallible creature.

This being premised, it is to be inquired whether instead of inclination or a leaning towards a Commonwealth, there is not in England a general dislike to it. If this be so, as I take it to be, by a very great disparity in numbers, it will be in vain to dispute the reason whilst humour is against it. Allowing the weight that is due to the argument which may be alleged for it, yet if the herd is against it the going about to convince them would have no other effect than to show that nothing can be more impertinent than good reasons, when they are misplaced or ill-timed.

I must observe that there must be some previous dispositions in all great changes to facilitate and to make way for them. I think it not at all absurd to affirm, that such resolutions are seldom made at all except by the general preparations of men's minds they are half made before it is plainly visible that men go about them.

Though it seemeth to me that this argument alone maketh all others unnecessary, yet I must take notice that besides what hath been said upon this subject, there are certain preliminaries to the first building a Commonwealth, some materials absolutely necessary for the carrying on such a fabric, which at present are wanting amongst us; I mean virtue, morality, diligence, or at least hypocrisy. Now this age is so plain dealing as not to dissemble so far as to an outward pretence of qualities which seem at present so unfashionable, and under so much discountenance. From hence we may draw a plain and natural inference that a Commonwealth is not fit for us, because we are not fit for a Commonwealth.

This being granted, the supposition of this form of government of England, with all its consequences as to the present question, must be excluded and Absolute Monarchy having been so too by the reasons at once alleged, it will without further examination fall to a Mixed Government, as we now are. I will not say that there is never to be any alteration; the constitution of the several parts that concur to make up the frame of the present government may be altered in many things, in some for the better, and in others perhaps for the worse, according as circumstances shall arise to induce a change, and as passion and interest shall have more or less influence upon the public councils; but still, if it remaineth in the whole so far a Mixed Monarchy, that there shall be a restraint upon the Prince as to the exercise of a despotic power, it is enough to make it a groundwork for the present question. It appeareth then that a bounded Monarchy is that kind of Government which will most probably prevail and continue in England; from whence it must follow (as hath been hinted before) that every considerable part ought to be so composed as the better to conduce to the preserving the harmony of the whole constitution. The Navy is of so great importance that it would be disparaged by calling it less than the life and soul of government.

Therefore to apply the argument to the subject we are upon; in case the Officers be all Tarpaulins, it would be in reality too great a tendency to a Commonwealth. Such a part of the constitution being democratically disposed may be suspected to endeavour to bring it into that shape; and where the influence must be so strong, the supposition will be the more justifiable. In short, if the Maritime Force, which is the only thing that can defend us, should be wholly directed by the lower sort of men, with an entire exclusion of the Nobility and Gentry, it will not be easy to answer the arguments supported by so great a probability, that such a scheme would not only lean towards a Democracy, but directly lead us into it.

Let us now examine the contrary proposition, viz., that all officers should be Gentlemen.

Here the objection lieth so fair, of its introducing an Arbitrary Government, that it is as little to be answered in that respect as the former is in the other. Gentlemen in a general definition will be suspected to lie more than other men under the temptations of being made instruments of unlimited power; their relations, their way of living, their taste of the entertainments of the Court, inspire an ambition that generally draweth their inclinations toward it, besides the gratifying of their interests. Men of quality are often taken with the ornaments of government, the splendour dazzleth them, so as that their judgments are surprised by it; and there will be always some that have so little remorse for invading other men's liberties, that it maketh them less solicitous to preserve their own.

These things throw them naturally into such a dependance as might give a dangerous bias; if they alone were in command at sea, it would make that great wheel turn by an irregular motion, and instead of being the chief means of preserving the whole frame, might come to be the chief instruments to discompose and dissolve it.

The two former exclusive propositions being necessarily to be excluded in this question, there remaineth no other expedient, neither can any other conclusion be drawn from the argument as it hath been stated, than that there must be a mixture in the Navy of Gentlemen and Tarpaulins, as there is in the constitution of the government, of power and liberty. This mixture is not to be so rigorously defined as to set down the exact proportion there is to be of each; the greater or lesser number must be directed by circumstances, of which the government is to judge, and which make it improper to set such bounds as that upon no occasion it shall on either side be lessened or enlarged. It is possible the men of Wapping may think they are injured, by giving them any partners in the Dominion of the Sea; they may take it unkindly to be jostled in their own element by men of such a different education that they may be said to be of another species; they will be apt to think it an usurpation upon them, and notwithstanding the instances that are against them, and which give a kind of prescription on the other side, they will not easily acquiesce in what they conceive to be a hardship to them.

But I shall in a good measure reconcile myself to them by what follows; viz., the Gentlemen shall not be capable of bearing office at sea, except they be Tarpaulins too; that is to say, except they are so trained up by a continued habit of living at sea, that they may have a right to be admitted free denizens of Wapping. Upon this dependeth the whole matter; and indeed here lieth the difficulty, because the Gentlemen brought up under the connivance of a looser discipline, and of an easier admittance, will take it heavily to be reduced within the fetters of such a new model; and I conclude, they will be so extremely averse to that which they call an unreasonable yoke upon them, that their original consent is never to be expected. But if it appeareth to be convenient, and which is more, that it is necessary for the preservation of the whole, that it should be so, the Government must be called in aid to suppress these first boilings of discontent; the rules must be imposed with such authority, and the execution of them must be so well supported, that by degrees their impatience will be subdued, and they will concur in an establishment to which they will every day be more reconciled.

They will find it will take away the objections which are now thrown upon them, of setting up for masters without having ever been apprentices – or at least, without having served out their time.

Mankind naturally swelleth against favour and partiality; their belief of their own merit maketh men object them to a prosperous competitor, even when there is no pretence for it; but when there is the least handle offered, to be sure it will be taken. So in this case, when a Gentleman is preferred at sea, the Tarpaulin is very apt to impute it to friend or favour; but if that Gentleman hath before his preferment passed through all the steps which lead to it, so that he smelleth as much of pitch and tar as those that were swaddled in sail-cloth, his having an escutcheon will be so far from doing him harm, that it will set him upon the advantage ground; it will draw a real respect to his quality when so supported, and give him an influence and authority infinitely superior to that which the mere seaman can ever pretend to.

When a Gentleman hath learned how to obey, he will grow very much fitter to command; his own memory will advise him not to inflict too rigorous punishments. He will better resist the temptations of authority (which are great) when he reflecteth how much he hath at other times wished it might be gently exercised, when he was liable to the rigour of it.

When the undistinguished discipline of a ship hath tamed the young mastership which is apt to arise from a Gentleman's birth and education, he then groweth proud in the right place, and valueth himself first upon knowing his duty, and then upon doing it.

In plain English, men of quality in their several degrees must either restore themselves to a better opinion, both for morality and diligence, or else quality itself will be in danger of being extinguished.

The original Gentleman is almost lost in strictness; when posterity doth not still further adorn by their virtue the escutcheon their ancestors first got for them by their merit, they deserve the penalty of being deprived of it.

To expect that quality alone should waft men up into places and employments is as unreasonable as to think that a ship, because it is carved and gilded, should be fit to go to sea without sails or tackling. But when a Gentleman maketh no other use of his quality than to incite him the more to his duty, it will give such a true and settled superiority, as must destroy all competition from those that are below him.

It is time now to go to the probationary qualifications of an officer at sea; and I have some to offer which I have digested in my thoughts, I hope impartially, that they may not be speculative notions, but things easy and practicable, if the directing powers will give due countenance and encouragement to the execution of them. But whilst I am going about to set them down, though this little Essay was made to no other end than to introduce them, I am upon better recollection induced to put a restraint upon myself, and rather retract the promise I made at the beginning, than, by advising the particular methods by which I conceive the good end that is aimed at may be obtained, to incur the imputation of the thing of the world of which I would least be guilty, which is of anticipating, by my private opinion, the judgment of the Parliament, or seeming out of my slender stock of reason to dictate to the supreme wisdom of the nation. They will, no doubt, consider the present establishments for discipline at sea, which are many of them very good, and if well executed, might go a great way in the present question. But I will not say they are so perfect, but that others may be added to make them more effectual, and that some more supplemental expedients may be necessary to complete what is yet defective; and whenever the Parliament shall think fit to take this matter into their consideration, I am sure they will not want for their direction the auxiliary reasons of any man without doors, much less of one whose thoughts are so entirely and unaffectedly resigned to whatever they shall determine in this, or anything else relating to the public.

SOME CAUTIONS OFFERED

EDITORIAL INTRODUCTION

This trenchant pamphlet was written in anticipation of a General Election in the autumn of 1695; Halifax died in April of that year, so this is almost certainly his last work. It was printed twice in 1695, in the *Miscellanies* in 1700, 1704 and 1717, and again in 1796. A. F. Pollard included it in a collection of *Political Pamphlets* in 1897, and it also recommended itself to George Orwell, who printed extracts from it in a collection called *British Pamphleteers*, published in 1948.

SOME CAUTIONS OFFERED TO THE CONSIDERATION OF THOSE WHO ARE TO CHOOSE MEMBERS TO SERVE IN THE ENSUING PARLIAMENT

I WILL make no other introduction, than that it is hoped the Counties and Boroughs will remember in general that besides other consequences they will have the credit of a good choice, or the scandal that belongeth to an ill one. The creators will be thought like their creatures, and therefore an ill choice will either be a disparagement of their understanding or their morals. There cannot be a fuller approbation of a thing than the choosing of it, so that the fault of the Members chosen, if known beforehand, will be judged to be of the growth of that County or Borough after such a solemn approbation of them. In short, those who send up their representatives to Westminster should take care they may be such as will do them right and their country honour.

Now to the particulars.

1. *A very extraordinary earnestness to be chosen is no very good symptom.* A desire to serve the nation in Parliament is an Englishman's ambition, always to be encouraged and never to be disapproved. A man may not only be willing to stand, but he may declare that willingness to his friends, that they may assist him, and by all the means becoming a modest and prudent man he may endeavour to succeed, and prevent the being disappointed in it.

But there is a wide difference between this and the raising a kind of petty war in the County or Corporation; entering the lists rather for a combat than an election, throwing fire-balls to put men into a heat, and omitting to spread no reports, whether true or false, which may give an advantage by laying a blemish upon a competitor.

These methods will ever be suspicious; it will never be thought a natural thing for men to take such extravagant pains for the mere sake of doing good to others. To be content to suffer something for a good end is that which many would do without any great repugnance; but where a man can honestly propose nothing to himself except troubles, charge and loss, by absence from his own affairs, to be so violent in the pursuit of so ill a bargain is not at all suited to the languishing virtue of mankind so corrupted. Such a self-denying zeal in such a self-seeking age is so little to be imagined that it may without injury be suspected.

Therefore when these blustering pretenders come upon the stage their natural temper and other circumstances ought to be very well considered before men trust them with the disposal of their money or their liberty. And I am apt to believe there could hardly be found one single man whose other qualifications would overbalance the objections that lie against such importunate suitors.

2. *Recommending letters ought to have no effect upon Elections.* In this I must distinguish; for though in strictness perhaps there should be no exception, yet in compliance with long practice, and out of an indulgence that is necessary in a time when mankind is too much loosened from severe rules to be kept close up to them, letters sent only from equal men, doing good men right by giving evidence on their behalf, offering them as fitly qualified when they really are so, and freeing them from unjust aspersions, may be still allowed.

The letters I mean[1] are from men of power, where it may be beneficial to comply and inconvenient to oppose.

Choice must not only be free from force but from influence, which is a degree of force. There must be no difficulty, no apprehension that a refusal will be ill taken or resented. The freeholders must be freemen too; they are to have no shackles upon their votes in an election, and the men who stand should carry their own letters of recommendation about them, which are their good character and behaviour in the world, without borrowing evidence, especially when it cometh from suspected hands.

Those who make use of these epistles ought to have no more advantage from them than the Muscovites have from the letters put into their hands when they are buried, to recommend them to St Nicholas. The first should as little get admittance for men into the

1. A reference back to the first sentence of the section.

Parliament, as these letters can introduce the bearers into heaven.

The scandal of such letters lieth first in the arrogant imposing of those that write them, and next in the wretched meanness of those that need them. Men must be fallen very low in their credit who upon such an occasion have a recourse to power to support it; their enemies could not give stronger evidence of their not being fit for that which they pretend to. And if the electors judge otherwise, they will be pretty sure in a little time to see their mistake, and to repent it.

3. *Non-attendance in former Parliaments ought to be a bar against the choice of men who have been guilty of it.* It is one of the worst kinds of non-residence, and the least to be excused; it is very hard that men should despise a duty which perhaps is the only ground of the respect that is paid to them. It is such a piece of sauciness for anyone to press for the honour of serving in Parliament and then to be careless in attending it, that in a House where there were so many Officers[2] the penalty had not been improper to have cashiered them for not appearing at the general muster.

If men forbear to come out of laziness, let them be gratified by taking their ease at home without interruption; if out of small cunning to avoid difficulties, and to escape from the inconvenience of voting in critical cases, let them enjoy that despicable pitch of wisdom, and never pretend to make a figure where the public is to be served.

If it would not be thought advisable to trust a man immediately after he hath been drawn out of a gaol, it may be as reasonable to look upon one who for his non-attendance in the House hath been sent for in custody, as a kind of bankrupt, which putteth him upon unequal terms with those who have been assiduous in the discharge of their duty. They who thought fit in one session to neglect the public business may be justly suspected, by their standing, in the next to intend their own.

Besides these more deliberate offenders, there are some who do

2. Army Officers; there were so many in the Parliament of 1690–95 that it was popularly known as the 'Officers' Parliament'. See also section 17 below.

not attend even when they are in the House; absent in their thoughts for want of comprehending the business that is doing, and therefore diverted from it by anything that is trivial. Such men are nuisances to a serious assembly; and when they are numerous it amounteth almost to a dissolution, it being scarce possible for good sense to be heard whilst a noise is made by the buzzing of these horse flies. The Roman Censors, who degraded a Senator for yawning whilst there was a debate, would have much more abundant matter here upon which they might exercise their jurisdiction.

To conclude this head, there are so few that ever mended in these cases, that after the first experiment it is not at all reasonable to take them upon a new trial.

4. *Men who are unquiet and busy in their natures are to give more than ordinary proofs of their integrity before the electing them into a public trust can be justified.* As a hot summer breedeth greater swarms of flies, so an active time breedeth a greater number of these shining gentlemen.

It is pretty sure that man who cannot allow themselves to be at rest will let nobody else be at quiet. Such a perpetual activity is apt by degrees to be applied to the pursuit of their private interest, and their thoughts being in a continual motion, they have not time to dwell long enough upon anything to entertain a scruple; so that they are generally at full liberty to do what is most convenient for them, without being fettered by any restraints. Nay further, whenever it happeneth that there is an impunity for cheating, these nimble gentlemen are apt to think it a disparagement to their understandings not to go into it.

I doubt[3] it is not a wrong to the present age to say that a knave is a less unpopular calling than it hath been in former times. And to say truth, it would be ingratitude in some men to turn honest, when they owe all they have to their knavery.

The People are in this respect unhappy; they are too many to do their own business; their numbers, which make their strength, are at the same time the cause of their weakness. They are too unwieldy to move, and for this reason nothing can ever redeem them from

3. fear.

this incurable impotency; so that they must have solicitors to pursue and look after their interests, who are too often disposed to dispense with the fidelity they owe to those that trust them, especially if the Government will pay their bills without abatement.

It is better these gentlemen's dexterity should be employed anywhere than in Parliament, where the ill consequence of their being Members is too much diffused, and not restrained to the County or Borough who shall be so unwary as to choose them.

5. *Great drinkers are less fit to serve in Parliament than is apprehended.* Men's virtue as well as their understanding is apt to be tainted by it. The appearance of it is sociable and well-natured, but it is by no means to be relied upon. Nothing is more frail than a man too far engaged in wet popularity. The habit of it maketh men careless of their business, and that naturally leadeth them into circumstances that make them liable to temptation. It is seldom seen that any principles have such a root as that they can be proof against the continual droppings of a bottle.

As to the faculties of the mind, there is not less objection; the vapours of wine may sometimes throw out sparks of wit, but they are like scattered pieces of ore, there is no vein to work upon. Such wit, even the best of it, is like paying great fines;[4] in which case there must of necessity be an abatement of the constant rent.

Nothing sure is a greater enemy to the brain than too much moisture, it can the least of anything bear the being continually steeped; and it may be said that thought may be resembled to some creatures which can live only in a dry country. Yet so arrogant are some men as to think they are so much masters of business as that they can play with it; they imagine they can drown their reason once a day and that it shall not be the worse for it, forgetting that by too often diving the understanding at last groweth too weak to rise up again.

I will suppose this fault was less frequent when Solon made it one of his laws that it was lawful to kill a magistrate if he was found drunk. Such a liberty taken in this age, either in the Parliament or out of it, would do terrible execution.

4. On renewal of a lease, that is.

I cannot but mention a Petition in the year 1647 from the County of Devon to the House of Commons, against the undue Election of Burgesses who are strong in wine and weak in wisdom. The cause of such Petitions is to be prevented by choosing such as shall not give handle for them.

6. *Wanting*[5] *men give such cause of suspicion wherever they deal, that surely the choosers will be upon their guard as often as such dangerous pretenders make their application to them.* Let the behaviour of such men be never so plausible and untainted, yet they who are to pitch upon those they are to trust with all they have may be excused if they do not only consider what they are but what they may be. As we pray ourselves we may not be led into temptation, we ought not by any means to thrust others into it, even though our own interest was not concerned; and sure when it is, the argument hath not less force.

If a man hath a small estate and a numerous family, where it happeneth that a man hath as many children as he hath tenants, it is not a recommending circumstance for his election. When it cometh to be the question with such a man, whether he shall be just to the public or cruel to his family, it is very possible the decision may be on the side of corrupted nature. It is a compliment to this age which it doth not deserve, to suppose men are so tied up to morality as that they cannot be pinched out of it; especially now, when it is called starving not to be embroidered or served on plate.

The men chosen to serve their country should not be laden with suits that may tempt them to assume privileges;[6] much less under such necessities as may more immediately prepare them for corruption. Men who need a Parliament for their own particular interest have more reason to offer their service than others have to accept of it; and though I do not doubt but there may be some whose virtue would triumph over their wants, let them be never so pressing, yet to expose the public to the hazard of being deceived is that which can never be justified by those that choose, and though it must be allowed possible for a wanting man to be

5. Needy. 6. The parliamentary privilege of freedom from arrest.

honest, yet it is impossible for a man to be wise that will depend upon it.

7. *There is a sort of men that have a tinsel wit, which makes them shine among those who cannot judge.* Club and coffee-house gentlemen, petty merchants of small conceits, who have an empty habit of prating without meaning; they always aim at wit[7] and generally make false fire.[8] Their business is less to learn than to set themselves out, which makes them choose to be with such as can only be witnesses of their small ingenuity rather than with such as might improve it.

There is a subordinate wit, as much inferior to a wit of business as a fiddler at a wake is to the lofty sound of an organ. Men of this size are in no degree suited to the business of redressing grievances and making laws.

There is a parliament wit to be distinguished from all other kinds, those who have it do not stuff their heads only with cavils and objections. They have a deliberate and an observing wit, a head turned to public things; men who place a greater pleasure in mending a fault than in finding it out. Their understanding directeth them to object in the right place, and not like those who go by no other rule than to conclude that must be the best counsel which was not taken.

These wholesale judges show such a gross and peevish ignorance, that it appeareth so openly in all they say or do that they give loud warning to all considering men not to choose them.

8. *The dislike of slight, airy men must not go so far as to recommend heaviness in opposition to it, especially where men are convicted of it by experience in former sessions.* As a lively coxcomb will seldom fail to lay in his claim for wit, so a blockhead is apt to pretend that his heaviness is a proof of his judgment.

Some have an universal lethargy spread upon their understand-

7. When reading this section, it should be remembered that in the seventeenth century 'wit' not only had its present meaning, but could also mean 'ingenuity', 'intellect', 'imagination' or 'judgement'.

8. We would say 'misfire'.

ing without exception, others have an insufficiency *quoad hoc* as in some cases men have *quoad hanc*; these last can never so turn their thoughts to public business as to give the attention that is necessary to comprehend it.

There are those who have such a thick shell upon their brains that their ignorance is impenetrable, and maketh such a stout resistance against common sense that it will never be subdued by it – true Heart of Oak ignorance that will never yield, let reason beat never so hard upon it; and though their kind neighbours have at several elections sent them up to school again they have still returned the same incurable dunces.

There is a false gravity that is a very ill symptom; and it may be said that as rivers which run very slowly have always the most mud at the bottom, so a solid stiffness in the constant course of a man's life is a sign of a thick bed of mud at the bottom of his brain.

A dull man is so near a dead man that he is hardly to be ranked in the list of the living; and as he is not to be buried whilst he is half alive, so he is as little to be employed whilst he is half dead.

Parliaments are now grown to be quite other things than they were formerly. In ancient times they were little more than great assizes; a roll of grievances, *Magna Charta* confirmed, privileges of Holy Church preserved, so many sacks of wool given, and away. Now there are traps and gins laid for the well-meaning country gentleman; he is to grapple with the cunning of men in town, which is not a little improved by being rewarded and encouraged; so that men whose good intentions are not seconded and supported by some degree of ability are as much the more dangerous as they are less criminal than cunning knaves. Their honest mistakes, for want of distinguishing, either give a countenance to, or at least lessen the scandal of the injurious things that are done to the public; and with leave asked for so odd an expression, their innocent guilt is as mischievous to the laws and liberties as the most deliberate malice of those that would destroy them.

9. *There is an abuse which daily increaseth, of sending such to Parliament as are scarce old enough to be sent to the University.*[9] I would not

9. There was no age restriction at all at this time.

in this restrain the definition of these boys to the age of twenty-one. If my opinion might take place, I should wish that none might be chosen into the House of Commons under thirty; and to make some equality I should from the same motives think it convenient that no Lord should have a vote in judicature under that age.

But to leave this digression, I cannot see why the choosers should not at least make it a rule among themselves not to send any man to represent them under the age of twenty five, which is the time of majority in most other places of the world.

Surely it is not that we are earlier plants than our neighbours; such supposition could neither be justified by our climate nor by the degree of latitude in which we are placed; I must therefore attribute it to the haste our ancestors had (and not without reason) to free themselves from the severity of wardships.

But whether this, or anything else, was the cause of our earlier stepping into man's estate, so it is now, that according to our laws, twenty one is the age of discretion; and the young man is then vested with a legal, how defective soever he may be in his natural understanding.

With all this, there ought to be a difference made between coming out of pupilage and leaping into legislatorship. It is perhaps inconvenient enough that a man should be so soon let loose to destroy his own estate; but it is yet worse that he should then have a power of giving away other men's.

The law must make general rules, to which there always will be some objections. If there were triers[10] appointed to judge when leading strings should be left off, many would wear them a very great while, and some perhaps with their gray hairs; there being no small number of old boys in all times and especially in this. It is necessary therefore to make exceptions to this general rule where the case so much requireth it as it doth in the matter in question.

The ground of sending these minors to Parliament ought not to recommend the continuance of it to those who are lovers of liberty, since it was by the authority and influence of great men that their stripling sons were first received by the humble depending boroughs

10. assessors.

or the complying counties. They called it, as many do still, the best school for young men. Now experience hath showed us that it is like a school only in this respect, that these youngsters when they are admitted deserve to be whipped in it.

If the House of Commons is a school, it must be for men of riper age; these are too young to learn there, and being elevated by a mistaken smattering in small politics, they grow too supercilious to learn anywhere else; so that instead of improving young promising plants, they are destroyed by being misplaced. If then they do themselves hurt by it, it is surer yet that they do the House no good by coming into it.

They were not green geese that are said to have saved the Capitol; they were certainly of full age, or else their cackling could not have been heard, so as to give warning.

Indeed it looked of late, when the fashion was to have long continued Parliaments, as if we might plant a boy in the House with a prospect that he might continue there till he had gray hairs; and that the same sapling might have such a root, as that he might grow up to be timber without being removed.[11]

If these young men had skill enough to pitch upon somebody in the House to whom they might resign their opinion, and upon whose judgment they might lean without reserve, there might be less objection. But to speak truth, they know as little how to choose as those did who elected them, so that there is no other expedient left than the letting them alone.

One may say, generally speaking, that a young man being too soon qualified for the serious business of Parliaments would really be no good symptom. It is a sign of too much phlegm and too little fire in the beginning of age, if men have not a little more heat than is convenient; for as they grow older they will run a hazard of not having so much as is necessary. The truth is, the vigour of youth is softened and misapplied when it is not spent either in war or close studies; all other courses have an idle mixture that cometh to nothing, and maketh them like trees which for want of pruning run up to wood, and seldom or never bear any fruit.

11. He is probably thinking of Charles II's Long Parliament, which lasted from May 1661 to January 1679.

To conclude this head, it must be owned that there is no age of our life which doth not carry arguments along with it to humble us, and therfore it would be well for the business of the world if young men would stay longer before they went into it, and old men not so long before they went out of it.

10. *Next to these may be ranked a sort of superfine Gentlemen, carpet-knights'*[12] *men whose heads may be said to be only appurtenances to their perukes, which entirely engross all their care and application.* Their understanding is so strictly appropriated to their dress that no part of it is upon pain of their utmost displeasure to be diverted to any other use.

It is not by this intended to recommend an affected clown, or to make it a necessary qualification for a Member of Parliament, that he must renounce clean linen or good manners; but surely a too earnest application to make everything sit right about them striketh too deep into their small stock of thoughts to allow it furniture for anything else.

To do right to these fine-spun Gentlemen, business is too coarse a thing for them, which maketh it an unreasonable hardship upon them to oppress them with it; so that in tenderness to them, no less than out of care to the public it is best to leave them to their tailors, with whom they will live in much better correspondence when the danger is prevented of their falling out about privileges.[13]

11. *Men of injustice and violence in their private dealings are not to be trusted by the People with a commission to treat for them in Parliament.* In the 4th of Edw. III the King commandeth in his writs not to choose any Knights who had been guilty of crime, or maintenance.[14] These warm men seldom fail to run into maintenance, taken in a larger extent.

It is an unnatural sound to come from a man that is arbitrary in his neighbourhood, to talk of laws and liberties at Westminster; he

12. A knight dubbed at Court, on a carpet, rather than on the field of battle.

13. That is, when they are no longer protected by parliamentary privilege against prosecution for debt.

14. The offence of supporting another man's suit at law by force or bribery.

is not a proper vehicle for such words, which ought never to be profaned.

An habitual breaker of the laws to be made one of the law-makers, is as if the benches in Westminster Hall should be filled with men out of Newgate. Those who are of this temper cannot change their nature out of respect to their country. Quite contrary, they will less scruple to do wrong to a nation, where nobody taketh it to himself, than to particular men to whose resentments they are more immediately exposed.

In short they lie under such strong objections, that the over-balance of better men cannot altogether purify an assembly where these unclean beasts are admitted.

12. *Excessive spenders and unreasonable savers are to be excluded, being both greedy from differing causes.* They are both of them diseases of infection, and for that reason are not to be admitted into public assemblies. A prodigal man must be greedy, because he thinketh he can never spend enough. The wretch must be so, because he will never think he can hoard enough.

The world first admireth men's wisdom for getting money, and then raileth at them if they do not throw it away, so that the prodigal man is only the less unpopular extreme; he is every jot as well prepared as the miser to fall out with his morals, when once a good temptation is offered him to lay them aside.

On the other side, some rich men are as eager to overtake those that are richer, as a running horse is to get to the racepost before the other that contendeth with him. Men often desire to heap rather because others have more than that they know what to do with that which they covet with so much impatience. So that it is plain the fancy hath as great a share in this imaginary pleasure of gathering as it hath in love, ambition, or any other passion.

It is pretty sure that as no man was ever the richer for having a good estate if he did not look after it, so neither will he be the honester if he hath never so much. Want of care will always create want of money; so that whether a man is a beggar because he never had any money or because he can never keep any it is all one to those who are to trust him.

Upon this head of prodigality, it may be no unreasonable caution to be afraid of those who in former service have been extravagantly liberal of the public money. Trusting is so hazardous a thing that it should never be done but where it is necessary, so that when trustees are found upon trial to be very lavish, even without examining into the causes of it, (which are generally very suspicious), it is a reasonable part of preventing wit to change hands, or else the choosers will pay the penalty that belongeth to good nature so misplaced, and the consequences will be attended with the aggravation of their not being made wiser by such a severe and costly warning.

13. *It would be of very great use to take a general resolution throughout the kingdom, that none should be chosen for a County but such as have either in possession or reversion a considerable estate in it; nor for a Borough, except he be resident, or that he hath some estate in the County, in present or expectancy.*[15] There have been eminent men of law who were of opinion, that in the case of a Burgess of a town not resident the court is to give judgment according to the statute, notwithstanding custom to the contrary. But not to insist now upon that, the prudential part is argument enough to set up a rule to abrogate an ill custom. There is not, perhaps, a greater cause of the corruption of Parliaments than by adopting Members who may be said to have no title by their births. The juries are by the law to be *ex vicineto*, and shall there be less care that the representatives of the People be so too?

Sure the interest of the County is best placed in the hands of such as have some share in it. The outliers are not so easily kept within the pale of the laws. They are often chosen without being known, which is more like choosing valentines[16] than Members of Parliament. The motive of their standing is more justly to be supposed

15. Medieval statutes obliged a Member to be resident in the County or Borough which elected him, and to have £600 of real or personal property there. They had not been enforced since the end of the Middle Ages, and an act of 1710 which obliged County Members to have £600 in real property and Borough Members £300 said nothing about residence. Halifax was very out-of-date, even by the standards of the backwoodsmen.

16. Valentines were chosen by lot.

that they may redress their own grievances, which they know, than those of the County, to which they are strangers. They are chosen at London to serve in Cornwall, &c. and are often parties, before they come to be representatives.

One would think the reproach it is for a County not to have men within their own circle to serve them in Parliament should be argument enough to reject these trespassers, without urging the ill consequences in other respects of their being admitted.

14. *As in some cases it is advisable to give a total exclusion to men not fitly qualified, so in others it is more proper to lay down a general rule of caution, with allowance of some exceptions where men have given such proofs of themselves as create a right to them to be distinguished.* Of this nature is that which I shall say concerning lawyers, who, by the same reason that they may be useful, may be also very dangerous. The negligence and want of application in gentlemen hath made them to be thought more necessary than naturally they are in Parliament. They have not only ingrossed the chair of the Speaker, but that of a committee is hardly thought to be well filled except it be by a man of the robe.[17] This maketh it worthy of the more serious reflection of all gentlemen, that it may be an argument to them to qualify themselves in parliamentary learning in such a manner as that they may rely upon their own abilities in order to the serving their country.

But to come to the point in question, it is not without precedent that practising lawyers have been excluded from serving in Parliament,[18] and, without following those patterns strictly, I cannot but think it reasonable that whilst a Parliament sitteth no Member of Parliament should plead at any bar. The reason of it is in many respects strong in itself, and is grown much stronger by the long sitting of Parliaments of late, but I will not dwell upon this; the matter now in question being concerning lawyers being elected, which I conceive should be done with so much circumspection that probably it would not often happen.

17. 'Gentlemen of the Long Robe' was the usual idiom, referring to a barrister's gown.

18. Under Edward III.

If lawyers have great practice, that ought to take them up; if not, it is no great sign of their ability, and at the same time giveth a suspicion that they may be more liable to be tempted.

If it should be so in fact, that no King ever wanted judges to soften the stiffness of the laws that were made so as to make them suit better with the reason of state and the convenience of the government, it is no injury now to suppose it possible for lawyers in the House of Commons so to behave themselves in the making of new laws as the better to make way for the having their robes lined with fur. They are men used to argue on both sides of a question, and if ordinary fees can inspire them with very good reasons in a very ill cause, that faculty exercised in Parliaments, where it may be better encouraged, may prove very inconvenient to those that choose them.

And therefore, without arraigning a profession that it would be scandalous for a man not to honour, one may, by a suspicion which is the more excusable when it is in the behalf of the People, imagine that the habit of taking money for their opinion may create in some such a forgetfulness to distinguish that they may take it for their vote.

They are generally men who by a laborious study hope to be advanced, they have it in their eye as a reward for the toil they undergo. This maketh them generally very slow and ill disposed (let the occasion never so much require it) to wrestle with that soil where preferment groweth.

Now if the supposition be in itself not unreasonable and that it should happen to be strengthened and confirmed by experience, it will be very unnecessary to say any more upon this article, but leave it to the electors to consider of it.

15. *I cannot forbear to put in a caveat against men tied to a Party.* There must in everybody be a leaning to that sort of men who profess some principles, more than to others who go upon a different Foundation; but when a man is drowned in a Party, plunged in it beyond his depth, he runneth a great hazard of being upon ill terms with good sense or morality, if not with both of them. Such a man can hardly be called a free agent, and for that reason is very

unfit to be trusted with the People's liberty, after he hath given up his own.

It is said that in some part of the Indies they do so affect little feet that they keep them squeezed while they are children, so that they stay at that small size after they are grown men. One may say something like this of men locked up in a Party; they put their thoughts into such a narrow mould that they can never be enlarged nor released from their first confinements.

Men in a Party have Liberty only for their motto; in reality they are greater slaves than anybody else would care to make them. A Party, even in times of peace, (though against the Original Contract and the Bill of Rights), sets up and continues the exercise of martial law; once enrolled, the man that quitteth, if they had their will, would be hanged for a deserter.

They communicate anger to one another by contagion, and it may be said that if too much light dazzleth the eyesight too much heat doth not less weaken the judgment. Heat reigneth in the fancy, and reason, which is a colder faculty of the brain, taketh more time to be heard than the other will allow.

The heat of a Party is like the burning of a fever, and not a natural warmth, evenly distributed to give life and vigour. There was a time indeed when anger showed a good sign of honesty, but that evidence is very much weakened by instances we have seen since the days of yore; and the public spirited choler hath been thrown off within time of memory, and lost almost all its credit with some people since they found that Governments thought fit to make their so doing a step to their preferment.

A strong, blustering wind seldom continues long in one corner. Some men knock loud only to be let in, the bustle they make is animated by their private interest. The outward blaze only is for religion and liberty; the true lasting fire, like that of the vestals which never went out, is an eagerness to get somewhat for themselves.

A House of Commons composed of such men would be more properly so many merchants incorporated in a regular company to make their particular adventures[19] than men sent from the People to serve and represent them.

There are some splenetic gentlemen who confine their favourable opinion within so narrow a compass that they will not allow it to any man that was not hanged in the late reigns.[20] Now by that rule one might expect they should rescue themselves from the disadvantage of being now alive and by abdicating a world so little worthy of them get a great name to themselves, with the general satisfaction of all those they would leave behind them.

Amongst the many other ill consequences of a stated[21] Party, it is none of the least that it tempteth low and insignificant men to come upon the stage, to expose themselves and to spoil business. It turneth a cypher into a figure, such an one as it is; a man in a Party is able to make a noise, let it be never so empty a sound. A weak man is easily blown out of his small senses by being mustered into a Party; he is flattered till he liketh himself so well that he taketh it extremely ill if he hath not an employment.

Nothing is more in fashion than for men to desire good places, and I doubt nothing is less so than to deserve them. From nobody to somebody is such a violent stride that Nature, which hath the negative voice, will not give its royal assent to it; so that when insufficient men aim at being in business, the worst of their enemies might out of malice to them pray for their preferment.

There could be no end, if one did not stop till this theme had no more matter to furnish. I will only say, nothing is more evident than that the good of the nation hath been sacrificed to the animosities of the several contending Parties; and without entering into the dispute which of them are more or less in the right, it is pretty sure that whilst these opposite sets of angry men are playing at football they will break all the windows, and do more hurt than their pretended zeal for the nation will ever make amends for.

In short, a man so engaged is retained before the People take him for their counsel; he hath such a reserve for his Party, that it is not advisable for those who would choose him to depend upon his

19. Trading venture or expedition.

20. Here, as elsewhere in this section, Halifax is venting his spleen against the extreme Whigs.

21. Formal, settled, coherent.

professions – all Parties assuming such a dispensing power that by their sovereign authority they cancel and dissolve any act or promise that they do not afterwards approve.

These things considered, those who will choose such men deserve whatever followeth.

16. *Pretenders to exorbitant merit in the late Revolution are not without objections against them when they stand to serve in Parliament.* It would not only be a low but a criminal kind of envy to deny a distinguishing justice to men who have been instrumental and active when the service of their Country required it, but there ought to be moderation in men's claims or else it is out of the power of our poor island to satisfy them. It is true, service of all kinds is grown much dearer, like a labourer's wages, which formerly occasioned several statutes to regulate them; but now the men who only carried mortar to the building, when it is finished think they are ill dealt with if they are not made master workmen. They presently cry out, 'The Original Contract is broken', if their merit is not rewarded at their own rate too.

Some will think there never ought to be an end of their rewards when indifferent judges would perhaps be puzzled to find out the beginning of their merit. They bring in such large bills that they must be examined; some bounds must be put to men's pretensions, else the nation, which is to pay the reckoning, will every way think it a scurvy thing to be undone, whether it be by being over-run by our enemies or by the being exhausted by our friends. There ought therefore to be deductions where they are reasonable, the better to justify the paying what remaineth.

For example, if any of these passionate lovers of the Protestant Religion should not think fit in their manner of living to give the least evidence of their morality, their claims upon that head might sure be struck off without any injustice to them. If there are any who set down great sums as a reward due to their zeal for rescuing Property from the jaws of Arbitrary Power, their pretensions may fairly be rejected if now they are so far from showing a care and tenderness of the laws that they look rather like counsel retained on the other side.

It is no less strange, than I doubt it is true, that some men should be so in love with their dear mistress *Old England*, with all her wrinkles, as out of an heroic passion to swim over to rescue her from being ravished; and when they have done the feat, the first thing after enjoyment is that they go about to strangle her. For the sake of true love it is not fit that such ungentle gallants should be too much encouraged; and their arrogance for having done well at first will have no right to be excused if their so doing ill at last doth not make them a little more modest. True merit, like a river, the deeper it is the less noise it maketh.

These loud proclaimers of their own deserts are not only to be suspected for their truth, but the electors are to consider that such meritorious men lay an assessment upon those that choose them. The public taxes are already heavy enough without the addition of these private reckonings. It is therefore the safer way not to employ men who will expect more for their wages than the mistaken boroughs that sendeth them up to Parliament could be sold for.

17. *With all due regard to the noblest of callings, Military Officers are out of their true element when they are misplaced in a House of Commons.*[22] Things in this world ought to be well suited. There are some appearances so unnatural that men are convinced by them without any other argument.

The very habit[23] in some cases recommendeth or giveth offence. If the judges upon the bench should, instead of their furs, which signify gravity and bespeak respect, be clothed like the jockeys at Newmarket, or wear jack-boots and steenkirks,[24] they would not in reality have less law, but mankind would be so struck with this unusual object that it would be a great while before they could think it possible to receive justice from men so accoutred.

It is to some degree the same thing in this case; such martial habits, blue coats, red stockings, &c. make them look very unlike grave senators. One would almost swear they were creatures apart, and of a differing species from the rest of the body.

22. See note to p. 167 above. 23. uniform.

24. Loose-ended cravats, as worn in the heat of the battle of Steenkirk, 1692, and fashionable for some years after.

In former times, when only the resident shopkeeper was to represent his Corporation, (which by the way is the law still at this day), the military looks of one of these sons of Mars would have stared the quaking Member down again to his borough. Now the number of them is so increased that the peaceable part of the House may lawfully swear they are in fear of their lives from such an awful appearance of men of war.

It maketh the room look like a guard-house by such an ill-suited mixture, but this is only the outside, the bark of the argument; the root goeth yet deeper against choosing such men, whose talents ought to be otherwise applied. Their two capacities are so inconsistent that men's undertaking to serve both the cures will be the cause in a little time that we shall neither have men of war nor men of business, good in their several kinds.

An Officer is to give up his liberty to obey orders; and it is necessarily incident to his calling that he should do so. A Member of Parliament is originally to be tender of his own liberty, that other men may the better trust him with theirs.

An Officer is to enable himself by his courage, improved by skill and experience, to support the laws (if invaded) when they are made; but he is not supposed to be at leisure enough to understand how they should be made. A Member of Parliament is to fill his thoughts with what may best conduce to the civil administration, which is enough to take up the whole man, let him be never so much raised above the ordinary level.

These two opposite qualifications, being placed in one man, make him such an ambiguous divided creature that he doth not know how to move.

It is best to keep men within their proper sphere; few men have understanding enough exactly to fill even one narrow circle, fewer are able to fill two; especially when they are both of so great compass, and that they are so contrary in their own natures. The wages [25] he hath as a Member and those he receiveth as an Officer, are paid for services that are very differing; and in the doubt which of them should be preferably performed it is likely the greater

25. Figurative. Borough Members were entitled to wages, but the last attempt to collect them had been made by an isolated eccentric in 1676.

salary may direct him, without the further inducements of complying most where he may expect most advantage by it.

In short, if his dependance is not very great it will make him a scurvy Officer; if it is great, it will make him a scurvier Member.

18. *Men under the scandal of being thought private pensioners are too fair a mark to escape being considered in reference to the point in question.* In case of plain evidence it is not to be supposed possible that men convicted of such a crime should ever again be elected; the difficulty is in determining what is to be done in case of suspicion.

There are suspicions so well grounded that they may pretend to have the force of proofs, provided the penalty goeth only to the forbearing to trust, but not extending it so far as to punish. There must be some things plain and express to justify the latter, but circumstances may be sufficient for the former; as where men have had such sudden cures of their ill humours and opposition to the Court that it is out of the way of ordinary methods of recovery from such distempers, which have a much slower progress; it must naturally be imputed to some specific that maketh such a quick alteration of the whole mass of blood.

Where men have raised their way of living, without any visible means to support them in it, a suspicion is justified, even by the example of the law, which in cases of this kind, though of an inferior nature, doth upon this foundation not only raise inferences but inflict punishments.

Where men are immoral, and scandalous in their lives, and dispense familiarly with the rules by which the world is governed, for the better preserving the bonds of human society, it must be a confidence very ill placed to conclude it impossible for such men to yield to a temptation well offered and pursued; when the truth is the habit of such *bons vivants*, which is the fashionable word, maketh a suspicion so likely that it is very hard not to believe it to be true.

If there should be nothing but the general report, even that is not to be neglected. Common fame is the only liar that deserveth to have some respect still reserved to it; though she telleth many an untruth she often hitteth right, and most especially when she speaketh ill of men. Her credit hath sometimes been carried too far when it hath gone to the divesting men of anything of which they were possessed, without more express evidence to justify such a proceeding.

If there was a doubt whether there ever was any corruption of this kind it would alter the question, but sure that will not bear the being controverted. We are told that Charles the Fifth sent over into England 1,200,000 crowns to be distributed amongst the leading men, to encourage them to carry on elections.[26] Here was the Protestant Religion to be bought out for a valuable consideration according to law, though not according to Gospel, which exalteth it above any price that can be set upon it. Now, except we had reason to believe that the virtue of the world is improved since that time, we can as little doubt that such temptations may be offered as that they may be received.

It will be owned that there is to be a great tenderness in suspecting, but it must be allowed at the same time that there ought not to be less in trusting, where the People are so much concerned; especially when the penalty upon the party suspected goeth no further than a suspension of that confidence which it is necessary to have in those who are to represent the nation in Parliament.

19. *I cannot omit the giving a caution against admitting men to be chosen who have places of any value.* There needeth the less to be said upon this article, the truth of the proposition being supported by such plain arguments.

Sure no man hath such a plentiful spring of thought as that all that floweth from it is too much to be applied to the business of Parliament. It is not less sure that a Member of Parliament, of all others, ought not to be exempted from the rule that no man should serve two masters. It doth so split a man's thoughts that no man can know how to make a fitting distribution of them to two such differing capacities. It exposeth men to be suspected and tempted more than is convenient for the public service, or for the mutual good opinion of one another which there ought to be in such an

26. In 1554.

assembly. It either giveth a real dependance upon the government, which is inconsistent with the necessity there is that a Member of Parliament should be disengaged; or at least it hath the appearance of it, which maketh them not look like freemen though they should have virtue enough to be so.

More reasons would lessen the weight of this last, which is that a Bill to this effect, commonly called the *Self-Denying Bill*, passed even this last House of Commons.[27] A greater demonstration of the irresistible strength of truth cannot possibly be given; so that a copy of that Bill in every County or Borough would hardly fail of discouraging such pretenders from standing, or at least it would prevent their success if their own modesty should not restrain them from attempting it.

20. *If distinctions may be made upon particular men, or remarks fixed upon their votes in Parliament, they must be allowed in relation to those gentlemen who for reasons best known to themselves thought fit to be against the Triennial Bill.*[28] The liberty of opinion is the thing in the world that ought least to be controlled, and especially in Parliament. But as that is an undoubted assertion, it is not less so, that when men sin against their own light, give a vote against their own thought, they must not plead privilege of Parliament against the being arraigned for it by others, after they are convicted of it by themselves.

There cannot be a man who in his definition of a House of Commons will state it to be an assembly that, for the better redressing of grievances the People feel, and for the better furnishing such supplies as they can bear, is to continue if the King so pleaseth for his whole reign. This could be as little intended as to throw all into one hand, and to renounce the claim to any liberty but so much as the sovereign authority would allow. It destroyeth the end of Parliaments, it maketh use of the letter of the law to extinguish the life of it.

27. A bill to exclude office-holders from Parliament passed the Commons in 1692 and was rejected by the Lords; a similar bill was vetoed by William III in 1693. They are usually known as 'Place Bills'.

28. A bill obliging the Crown to hold a General Election every three years passed both Houses in January 1693 and was vetoed by the King.

It is in truth some kind of disparagement to so plain a thing that so much has been said and written upon it; and one may say, it is such an affront to these gentlemen's understandings to censure this vote only as a mistake that as the age goeth it is less discredit to them to call it by its right name; and if that is rightly understood by those who are to choose them, I suppose they will let them exercise their liberty of conscience at home, and not make men their trustees who in this solemn instance have such an unwillingness to surrender.

It must be owned that this Bill hath met with very hard fortune, and yet that doth not in the least diminish the value of it. It had in it such a root of life that it might be said it was not dead but sleeped; and we see that the last session it was revived and animated by the royal assent, when once fully informed of the consequence as well as of the justice of it.[29]

In the meantime, after having told my opinion who ought not to be chosen, if I should be asked who ought to be, my answer must be, choose Englishmen; and when I have said that, to deal honestly, I will not undertake that they are easy to be found.

29. William III also insisted on the removal of the coercive machinery which would have dissolved Parliament and summoned another without the intervention of the Crown. This was in the session 1694–5, and since Halifax died on 5 April 1695, a month before the session ended, this paragraph was probably added by the editor or printer.

POLITICAL THOUGHTS AND REFLECTIONS

EDITORIAL INTRODUCTION

The *Political, Moral and Miscellaneous Reflections* were published in 1750, together with *A Character of King Charles II*, from a manuscript in the hands of his granddaughter, Lady Burlington, which has not survived. In the absence of the manuscript it is almost impossible to date them. They may have been composed deliberately towards the end of his life, or they may have been jotted down from time to time over the years. Halifax often made notes on small pieces of paper, one or two remarks or anecdotes to a piece, and it is possible that they were assembled and divided into subjects by Lady Burlington or an amanuensis; this would explain the confusion that exists here and there.[1]

1. p. 192 below, for instance. For a description of Halifax's surviving loose notes, see Foxcroft, ii, 201.

POLITICAL THOUGHTS AND REFLECTIONS

Of Fundamentals

EVERY Party, when they find a maxim for their turn, they presently[2] call it a *Fundamental.* They think they nail it with a peg of iron, whereas in truth they only tie it with a wisp of straw.

The word soundeth so well that the impropriety of it hath been the less observed. But as weighty as the word appeareth, no feather hath been more blown about in the world than this word *Fundamental.*

It is one of those mistakes that at some times may be of use, but it is a mistake still.

Fundamental is used as men use their friends; they commend them when they have need of them, and when they fall out, find a hundred objections to them.

Fundamental is a pedestal that men set everything upon that they would not have broken. It is a nail everybody would use to fix that which is good for them; for all men would have that principle to be immoveable that serves their use at the time.

Everything that is created is mortal, *ergo* all fundamentals of human creation will die.

A true fundamental must be like the foundation of a house; if it is undermined the whole house falleth.

The fundamentals in divinity have been changed in several ages of the world. They have made no difficulty in the several Councils,[3] to destroy and excommunicate men for asserting things that at other times were called fundamentals.

Philosophy, astronomy, &c. have changed their fundamentals as the men of art[4] no doubt called them at the time – motion of the earth, &c.

Even in morality one may more properly say, there *should be* fundamentals allowed, than that there *are* any which in strictness

2. immediately. 3. of the Church. 4. skill, intelligence.

can be maintained. However, this is the least uncertain foundation; fundamental is less improperly applied here than anywhere else. Wise and good men will in all ages stick to some fundamentals, look upon them as sacred, and preserve an inviolable respect for them; but mankind in general make morality a more malleable thing than it ought to be.[5]

There is then no certain fundamental but in Nature, and yet there are objections too. It is a fundamental in nature that the son should not kill the father, and yet the Senate of Venice gave a reward to a son who brought in his father's head according to a proclamation.

It is a fundamental that where a man intendeth no hurt he should receive none, yet manslaughter, &c. are cases of mercy. The great punishments upon self-murder are arguments that it was rather a tempting sin to be discouraged than an unnatural act.

That a boy under ten shall not suffer death; yet where *malitia supplet ætatem*,[6] otherwise.

That there were witches – much shaken of late.

That the King is not to be deceived in his grant – the practical fundamental the contrary.[7]

That what is given to God cannot be alienated. Yet in practice it is, by treaties, &c. and even by the Church itself, when they get a better bargain by it.

I can make no other definition of a true fundamental than this: *viz*. That whatever a man hath a desire to do or to hinder, if he hath uncontested and irresistible power to effect it, that he will certainly do it. If he thinketh he hath that power, though he hath it not, he will certainly go about it.

Some would define a fundamental to be the settling the laws of nature and common equity in such a sort as that they may be well

5. The next fifteen paragraphs are printed in no sensible sort of order in the 1750 edition, (1-11-3-2-4-5-6-7-8-9-10-12-14-13-15). Foxcroft rearranged them drastically, and not entirely to her satisfaction; I have made a new attempt, but I would not claim that it is completely successful.

6. Where the child was found to be able to distinguish right from wrong.

7. It was an axiom in law that if the King made a grant on the basis of false or mistaken information that grant was automatically voided.

administered: even in this case there can be nothing fixed but it must vary for the good of the whole.

Salus populi[8] is an unwritten law, yet that doth not hinder but that it is sometimes very visible; and as often as it is so it supersedeth all other laws, which are subordinate things compared.

A Constitution cannot make itself; somebody made it, not at once but at several times. It is alterable, and by that draweth nearer perfection; and without suiting itself to differing times and circumstances it could not live. Its life is prolonged by changing seasonably the several parts of it at several times.

Neither King nor People would now like just the original Constitution, without any varyings.

The reverence that is given to a fundamental, in a general unintelligible notion, would be much better applied to that Supremacy or Power which is set up in every nation in differing shapes, that altereth the Constitution as often as the good of the People requireth it.

If Kings are only answerable to God, that doth not secure them even in this world; since if God upon the appeal thinketh fit not to stay, he maketh the People his instruments.

I am persuaded that wherever any single man had power to do himself right upon a deceitful trustee, he would do it. That thought well digested would go a great way towards the discouraging invasions upon rights, &c.

I lay down then as a fundamental, 1st, that in every constitution there is some power which neither will nor ought to be bounded.

2. That the King's prerogative should be as plain a thing as the people's obedience.

3. That a power which may by parity of reason destroy the whole laws, can never be reserved by the laws.

4. That in all limited governments it must give the governor power to hurt, but it can never be so interpreted as to give him power to destroy, for then in effect it would cease to be a limited government.

8. *Salus populi suprema lex*, the safety of the people is the supreme law.

5. That severity be rare and great; for as Tacitus[9] sayeth of Nero, 'Frequent punishments made the People call even his justice cruelty.'

6. That it is necessary to make the instruments of power easy, for power is hard enough to be digested by those under it at the best.

7. That the People are never so perfectly backed[10] but that they will kick and fling if not stroked at seasonable times.

8. That a Prince must think if he loseth his people he can never regain them. It is both wise and safe to think so.

9. That Kings assuming prerogative teach the People to do so too.

10. That prerogative is a trust.

11. That they are not the King's laws, nor the Parliament's Laws, but the Laws of England, in which, after they have passed by the Legislative Power, the People have the property,[11] and the King the executive part.

12. That no abilities should qualify a noted knave to be employed in business. A knave can by none of his dexterities make amends for the scandal he bringeth upon the Crown.

13. That those who will not be bound by the laws rely upon crimes: a third way was never found in the world to secure any government.

14. That a seaman be a seaman; a cabinet-counsellor a man of business; an officer, an officer.

15. In corrupted governments the place is given for the sake of the man; in good ones the man is chosen for the sake of the place.

16. That crowds at Court are made up of such as would deceive. The real worshippers are few.

17. That *Salus populi* is the greatest of all fundamentals, yet not altogether an immoveable one. It is a fundamental for a ship to ride at anchor when it is in port, but if a storm cometh the cable must be cut.

18. Property is not a fundamental right in one sense, because in the beginning of the world there was none; so that property itself was an innovation introduced by laws.

Property is only secured by trusting it in the best hands, and

9. *Annals*, bk. 15, c. 44. 10. Mounted, in the sense of mounting a horse.
11. Propriety, or ownership.

those are generally chosen who are least likely to deceive; but if they should, they have a legal authority to abuse as well as use the power with which they are trusted, and there is no fundamental can stand in their way, or be allowed as an exception to the authority that was vested in them.

19. *Magna Carta* would fain be made to pass for a fundamental, and Sir Edward Coke would have it that the Grand Charter was for the most part declaratory of the principal grounds of the fundamental Laws of England.[12]

If that referreth to the Common Law, it must be made out that everything in *Magna Carta* is always and at all times necessary in itself to be kept, or else the denying a subsequent Parliament the right of repealing any law doth by consequence deny the preceding Parliament the right of making it. But they are fain to say it was only a declarative law, which is very hard to be proved. Yet suppose it, you must either make the Common Law so stated a thing that all men know it beforehand, or else universally acquiesce in it whenever it is alleged, from the affinity it hath to the Law of Nature. Now I would fain know whether the Common Law is capable of being defined, and whether it doth not hover in the clouds like the prerogative, and bolteth out like lightning to be made use of for some particular occasion? If so, the government of the world is left to a thing that cannot be defined, and if it cannot be defined you know not what it is; so that the supreme appeal is we know not what. We submit to God Almighty though he is incomprehensible, and yet he hath set down his methods; but for this world there can be no government without a stated rule, and a supreme power not to be controlled neither by the dead nor the living.

The laws under the protection of the King govern in the ordinary administration; the extraordinary power is in Acts of Parliament, from whence there can be no appeal but to the same power at another time.

To say a power is supreme and not arbitrary is not sense. It is acknowledged supreme and therefore, &c.

12. The great Jacobean jurist set the seal of his authority on this interpretation, but it had been common form long before; see Faith Thomson, *Magna Carta in English History*.

If the Common Law is supreme, then those are so who judge what is the Common Law; and if none but the Parliament can judge so, there is an end of the controversy. There is no fundamental, for the Parliament may judge as they please; that is, they have the authority, but they may judge against right their power is good, though their act is ill. No good man will outwardly resist the one, or inwardly approve the other.

There is then no other fundamental but that every supreme power must be arbitrary.

Fundamental is a word used by the laity, as the word sacred is by the clergy, to fix everything to themselves they have a mind to keep, that nobody else may touch it.

Of PRINCES

A prince who will not undergo the difficulty of understanding must undergo the danger of trusting.

A wise prince may gain such an influence that his countenance would be the last appeal. Where it is not so, in some degree his authority is precarious.

A prince must keep up the power of his countenance, which is not the least of his prerogatives.

The conscience as well as the prerogative of a king must be restrained or loosened as is best for his people.

It may without scandal be made of stretching leather, but it must be drawn by a steady hand.

A King that lets intercession prevail will not be long worshipped.

A prince used to war getteth a military logic that is not very well suited to the civil administration.

If he maketh war successfully, he groweth into a demi-god; if without success, the world throweth him as much below humanity as they had before set him above it.

A hero must be sometimes allowed to make bold strokes, without being fettered by strict reason.

He is to have some generous irregularities in his reasoning, or else he will not be a good thing of his kind.

PRINCES: *their Rewards of Servants*

When a prince giveth any man a very extravagant reward it looketh as if it was rather for an ill thing than a good one.

Both the giver and receiver are out of countenance where they are ill suited and ill applied.

Serving princes will make men proud at first, and humble at last.

Resolving to serve well, and at the same time resolving to please, is generally resolving to do what is not to be done.

A man that will serve well must often rule the master so hard that it will hurt him.

It is thought an unsociable quality in a Court to do one's duty better than other men.

Nothing is less forgiven than setting patterns men have no mind to follow.

Men are so unwilling to displease a prince that it is as dangerous to inform him right as to serve him wrong.

Where men get by pleasing and lose by serving, the choice is so easy that nobody can miss it.

PRINCES: *their Secrets*

Men are so proud of princes' secrets that they will not see the danger of them.

When a prince trusteth a man with a dangerous secret, he would not be sorry to hear the bell toll for him.

Love of the Subjects to a PRINCE

The heart of the subjects yieldeth but a lean crop where it is not cultivated by a wise prince.

The good-will of the governed will be starved if it is not fed by the good conduct of the governors.

Suffering for PRINCES

Those who merit because they suffered are so very angry with those that made them suffer, that though their services may deserve employment their temper[13] rendereth them unfit for it.

Of MINISTERS

The world dealeth with Ministers of State as they do with ill fiddlers, ready to kick them downstairs for playing ill, though few of the fault-finders understand their music enough to be good judges.[14]

A Minister who undertaketh to make his master very great, if he faileth, is ruined for his folly; if he succeedeth, he is feared for his skill.

A good statesman may sometimes mistake as much by being too humble as by being too proud; he must take upon him in order to do his duty, and not in order to the setting himself out.

A Minister is not to plead the King's command for such things as he may in justice be supposed to have directed.

It is dangerous to serve where the master hath the privilege not to be blamed.

It is hard for a Prince to esteem the parts of a Minister without either envying or fearing them; and less dangerous for a Minister to show all the weakness than all the strength of his understanding.

There are so many things necessary to make up a good Minister that no wonder there are so few of them in the world.

There is hardly a rasher thing than for a man to venture to be a good Minister.

A Minister of State must have a spirit of liberal economy, not a restrained frugality.

13. Temperament.

14. Halifax had two outstanding examples before him: the first Earl of Clarendon, Lord Chancellor, who was dismissed in 1667 and exiled for the rest of his life; and the Earl of Danby, Lord Treasurer, who was impeached in 1679 and spent nearly five years in the Tower.

He must enlarge his family soul, and suit it to the bigger compass of a kingdom.

A Prince should be asked, why he will do a thing, but not why he hath done it.

If the boys were to choose a schoolmaster, it should be one that would not whip them; the same thing if the Courtiers were to choose a Minister.

They would have a great many play days, no rods, and leave to rob orchards. – The parallel will hold.

Wicked MINISTERS

A cunning Minister will engage his master to begin with a small wrong step, which will insensibly engage him in a great one.[15]

A man that hath the patience to go by steps may deceive one much wiser than himself.

State business is a cruel trade; good nature is a bungler in it.

Instruments of STATE MINISTERS

Men in business are in as much danger from those that work under them as from those that work against them.

When the instruments bend under the weight of their business, it is like a weak-legged horse that brings his rider down with him.

As when they are too weak they let a man fall, so when they are too strong they throw him off.

If men of business did not forget how apt their tools are to break or fail, they would shut up shop.

They must use things called men under them who will spoil the best scheme that can be drawn by human understanding.

Tools that are blunt cannot cut at all, and those that are sharp are apt to cut in the wrong place.

15. Halifax detested his brother-in-law, the Earl of Sunderland, and may have had him in mind. He was popularly blamed for encouraging James II in his extreme pro-Catholic policy, and thus bringing on the Revolution of 1688.

Great difference between a good tool and a good workman.

When the tools will be workmen they cut their own fingers, and everybody elses.

Of the PEOPLE

There is more strength in union that in number; witness the People, that in all ages have been scurvily used because they could so seldom agree to do themselves right.

'The more the weaker' may be as good a proverb as 'The more the merrier'.

A People can no more stand without Government than a child can go without leading strings; as old and as big as a nation is, it cannot go by itself, and must be led. The numbers that make its strength are at the same time the cause of its weakness and incapacity of acting.

Men have so discovered themselves to one another that union is become a mere word, in reality impracticable.

They trust, or suspect, not upon reason but ill-grounded fame; they would be at ease, saved, protected, &c. and give nothing for it.

The lower sort of men must be indulged the consolation of finding fault with those above them; without that, they would be so melancholy that it would be dangerous, considering their numbers.

They are too many to be told of their mistakes, and for that reason they are never to be cured of them.

The body of the People are generally either so dead that they cannot move, or so mad that they cannot be reclaimed; to be neither all in a flame nor quite cold requireth more reason than great numbers can ever attain.

The People can seldom agree to move together against a Government, but they can to sit still and let it be undone.

Those that will be martyrs for the People must expect to be repayed only by their vanity, or their virtue.

A man that will head the mob is like a bull let loose, tied about with squibs and crackers.

He must be half mad that goeth about it, yet at some times it shall be too hard for all the wise men in a kingdom; for though good sense speaketh against madness, yet it is out of countenance whenever it meets it.

It would be a greater reproach to the People that their favour is short-lived, if their malice was not so too.

The thoughts of the People have no regular motion, they come out by starts.

There is an accumulative cruelty in a number of men, though none in particular are ill-natured.

The angry buzz of a multitude is one of the bloodiest noises in the world.

Of GOVERNMENT

An exact administration and good choice of proper instruments doth insensibly make the Government in a manner absolute without assuming it.

The best definition of the best Government is, that it hath no inconveniences but such as are supportable – but inconveniences there must be.

The interest of the governors and the governed is in reality the same, but by mistakes on both sides it is generally very differing. He who is a Courtier by trade, and the Country Gentleman who will be popular, right or wrong, help to keep up this unreasonable distinction.

There are as many apt to be angry at being well, as at being ill governed. For most men, to be well governed, must be scurvily used.[16]

As mankind is made, the keeping it in order is an ill-natured office.

16. These remarks on the people contradict what he wrote in CT, p. 59 above, and also some of his notes of speeches made in the early nineties. For instance, he wrote of the Triennial Act of 1694: 'The true Government of England is founded in good measure upon a great confidence in the People; it is not very natural to distrust those we intend to be kind to'. Foxcroft, *Character*, p. 322.

It is like a great galley, where the officers must be whipping with little intermission if they will do their duty.

It is in a disorderly Government as in a river, the lightest things swim at the top.

A nation is best to be judged by the Government it is under at the time. Mankind is moulded to good or ill, according as the power over it is well or ill directed. A nation is a mass of dough, it is the Government that kneadeth it into form.

Where learning and trade flourish in a nation they produce so much knowledge, and that so much equality among men that the greatness of dependencies is lost, but the nation in general will be the better for it. For if the Government be wise, it is the more easily governed; if not, the bad Government is the more easily overturned, by men's being more united against it than when they depended upon great men, who might sooner be gained over and weakened by being divided.

There is more reason for allowing luxury in a Military Government than in another; the perpetual exercise of war not only excuseth but recommendeth the entertainments in the winter. In another it groweth into a habit of uninterrupted expenses and idle follies, and the consequences of them to a nation become irrecoverable.

Clergy

If the Clergy did not live like temporal men, all the power of Princes could not bring them under the temporal jurisdiction.

They who may be said to be of God Almighty's household should show by their lives that he hath a well-disciplined family.

The Clergy, in this sense, of divine institution; that God hath made mankind so weak that it must be deceived.

Religion

It is a strange thing that the way to save men's souls should be such a cunning trade as to require a skilful master.

The time spent in praying to God might be better employed in deserving well from him.

Men think praying the easier task of the two, and therefore choose it.

The People would not believe in God at all if they were not permitted to believe wrong in him.

The several sorts of religion in the world are little more than so many spiritual monopolies.

If their interests could be reconciled, their opinions would be so too.

Men pretend to serve God Almighty, who doth not need it, but make use of him because they need him.

Factions are like pirates that set out false colours; when they come near a booty religion is put under deck.

Most men's anger about religion is as if two men should quarrel for a lady they neither of them care for.

Of PREROGATIVE, POWER *and* LIBERTY

A Prerogative that tendeth to the dissolution of all laws must be void in itself, *felo de se*; for a Prerogative is a law. The reason of any law is, that no man's will should be a law.

The King is the life of the law, and cannot have a Prerogative that is mortal to it.

The law is to have a soul in it or it is a dead thing. The King is by his sovereign power to add warmth and vigour to the meaning of the law. We are by no means to imagine there is such an antipathy between them that the Prerogative, like a basilisk, is to kill the law whenever it looks upon it.

The Prince hath very rarely use of his Prerogative, but hath constantly a great advantage by the laws.

They attribute to the Pope indeed, that all the laws of the Church are in his breast; but then he hath the Holy Ghost for his learned counsel, &c.

The People's obedience must be plain, and without evasions. The Prince's Prerogative should be so too.

King Charles the First made this Answer to the Petition of Right – to the observation whereof he held himself obliged in conscience, as well as of his Prerogative –'That the People's liberties strengthen the King's Prerogative, and the King's Prerogative is to defend the People's liberties.'[17]

That Prince's declarations allow the original of Government to come from the People. Prerogative never yet pretended to repealing.

The first ground of Prerogative was to enable the Prince to do good, not to do everything.

If the ground of a King's desire of power be his assurance of himself that he will do no hurt by it, it is not an argument for subjects to desire to keep that which they will never abuse?

It must not be such a Prerogative as giveth the Government the rickets; all the nourishment to go to the upper part, and the lower starved.

As a Prince is in danger who calleth a stronger than himself to his assistance, so when Prerogative useth necessity for an argument it calleth in a stronger thing than itself. The same reason may overturn it. Necessity too is so plain a thing that everybody sees it, so that the Magistrate hath no great privilege in being the judge of it. Necessity therefore is a dangerous argument for Princes, since wherever it is real it constitutes every man a Magistrate, and gives as great a power of dispensing to every private man as a Prince can claim.

It is not so proper to say that Prerogative justifieth force, as that force supporteth Prerogative. They have not been such constant friends but that they have had terrible fallings out.

All powers are of God; and between permission and appointment, well considered, there is no real difference.

In a limited monarchy, Prerogative and liberty are as jealous of one another as any two neighbouring states can be of their respective encroachments.

They ought not to part for small bickerings, and must bear little jealousies without breaking for them.

Power is so apt to be insolent, and liberty to be saucy, that they are very seldom upon good terms.

They are both so quarrelsome that they will not easily enter into

17. The Petition of Right in 1628 obliged Charles to abandon imprisonment without trial, taxation without parliamentary consent, forced billeting of troops and the subjection of civilians to martial law.

a fair treaty. For indeed it is hard to bring them together; they ever quarrel at a distance.

Power and liberty are respectively managed in the world in a manner not suitable to their value and dignity.

They are both so abused that it justifieth the satires that are generally made upon them, and they are so in possession of being misapplied, that instead of censuring their being abused it is more reasonable to wonder whenever they are not so.

They are perpetually wrestling, and have had their turns when they have been thrown to have their bones broken by it.

If they were not both apt to be out of breath, there would be no living.

If Prerogative will urge reason to support it, it must bear reason when it resisteth it.

It is a diminution instead of a glory, to be above treating upon equal terms with reason.

If the People were designed to be the sole property of the supreme Magistrate, sure God would have made them of a differing and subordinate species; as he hath the beasts, that by the inferiority of their nature they might the better submit to the dominion of mankind.

If none were to have liberty but those who understand what it is, there would not be many freed men in the world.

When the People contend for their liberty they seldom get anything by their victory but new masters.

Liberty can neither be got nor kept but by so much care, that mankind generally are unwilling to give the price for it. And therefore, in the contest between ease and liberty the first hath generally prevailed.

Of LAWS

Laws are generally not understood by three sorts of persons, *viz.* by those that make them, by those that execute them, and by those that suffer if they break them.

Men seldom understand any laws but those they feel.

Precepts, like fomentations, must be rubbed into us – and with a rough hand too.

If the laws could speak for themselves they would complain of the lawyers in the first place.

There is more learning now required to explain a law made, than went to the making it.

The law hath so many contradictions, and varyings from itself, that the law may not improperly be called a lawbreaker.

It is become too changeable a thing to be defined; it is made little less a mystery than the Gospel.

The clergy and the lawyers, like the freemasons, may be supposed to take an oath not to tell the secret.

The men of law have a bias to their calling in the interpretations they make of the law.

Of PARLIAMENTS

The Parliaments are so altered from their original constitution that between the Court and the Country the House, instead of being united, is like troops of a contrary party facing one another, and watching their advantage.

Even the well-meaning men who have good sense, too, have their difficulties in an assembly; what they offer honestly for a good end will be skilfully improved for an ill one.

It is strange that a gross mistake should live a minute in an assembly; one would expect that it should be immediately stifled by their discerning faculties. But practice convinceth that a mistake is nowhere better entertained.

In Parliaments, men wrangle on behalf of liberty that do as little care for it as they deserve it.

Where the People in Parliament give a good deal of money in exchange for anything from the Crown a wise Prince can hardly have an ill bargain. The present gift begetteth more; it is a politic kind of generation; and whenever a Parliament does not bring forth it is the unskilfulness of the Government that is the cause of the miscarriage.

Parliaments would bind and limit one another, and enact that such and such things shall not be made precedents. There is not a word of sense in this language, which yet is to be understood the sense of the nation, and is printed as solemnly as if it was sense.

Of PARTIES[18]

The best Party is but a kind of a conspiracy against the rest of the nation. They put everybody else out of their protection. Like the Jews to the Gentiles, all others are the offscourings of the world.

Men value themselves upon their principles, so as to neglect practice, abilities, industry, &c.

Party cutteth off one half of the world from the other, so that the mutual improvement of men's understanding by conversing, &c. is lost, and men are half undone when they lose the advantage of knowing what their enemies think of them.

It is like faith without works; they take it for a dispensation from all other duties, which is the worst kind of dispensing power.

It groweth to be the master thought; the eagerness against one another at home, being a nearer object, extinguisheth that which we ought to have against our foreign enemies; and few men's understandings can get above overvaluing the danger that is nearest in comparison of that more remote.

It turneth all thought into talking instead of doing. Men get a habit of being unuseful to the public by turning in a circle of wrangling and railing, which they cannot get out of. And it may be remarked that a speculative coxcomb is not only unuseful, but mischievous; a practical coxcomb under discipline may be made use of.

It maketh a man thrust his understanding in a corner, and confine it till by degrees he destroys it.

Party is generally an effect of wantonness, peace and plenty, which beget humour, pride, &c. and that is called zeal and public spirit.

They forget insensibly that there is anybody in the world but themselves, by keeping no other company; so they miscalculate cruelly. And thus Parties mistake their strength by the same reason that private men overvalue themselves; for we by finding fault with others build up a partial esteem of ourselves upon the founda-

18. The terms 'Whig' and 'Tory' arose during the Exclusion Crisis, in 1679 or 1680, and in Halifax's old age their use was habitual, though historians differ as to their meaning and few would credit the Whig or Tory party with the cohesion and powers of discipline which he ascribes to them. He would also be thinking of larger, looser organizations like the 'High Church Party' and the 'Country Party'.

tion of their mistakes. So men in Parties find faults with those in the Administration, not without reason, but forget that they would be exposed to the same objections, and perhaps greater, if it was their adversary's turn to have the fault-finding part.

There are men who shine in a faction, and make a figure by opposition, who would stand in a worse light if they had the preferments they struggle for.

It looketh so like courage – but nothing that is *like* is *the same* – to go to the extreme, that men are carried away with it, and blown up out of their senses by the wind of popular applause.

That which looketh bold is a great object that the People can discern; but that which is wise is not so easily seen. It is one part of it that it is not seen but at the end of a design. Those who are disposed to be wise too late, are apt to be valiant too early.

Most men enter into a Party rashly, and retreat from it as shamefully. As they encourage one another at first, so they betray one another at last; and because every qualification is capable of being corrupted by the excess, they fall upon the extreme to fix mutual reproaches upon one another.

Party is little less than an inquisition, where men are under such a discipline in carrying on the common cause as leaves no liberty of private opinion.

It is hard to produce an instance where a Party did ever succeed against a Government, except they had a good handle given them.

No original Party ever prevailed in a turn; it brought up something else, but the first projectors were thrown off.

If there are two Parties, a man ought to adhere to that which he disliketh least, though in the whole he doth not approve it; for whilst he doth not list himself in one or the other Party he is looked upon as such a straggler that he is fallen upon by both. Therefore a man under such a misfortune of singularity is neither to provoke the world, nor disquiet himself by taking any particular station.[19]

19. Macaulay may have had this passage in mind when he wrote: 'The party to which he at any moment belonged was the party which, at that moment, he liked least'. See Introduction, p. 23 above.

It becometh him to live in the shade, and keep his mistakes from giving offence; but if they are his opinions he cannot put them off as he doth his clothes. Happy those who are convinced so as to be of the general opinions.

Ignorance maketh most men go into a Party, and shame keepeth them from getting out of it.

More men hurt others they do not know why than for any reason.

If there was any Party entirely composed of honest men, it would certainly prevail; but both the honest men and the knaves resolve to turn one another off when the business is done.

They by turns defame all England, so nobody can be employed that hath not been branded; there are few things so criminal as a place.

Of Courts

The Court may be said to be a company of well-bred fashionable beggars.

At Court, if a man hath too much pride to be a creature,[20] he had better stay at home. A man who will rise at Court must begin by creeping upon all-fours. A place at Court, like a place in Heaven, is to be got by being much upon one's knees.

There are hardly two creatures of a more differing species than the same man when he is pretending to a place and when he is in possession of it.

Men's industry is spent in receiving the rents of a place; there is little left for discharging the duty of it.

Some places have such a corrupting influence upon the man that it is a supernatural thing to resist it.

Some places lie so fair to entertain corruption that it looketh like renouncing a due perquisite not to go into it.

If a getting fool would keep out of business, he would grow richer in a Court than a man of sense.

20. 'Creature' had the meaning 'dependant', a man entirely 'created' by his patron.

One would wonder that in a Court where there is so little kindness there should be so much whispering.

Men must brag of kind letters from Court, at the same time that they do not believe one word of them.

Men at Court think so much of their own cunning that they forget other men's.

After a Revolution[21] you see the same men in the Drawing Room, and within a week the same flatterers.

Of Punishment

Wherever a Government knows when to show the rod, it will not often be put to use it. But between the want of skill and the want of honesty faults generally either escape punishment or are mended to no purpose.

Men are not hanged for stealing horses but that horses may not be stolen.

Wherever a knave is not punished, an honest man is laughed at.

A cheat to the public is thought infamous, and yet to accuse him is not thought an honourable part. What a paradox! It is an ill method to make the aggravation of the crime a security against the punishment, so that the danger is not to rob but not to rob enough.

Treason must not be inlaid work of several pieces, it must be an entire piece of itself. Accumulative in that case is a murdering word, that carrieth injustice, and no sense in it.[22]

An inference, though never so rational, should go no farther than to justify a suspicion, not so far as to inflict a punishment. Nothing is so apt to break with stretching as an inference, and nothing so ridiculous as to see how fools will abuse one.

21. This may refer to the Revolution of 1688, but 'revolution' was a much weaker word in the seventeenth century than it is today; it could mean just 'change', or a 'revolution' of Fortune's wheel.

22. The doctrine that a large number of actions, none of them in themselves treasonable, could amount to treason by accumulation had been pressed, without success, in the impeachment of the Earl of Strafford in 1641. Halifax may be thinking of a more recent case, but though in the great treason trials of Charles II the judges were willing to accept strained or circumstantial evidence, and in the case of Algernon Sydney they accepted a manuscript book as treasonable, the question of accumulation did not arise.

MORAL THOUGHTS AND REFLECTIONS

MORAL THOUGHTS AND REFLECTIONS

Of the World

It is from the shortness of thought that men imagine there is any great variety in the World.

Time hath thrown a veil upon the faults of former ages, or else we should see the same deformities we condemn in the present times.

When a man looketh upon the rules that are made he will think there can be no faults in the World; and when he looketh upon the faults there are so many he will be tempted to think there are no rules.

They are not to be reconciled, otherwise than by concluding that which is called frailty is the incurable nature of mankind.

A man that understandeth the World must be weary of it, and a man who doth not for that reason ought not to be pleased with it.

The uncertainty of what is to come is such a dark cloud that neither reason nor religion can quite break through it; and the condition of mankind is to be weary of what we do know and afraid of what we do not.

The World is beholden to generous mistakes for the greatest part of the good that is done in it.

Our vices and virtues couple with one another, and get children that resemble both their parents.

If a man can hardly enquire into a thing he undervalueth, how can a man of good sense take pains to understand the World?

To understand the World, and to like it, are two things not easily to be reconciled.

That which is called an able man is a great over-valuer of the World, and all that belongeth to it.

All that can be said of him is, that he maketh the best of the general mistake.

It is the fools and the knaves that make the wheels of the World turn. They *are* the World; those few who have sense or honesty sneak up and down single, but never go in herds.

To be too much troubled is a worse way of over-valuing the World than the being too much pleased.

A man that steps aside from the World, and hath leisure to observe it without interest or design, thinks all mankind as mad as they think him for not agreeing with them in their mistakes.

Of AMBITION

The serious folly of wise men in over-valuing the World is as contemptible as anything they think fit to censure.

The first mistake belonging to business[1] is the going into it.

Men make it such a point of honour to be fit for business that they forget to examine whether business is fit for a man of sense.

There is reason to think the most celebrated philosophers would have been bunglers at business; but the reason is because they despised it.

It is not a reproach but a compliment to learning to say that great scholars are less fit for business, since the truth is, business is so much a lower thing than learning that a man used to the last cannot easily bring his stomach down to the first.

The Government of the World is a great thing, but it is a very coarse one, too, compared with the fineness of speculative knowledge.

The dependance of a great man upon a greater is a subjection that lower men cannot easily comprehend.

Ambition hath no mean, it is either upon all fours or upon tiptoes.

Nothing can be humbler than ambition when it is so disposed.

Popularity is a crime from the moment it is sought; it is only a virtue where men have it whether they will or no.

It is generally an appeal to the People from the sentence given by men of sense against them.

It is stepping very low to get very high.

Men by habit make irregular stretches of power, without discerning the consequence and extent of them.

Eagerness is apt to overlook consequences, it is loth to be

1. public business, or politics.

stopped in its career; for when men are in great haste they see only in a straight line.

Of CUNNING *and* KNAVERY

Cunning is so apt to grow into knavery that an honest man will avoid the temptation of it. But men in this age are half bribed by the ambition of circumventing, without any other encouragements; so proud of the character of being able men that they do not care to have their dexterity confined.

In this age, when it is said of a man, 'He knows how to live', it may be implied he is not very honest.

An honest man must lose so many occasions of getting that the World will hardly allow him the character of an able one.

There is however more wit[2] requisite to be an honest man than there is to be a knave.

The most necessary thing in the World, and yet the least usual, is to reflect that those we deal with may know how to be as arrant knaves as ourselves.

The eagerness of a knave maketh him often as catchable, as ignorance maketh a fool.

No man is so much a fool as not to have wit enough sometimes to be a knave; nor any so cunning a knave, as not to have the weakness sometimes to play the fool.

The mixture of fool and knave maketh up the parti-coloured creatures that make all the bustle in the World.

There is not so pleasant a quarry as a knave taken in a net of his own making.

A knave leaneth sometimes so hard upon his impudence that it breaketh and lets him fall.

Knavery is in such perpetual motion that it hath not always leisure to look to its own steps; it is like sliding upon skates, no motion so smooth or swift, but none gives so terrible a fall.

A knave loveth self so heartily that he is apt to overstrain it; by never thinking he can get enough he gets so much less. His thought is like wine that fretteth with too much fermenting.

2. intelligence.

The knaves in every Government are a kind of corporation; and though they fall out with one another, like all beasts of prey, yet upon occasion they unite to support the common cause.

It cannot be said to be such a corporation as the Bank of England,[3] but they are a numerous and formidable body, scarce to be resisted; but the point is, they can never rely upon one another.

Knaves go chained to one another like slaves in the galleys, and cannot easily untie themselves from their company. Their promises and honour indeed do not hinder them, but other entangling circumstances keep them from breaking loose.

If knaves had not foolish memories, they would never trust one another so often as they do.

Present interest, like present love, maketh all other friendship look cold to it, but it faileth in the holding.

When one knave betrayeth another, the one is not to be blamed nor the other to be pitied.

When they complain of one another as if they were honest men, they ought to be laughed at as if they were fools.

There are some cunning men who yet can scarce be called rational creatures; yet they are often more successful than men of sense, because those they have to deal with are upon a looser guard, and their simplicity maketh their knavery unsuspected.

There is no such thing as a venial sin against morality, no such thing as a small knavery. He that carries a small crime easily will carry it on when it grows to be an ox. But the little knaves are the greater of the two, because they have less the excuse of temptation.

Knavery is so humble, and merit so proud, that the latter is thrown down because it cannot stoop.

Of FOLLY *and* FOOLS

There are five Orders of fools, as of building:[4] 1. the blockhead, 2. coxcomb, 3. vain blockhead, 4. grave coxcomb, and 5. the half-witted fellow; this last is of the composite order.

3. Founded April 1694.

4. The five classical orders of architecture are the Tuscan, the Doric, the Ionic, the Corinthian and the Composite.

The follies of grave men have the precedence of all others, a ridiculous dignity, that gives them a right to be laughed at in the first place.

As the masculine wit is the strongest, so the masculine impertinence[5] is the greatest.

The consequence of a half-wit is a half-will, there is not strength enough in the thought to carry it to the end.

A fool is naturally recommended to our kindness by setting us off by the comparison. Men are grateful to fools for giving them the pleasure of condemning them.

But folly hath a long tail that is not seen at first. For every single folly hath a root out of which more are ready to sprout; and a fool hath so unlimited a power of mistaking that a man of sense can never comprehend to what degree it may extend.

There are some fools so low that they are preferred when they are laughed at. Their being named putteth them in the list of men, which is more than belongeth to them.

One should no more laugh at a contemptible fool than at a dead fly.

The dissimulation of a fool should come within the Statute of stabbing.[6] It giveth no warning.

A fool will be rude from the moment he is allowed to be familiar; he can make no other use of freedom than to be unmannerly.

Weak men are apt to be cruel, because they stick at nothing that may repair the ill effect of their mistakes.

Folly is often more cruel in the consequence than malice can be in the intent.

Many a man is murdered by the well-meant mistakes of his unthinking friends.

A weak[7] friend, if he will be kind, ought to go no farther than wishes; if he proffereth either to say or to do it is dangerous.

A man had as good go to bed to a razor as to be intimate with a foolish friend.

5. folly.
6. 1 Jac. I c. 8 made stabbing a capital offence if the victim had not drawn.
7. weak-minded.

Mistaken kindness is little less dangerous than premeditated malice.

A man hath not the relief of being angry at the blows of a mistaken friend.

A busy fool is fitter to be shut up than a downright madman.

A man that hath only wit enough not to do hurt committeth a sin if he aimeth at doing good.

His passive understanding must not pretend to be active.

It is a sin against nature for such a man to be meddling.

It is hard to find a blockhead so wise as to be upon the defensive; he will be sallying, and then he is sure to be ill used.

If a dull fool can make a vow and keep it, never to speak his own sense or do his own business, he may pass a great while for a rational creature.

A blockhead is as ridiculous when he talketh as a goose is when it flieth.

The grating a gridiron is not a worse noise than the jingling of words is to a man of sense.

It is ill-manners to silence a fool, and cruelty to let him go on.

Most men make little other use of their speech than to give evidence against their own understanding.

A great talker may be a man of sense, but he cannot be one who will venture to rely upon him.

There is so much danger in talking that a man strictly wise can hardly be called a sociable creature.

The great expense of words is laid out in setting ourselves out, or deceiving others; to convince them requireth but a few.

Many words are always either suspicious or ridiculous.

A fool hath no dialogue within himself, the first thought carrieth him, without the reply of a second.

A fool will admire or like nothing that he understands, a man of sense nothing but what he understands.

Wise men gain, and poor men live, by the superfluities of fools.

Till follies become ruinous, the World is better with than it would be without them.

A fool is angry that he is the food of a knave, forgetting that it is the end of his creation.

Of Hope

Hope is a kind cheat; in the minute of our disappointment we are angry, but upon the whole matter there is no pleasure without it.

It is so much a pleasanter thing than truth to the greatest part of the world that it hath all their kindness; the other only hath their respect.

Hope is generally a wrong guide, though it is very good company by the way. It brusheth through hedge and ditch till it cometh to a great leap, and there it is apt to fall and break its bones.

It would be well if hopes carried men only to the top of the hill, without throwing them afterwards down the precipice.

The hopes of a fool are blind guides, those of a man of sense doubt often of their way.

Men should do with their hopes as they do with tame fowl, cut their wings that they may not fly over the wall.

A hoping fool hath such terrible falls that his brains are turned, though not cured by them.

The hopes of a fool are bullets he throws into the air, that fall down again and break his skull.

There can be no entire disappointment to a wise man, because he maketh it a cause of succeeding another time. A fool is so unreasonably raised by his hopes that he is half dead by a disappointment; his mistaken fancy draweth him so high, that when he falleth he is sure to break his bones.

Of Anger

Anger is a better sign of the heart than of the head; it is a breaking out of the disease of honesty. Just anger may be as dangerous as it could be if there was no provocation to it; for a knave is not so nice a casuist but that he will ruin, if he can, any man that blameth him.

Where ill-nature is not predominant anger will be short-breathed, it cannot hold out a long course. Hatred can be tired and cloyed as well as love; for our spirits, like our limbs, are tired with being long in one posture.

There is a dignity in good-sense that is offended and defaced by anger.

Anger is never without an argument, but seldom with a good one.

Anger raiseth invention but it overheateth the oven.

Anger, like drink, raiseth a great deal of unmannerly wit.

True wit must come by drops; anger throweth it out in a stream, and then it is not likely to be of the best kind.

Ill language punisheth anger by drawing a contempt upon it.

Of Apologies

It is a dangerous task to answer objections, because they are helped by the malice of mankind.

A bold accusation doth at first draw such a general attention, that it gets the world on its side.

To a man who hath a mind to find a fault, an excuse generally giveth farther hold.

Explaining is generally half confessing.

Innocence hath a very short style.

When a jealousy[8] of any kind is once raised, it is as often provoked as cured by any arguments, let them be never so reasonable.

When laziness letteth things alone, it is a disease; but when skill doth it, it is a virtue.

Malice may help a fool to aggravate, but there must be skill to know how to extenuate.

To lessen an object that at the first sight giveth offence requireth a dexterous hand; there must be strength as well as skill to take off the weight of the first impression.

When a man is very unfortunate, it looketh like a saucy thing in him to justify himself.

A man must stoop sometimes to his ill star, but he must never lie down to it.

The vindications men make of themselves to posterity would hardly be supported by good sense, if they were not of some advantage to their own families.

8. suspicion.

The defending an ill thing is more criminal than the doing it, because it wanteth the excuse of its not being premeditated.

An advocate for injustice is like a bawd that is worse than her client who committeth the sin.

There is hardly any man so strict as not to vary a little from truth when he is to make an excuse.

Not telling all the truth is hiding it, and that is comforting or abetting a lie.

A long vindication is seldom a skilful one.

Long doth at least imply doubtful in such a case.

A fool should avoid the making an excuse as much as the committing a fault; for a fool's excuse is always a second fault; and whenever he will undertake either to hide or mend a thing, he proclaimeth and spoileth it.

Of Malice *and* Envy

Malice is a greater magnifying-glass than kindness.

Malice is of a low stature, but it hath very long arms. It often reacheth into the next world, death itself is not a bar to it.

Malice, like lust, when it is at the height doth not know shame.

If it did not sometimes cut itself with its own edge it would destroy the world.

Malice can mistake by being keen as well as by being dull.

When malice groweth critical, it loseth its credit.

It must go under the disguise of plainness, or else it is exposed.

Anger may have some excuse for being blind, but malice none; for malice hath time to look before it.

When malice is overgrown, it cometh to be the highest degree of impertinence. For that reason it must not be fed and pampered, which is apt to make it play the fool. But where it is wise and steady there is no precaution that can be quite proof against it.

Ill-will is seldom cured on a sudden, it must go off by degrees, by insensible transpiration.[9]

Malice may be sometimes out of breath, envy never. A man may make peace with hatred, but never with envy.

9. evaporation.

No passion is better heard by our will, than that of envy; no passion is admitted to have audience with less exception.

Envy taketh the shape of flattery, and that maketh men hug it so close that they cannot part with it.

The sure way to be commended is to get into a condition of being pitied; for envy will not give its leave to commend a man till he is miserable.

A man is undone when envy will not vouchsafe to look upon him.

Yet after all, envy doth virtue as much good as hurt, by provoking it to appear. Nay, it forcibly draweth out and inviteth virtue, by giving it a mind to be revenged of it.

Of Vanity

The world is nothing but vanity cut out into several shapes.

Men often mistake themselves, but they never forget themselves.

A man must not so entirely fall out with vanity as not to take its assistance in the doing great things.

Vanity is like some men, who are very useful if they are kept under, and else not to be endured.

A little vanity may be allowed in a man's train, but it must not sit down at table with him.

Without some share of it, men's talents would be buried like ore in a mine unwrought.

Men would be less eager to gain knowledge if they did not hope to set themselves out by it.

It showeth the narrowness of our nature, that a man that intendeth any one thing extremely hath not thought enough left for anything else.

Our pride maketh us over-value our stock of thought, so as to trade much beyond what it is able to make good.

Many aspire to learn what they can never comprehend, as others pretend to teach what they themselves do not know.

The vanity of teaching often tempteth a man to forget he is a blockhead.

Self-conceit driveth away the suspecting how scurvily others think of us.

Vanity cannot be a friend to truth, because it is restrained by it; and vanity is so impatiently desirous of showing itself that it cannot bear the being crossed.

There is a degree of vanity that recommendeth; if it goeth further it exposeth.

So much as to stir the blood to do commendable things, but not so much as to possess the brain, and turn it round.

There are as many that are blown up by the wind of vanity as are carried away by the stream of interest.

Everybody hath not wit enough to act out of interest, but everybody hath little enough to do it out of vanity.

Some men's heads are as easily blown away as their hats.

If the commending others well did not recommend ourselves, there would be few panegyrics.

Men's vanity will often dispose them to be commended into very troublesome employments.

The desiring to be remembered when we are dead is to so little purpose that it is fit men should, as they generally are, be disappointed in it. Nevertheless, the desire of leaving a good name behind us is so honourable to ourselves and so useful to the world that good sense must not be heard against it.

Heraldry is one of those foolish things that may yet be too much despised.

The contempt of scutcheons[10] is as much a disease in this age as the over-valuing them was in former times.

There is a good use to be made of the most contemptible things, and an ill one of those that are the most valuable.

Of Money

If men considered how many things there are that riches cannot buy, they would not be so fond of them.

The things to be bought with money are such as least deserve the giving a price for them.

10. coats-of-arms.

Wit and money are so apt to be abused that men generally make a shift to be the worse for them.

Money in a fool's hand exposeth him worse than a pied coat.

Money hath too great a preference given to it by states, as well as by particular men.

Men are more the sinews of war than money.

The third part of an army must be destroyed before a good one can be made out of it.

They who are of opinion that money will do everything may very well be suspected to do everything for money.

False LEARNING

A little learning misleadeth, and a great deal often stupifieth the understanding.

Great reading without applying it is like corn heaped that is not stirred, it groweth musty.

A learned coxcomb dyeth his mistakes in so much a deeper colour; a wrong kind of learning serveth only to embroider his errors.

A man that hath read without judgment is like a gun charged with goose-shot let loose upon the company.

He is only well furnished with materials to expose himself, and to mortify those he liveth with.

The reading of the greatest scholars, if put into a limbeck,[11] might be distilled into a small quantity of essence.

The reading of most men is like a wardrobe of old clothes that are seldom used.

Weak men are the worse for the good sense they read in Books, because it furnisheth them only with more matter to mistake.

11. a retort.

Of Company

Men that cannot entertain themselves want[12] somebody, though they care for nobody.

An impertinent[13] fellow is never in the right, but in his being weary of himself.

By that time men are fit for company they see the objections to it.

The company of a fool is dangerous as well as tedious.

It is flattering some men to endure them.

Present[14] punishment attendeth the fault.

A following wit will be welcome in most companies; a leading one lieth too heavy for envy to bear.

Out-doing is so near reproaching that it will generally be thought very ill company.

Anything that shineth doth in some measure tarnish everything that standeth next to it.

Keeping much company generally endeth in playing the fool or the knave with them.

Of Friendship

Friendship cometh oftener by chance than by choice, which maketh it generally so uncertain.

It is a mistake to say a friend can be bought.

A man may buy a good turn, but he cannot buy the heart that doth it.

Friendship cannot live with ceremony, nor without civility.

There must be a nice diet observed to keep friendship from falling sick; nay, there is more skill necessary to keep a friend than there is to reclaim an enemy.

Those friends who are above interest are seldom above jealousy.

It is a misfortune for a man not to have a friend in the world, but for that reason he shall have no enemy.

In the commerce of the World men struggle little less with their friends than they do with their enemies.

12. lack. 13. foolish. 14. immediate.

Esteem ought to be the ground of kindness, and yet there are no friends that seldomer meet.

Kindness is apt to be as afraid of esteem, as that is to be ashamed of kindness.

Our kindness is greatest to those that will do what we would have them, in which our esteem cannot always go along.

MISCELLANEOUS THOUGHTS AND REFLECTIONS

MISCELLANEOUS THOUGHTS AND REFLECTIONS

Of Advice and Correction

The rule of doing as we would be done by is never less observed than it is in telling others their faults. But men intend more to show others that they are free from the fault, than to dissuade them from committing it. They are so pleased with the prudent shape of an adviser, that it raiseth the value they have of themselves, whilst they are about it.

Certainly, to give advice to a friend, either asked or unasked, is so far from a fault that it is a duty; but if a man loves to give advice it is a sure sign that he himself wanteth it.

A man whilst he is advising putteth his understanding upon tiptoes, and is unwilling to bring it down again.

A weak man had rather be thought to know than know, and that maketh him so impatient to be told of a mistake.

He who will not be the better for other men's faults hath no cure left for his own.

But he that can probe himself to cure his own faults, will seldom need either the surgery of his friends or of his enemies.

Of Alterations

In a corrupted age the putting the world in order would breed confusion.

A rooted disease must be stroked away rather than kicked away.

As soon as men have understanding enough to find a fault, they have enough to see the danger of mending it.

Desiring to have anything mended is venturing to have it spoiled; to know when to let things alone is a high pitch of good sense. But a fool hath an eagerness, like a monkey in a glass shop. to break everything in the handling.

Curing and mending are generally mere words of art not to be

1. Advertisements.

relied upon. They are set out in bills,[1] but the mountebanks only get by them.

Bashfulness

Great bashfulness is oftener an effect of pride than of modestry.

Modesty is oftener mistaken than any other virtue.

Boldness

Wise venturing is the most commendable part of human prudence.

It is the upper storey of prudence, whereas perpetual caution is a kind of underground wisdom that doth not care to see the light.

It is best for great men to shoot over, and for lesser men to shoot short.

Borrowers of Opinions

Men who borrow their opinions can never repay their debts. They are beggars by nature, and can therefore never get a stock to grow rich upon.

A man who hath not a distinguishing head is safest by not minding what anybody sayeth. He had better trust to his own opinion, than spoil another man's for want of apprehending it.

Candour

It is some kind of scandal not to bear with the faults of an honest man. It is not loving honesty enough to allow it distinguishing privileges.

There are some decent faults which may pretend to be in the lower rank of virtues; and surely where honour or gratitude are the motives, censure must be a good deal silenced.

Of Caution and Suspicion

Men must be saved in this world by their want of faith.

A man that getteth care into his thoughts cannot properly be said to trade without a stock.

Care and right thought will produce crops all the year without staying for the seasons.

1. advertisements.

A man is to go about his own business as if he had not a friend in the world to help him in it.

He that relieth upon himself will be oppressed by others with offers of their service.

All are apt to shrink from those that lean upon them.

If men would think how often their own words are thrown at their heads, they would less often let them go out of their mouths.

Men's words are bullets that their enemies take up and make use of against them.

A man watches himself best when others watch him too.

It is as necessary for us to suppress our reason when it offendeth, as our mistakes when they expose us.

In an unreasonable age a man's reason let loose would undo him.

A wise man will do with his reason as a miser doth with his money, hoard it, but be very sparing in the expense of it.

A man that should call everything by its right name would hardly pass the streets without being knocked down as a common enemy.

A man cannot be more in the wrong than to own without distinction the being in the right.

When a man is very kind or very angry there is no sure guard but silence upon that subject.

A man's understanding is easily shoved out of its place by warm thoughts of any kind.

We are not so much masters of our heat as to have enough to warm our thoughts, and not so much as to set them on fire.

A great enemy is a great object that inviteth precaution, which maketh him less dangerous than a mean one.

An old man concludeth from his knowing mankind that they know him too, and that maketh him very wary.

On the other hand, it must be allowed that a man's being deceived by knaves hath often this ill effect, that it maketh him too jealous of honest men.

The mind, like the body, is subject to be hurt by everything it taketh for a remedy.

There are some such very great foreseers, that they grow into the vanity of pretending to see where nothing is to be seen.

He that will see at too great a distance, will sometimes mistake a bush for a horse. The prospect of a wise man will be bounded.

A man may so overdo it in looking too far before him, that he may stumble the more for it.

And, to conclude, he that leaveth nothing to chance will do few things ill, but he will do very few things.

Suspicion is rather a virtue than a fault, as long as it doth like a dog that watcheth, and doth not bite.

A wise man, in trusting another, must not rely upon his promise against his nature.

Early suspicion is often an injury, and late suspicion is always a folly.

A wise man will keep his suspicions muzzled, but he will keep them awake.

There can no rules be given to suspicion, no more than to love.

Suspicion taketh root, and beareth fruit, from the moment it is planted.

Suspicion seldom wanteth food to keep it up in health and vigour. It feedeth upon everything it seeth, and is not curious in its diet.

Suspicion doth not grow up to an injury till it breaketh out.

When our suspicion of another man is once discovered by him, there ought to be an end of all further commerce.

He that is never suspected is either very much esteemed, or very much despised.

A man's interest is not a sufficient ground to suspect him, if his nature doth not concur in it.

A weak man hath less suspicion than a wise one, but when he hath it he is less easily cured.

The remedies as often increase the disease as they do allay it and a fool valueth himself upon suspecting at a venture.

Cheats

Many men swallow the being cheated, but no man could ever endure to chew it.

Few men would be deceived if their conceit of themselves did not help the skill of those that go about it.

Complaint

Complaining is a contempt upon oneself. It is an ill sign both of a man's head and of his heart.

A man throweth himself down whilst he complaineth; and when a man throweth himself down, nobody careth to take him up again.

Content

Content layeth pleasure, nay virtue, in a slumber, with few and faint intermissions.

It is to the mind like moss to a tree, it bindeth it up so as to stop its growth.

Converts

The impudence of a bawd is modesty compared with that of a convert.

A convert hath so much to do to gain credit that a man is to think well before he changeth.

Desires

Men generally state their wants by their fancy, and not by their reason.

The poor young children are whipped and beaten by the old ones, who are much more inexcusably impertinent.

Not having things is a more proper expression for a man of sense than his wanting them.

Where sense is wanting everything is wanting.

A man of sense can hardly want, but for his friends and children that have none.

Most men let their wishes run away with them. They have no mind to stop them in their career, the motion is so pleasing.

To desire what belongeth to another man is misprision of robbery.

Men are commanded not to covet, because when they do they are very apt to take.

Difficulty

A difficulty raiseth the spirits of a great man, he hath a mind to wrestle with it and give it a fall.

A man's mind must be very low, if the difficulty doth not make a part of his pleasure.

The pride of compassing may more than compare with the pleasure of enjoying.

Dissembling

Nothing so ridiculous as a false philosopher, and nothing so rare as a true one.

Men take more pains to hide than to mend themselves.

Dreams

Men's pride, as well as their weakness, disposeth them to rely upon dreams, from their thinking themselves of such importance as to have warning of what is to befall them.

The enquiry into a dream is another dream.

Drunkenness

It is a piece of arrogance to dare to be drunk, because a man showeth himself without a veil.

Experience

The best way to suppose what may come is to remember what is passed.

The best qualification of a prophet is to have a good memory.

Experience maketh more prophets than revelation.

The knowledge that is got without pains is kept without pleasure.

The struggling for knowledge hath a pleasure in it like that of wrestling with a fine woman.

Extremes

Extremity is always ill, that which is good cannot live a moment with it.

Anybody that is fool enough will be safe in the world, and anybody that can be knave enough will be rich in it.

The generality of the world falleth into an insufficient mean that exposeth them more than an extreme on either side.

Faculties of the Mind

Though memory and invention are not upon good terms, yet when the first is loaded, the other is stifled.

The memory hath claws by which it holdeth fast; but it hath no wings, like the invention, to enable it to fly.

Some men's memory is like a box where a man should mingle his jewels with his old shoes.

There ought to be a great difference between the memory and the stomach; the last is to admit everything, the former should have the faculty of rejecting.

It is a nice mean between letting the thought languish for want of exercise, and tiring it by giving it too much.

A man may dwell so long upon a thought that it may take him prisoner.

The hardest thing in the world is to give the thoughts due liberty, and yet retain them in due discipline.

They are libertines that are apt to abuse freedom, and do not well know how to bear restraint.

A man that excels in any one thing has a kind of arbitrary power over all that hear him upon that subject, and no man's life is too short to know any one thing perfectly.

The modern wit is rather to set men out, than to make them of any use.

Some men have acted courage who had it not, but no man can act wit if nature doth not teach him his part. True wit is always revenged upon any false pretender that meddleth with it.

Wit is the only thing that men are willing to think they can ever have enough of.

There is a happy pitch of ignorance that a man of sense might pray for.

A man that hath true wit will have honour too, not only to adorn, but to support it.

Families

The building up a family is a manufacture very little above the building a house of cards.

Time and accidents are sure to furnish a blast to blow it down.

No house wanteth new tiling so often as a family wants repairing.

The desire of having children is as much the effect of vanity as of good nature.

We think our children a part of ourselves, though as they grow up they might very well undeceive us.

Men love their children, not because they are promising plants, but because they are theirs.

They cannot discredit the plant without disparaging the soil out of which it came.

Pride in this, as in many other things, is often mistaken for love.

As children make a man poor in one sense, so in another they enforce care, and that begetteth riches.

Love is presently out of breath when it is to go up hill from the children to the parents.

Fear

'Tis good to have men in awe, but dangerous to have them afraid of us.

The mean is so nice that the hitting upon it is oftener the effect of chance than of skill.

A degree of fear sharpeneth, the excess of it stupifieth.

It is as scandalous not to fear at some times, as it can be to be afraid of others.

Flattery

Folly begets want, and want flattery; so that flattery, with all its wit, is the grandchild of folly.

Were it not for bunglers in the manner of doing it, hardly any man would ever find out he was laughed at.

And yet, generally speaking, a trowel is a more effectual instrument than a pencil for flattery.

Men generally do so love the taste of flattery, their stomach can never be overcharged with it.

There is a right reverend flattery that hath the precedence of all other kinds of it.

This mitred flattery is of all others the most exalted. It ever groweth in proportion, and keepeth pace with power. There is a noble stroke of it in the Articles sent to Princess Mary from Henry VIII: 'Such is his Majesty's Gracious and Divine Nature – showing mercy to such as repentantly cry and call for the same.'[2]

Forgetfulness

Forgetting is oftener an aggravation than an excuse.

The memory will seldom be unmannerly but where it is unkind.

Good manners

There needeth little care to polish the understanding; if true means were used to strengthen it, it will polish itself.

Good manners is such a part of good sense that they cannot be divided; but that which a fool calleth good breeding is the most unmannerly thing in the world.

Right good manners require so much sense that there is hardly any such thing in the world.

Good nature

Good nature is rather acted than practised in the world.

Good nature to others is an inseparable part of justice.

Good will

Good will, like grace, floweth where it listeth.

Men mean so very well to themselves, that they forget to mean well to anybody else.

Heat

Good sense will allow of some intermitting fevers, but then the fit must be short.

2. An authentic quotation of 1536.

Honesty

He that can be quite indifferent when he seeth another man injured hath a lukewarm honesty that a wise man will not depend upon.

He that is not concerned when he seeth an ill thing done to another will not be very eager to do a good one himself.

Hypocrisy

There is so much wit necessary to make a skilful hypocrite that the faculty is fallen amongst bunglers, who make it ridiculous.

Injuries

An injury may more properly be said to be postponed, than to be forgiven. The memory of it is never so subdued, but that it hath always life in it.

The memory of an enemy admitteth no decay but age.

Could we know what men are most apt to remember, we might know what they are most apt to do.

It is a general fault that we dislike men only for the injuries they do to us, and not for those they do to mankind. Yet it will be hard to give a good reason why a man who hath done a deliberate injury to one, will not do it to another.

The memory and the conscience never did, nor never will agree about forgiving injuries.

Nature is second to the memory, and religion to the conscience. When the second fight, the latter is generally disarmed.

Integrity

A man in a corrupted age must make a secret of his integrity, or else he will be looked upon as a common enemy. He must engage his friends not to speak of it, for he setteth himself for a mark to be ill used.

Justice

As far as keeping distance is a sign of respect, mankind hath a great deal for justice.

They make up in ceremony what they want in good will to it.

Where the generality are offenders, justice cometh to be cruelty.

To Love, and be in Love different

To love and to be in love with anything are things as differing as good sense and impertinence.

When we once go beyond bare liking we are in danger of parting with good sense, and it is not easy for good sense to get so far as liking.

Lucre

When by habit a man cometh to have a bargaining soul, its wings are cut, so that it can never soar.

It bindeth reason an apprentice to gain, and instead of a director, maketh it a drudge.

Lying

The being kind to a liar is abetting a treason against mankind. A man is to inform the first magistrate, that he may be clapped up.

Lies are embroidered with promises and excuses.

A known liar should be outlawed in a well-ordered Government.

A man that renounceth truth runneth away from his trial in the world.

The use of talking is almost lost in the world by the habit of lying.

A man that doth not tell all the truth ought to be hanged for a clipper.

Half the truth is often as arrant a lie as can be made. It is the more dexterous, but not the less criminal kind of lying.

Names

Names to men of sense are no more than fig-leaves; to the generality they are thick coverings that hide the nature of things from them.

Fools turn good sense upon its head, they take names for things, and things only for names.

Partiality

It is a general mistake to think the men we like are good for everything, and those we do not, good for nothing.

Patience

A man who is master of patience is master of everything else.

He that can tell how to bear in the right place is master of everybody he dealeth with.

Positiveness

Positive is the perfection of coxcomb, he is then come to his full growth.

Prosperity

It showeth men's nature, that when they are pampered in any kind, they are very apt to play jadish tricks.

One of the tricks of any creature that is wanton, is to kick what is next them.

Quiet

Everything that doth us good is so apt to do us hurt too, that it is a strong argument for men to be quiet.

If men would think more, they would act less.

The greatest part of the business of the world is the effect of not thinking.

Reason and Passion

Most men put their reason out to service to their will.

The master and the man are perpetually falling out.

A third man will hazard a beating, if he goes about to part them.

Nothing hath an uglier look to us than reason, when it is not of our side.

We quarrel so often with it that it maketh us afraid to come near it.

A man that doth not use his reason is a tame beast; a man that abuses it is a wild one.

Reputation

It is a self-flattering contradiction, that wise men despise the opinion of fools, and yet are proud of having their esteem.

Self-love

Self-love rightly defined is far from being a fault.

A man that loveth himself right will do everything else right.

Shame

A man who doth not think he is punished when he is blamed, is too much hardened to be ever reformed.

The court of shame hath of late lost much of its jurisdiction. It ought by right both to judge in the first instance, and to exclude all appeals from it.

Shame is a disease of the last age; this seemeth to be cured of it.

Singularity

Singularity may be good sense at home, but it must not go much abroad.

It is a commendation to be that which a crowd of mistaken fools call singular.

There can hardly be a severer thing said to a man in this age, than that he is like the rest of the world.

Slander

Slander would not stick if it had not always something to lay hold of.

A man who can allow himself the liberty to slander hath the world too much at his mercy.

But the man that despiseth slander deserveth it.

Speakers in Public

Speakers in public should take more pains to hold in their invention than to raise it.

Invention is apt to make such sallies that it cannot secure its retreat.

He that will not make a blot will be pretty sure in his time to give a stroke.

A patient hearer is a sure speaker.

Men are angry when others do not hear them, yet they have more reason to be afraid when they do.

Time the loss of it

Mispending a man's time is a kind of self-homicide, it is making life to be of no use.

Truth

Truth is not only stifled by ignorance, but concealed out of caution or interest, so if it had not a root of immortality it must have been long since extinguished.

Wisdom

The most useful part of wisdom is for a man to give a good guess, what others think of him.

It is a dangerous thing to guess partially, and a melancholy thing to guess right.

Nothing would more contribute to make a man wise than to have always an enemy in his view.

A wise man may have more enemies than a weak one, but he will not so much feel the weight of them. Indeed, the being wise doth either make men our friends or discourage them from being our enemies.

Wisdom is only a comparative quality, it will not bear a single definition.

Youth

A man hath too little heat, or wit, or courage, if he hath not sometimes more than he should.

Just enough of a good thing is always too little.

Long life giveth more marks to shoot at, and therefore old men are less well thought of than those who have not been so long upon the stage.

Other men's memories retain the ill, whilst the good things done by an old man easily slip out of them.

Old men have in some degree their reprisals upon younger, by making nicer observations upon them by virtue of their experience.

A CHARACTER OF KING CHARLES II

EDITORIAL INTRODUCTION

This work was first published in 1750, from a manuscript in the hands of Halifax's granddaughter, Dorothy, Countess of Burlington, which has not survived. One phrase (p. 266 below) strongly suggests that it was written after 1688.

A CHARACTER OF KING CHARLES II

1. *Of his* Religion

A character differeth from a picture only in this, every part of it must be like, but it is not necessary that every feature should be comprehended in it, as in a picture, only some of the most remarkable.

This Prince at his first entrance into the world had adversity for his introducer, which is generally thought to be no ill one but in his case it proved so, and laid the foundation of most of those misfortunes or errors that were the causes of the great objections made to him.

The first effect it had was in relation to his Religion.

The ill-bred familiarity of the Scotch divines[1] had given him a distaste of that part of the Protestant religion. He was left then to the little remnant of the Church of England in the Faubourg St. Germain, which made such a kind of figure as might easily be turned in such a manner as to make him lose his veneration for it. In a refined country, where religion appeared in pomp and splendour, the outward appearance of such unfashionable men was made an argument against their religion; and a young Prince not averse to raillery was the more susceptible of a contempt for it.

The company he kept, the men in his pleasures, and the arguments of state that he should not appear too much a Protestant whilst he expected assistance from a Popish Prince; all these, together with a habit encouraged by an application to his pleasures, did so loosen and untie him from his first impressions that I take it for granted after the first year or two he was no more a Protestant. If you ask me what he was, my answer must be that he was of the religion of a young Prince in his warm blood, whose enquiries were more applied to find arguments against believing than to lay any settled foundations for acknowledging Providence, mysteries, &c. A general creed, and no very long one, may be presumed to be

1. A reference to his visit to Scotland, 1649–51.

the utmost religion of one whose age and inclination could not well spare any thoughts that did not tend to his pleasures.

In this kind of indifference or unthinkingness, which is too natural in the beginnings of life to be heavily censured, I will suppose he might pass some considerable part of his youth. I must presume, too, that no occasions were lost during that time to insinuate everything to bend him towards Popery. Great art without intermission, against youth and easiness, which are seldom upon their guard, must have its effect. A man is to be admired if he resisteth, and therefore cannot reasonably be blamed if he yieldeth to them. When the critical minute was, I'll not undertake to determine; but certainly the inward conviction doth generally precede the outward declarations – at what distances dependeth upon men's several complexions and circumstances; no stated period can be fixed.

It will be said that he had not religion enough to have conviction; that is a vulgar error. Conviction indeed is not a proper word but where a man is convinced by reason, but in the common acceptation it is applied to those who cannot tell why they are so. If men can be at least as positive in a mistake as when they are in the right, they may be as clearly convinced when they do not know why as when they do.

I must presume that no man of the King's age and his methods of life could possibly give a good reason for changing the religion in which he was born, let it be what it will. But our passions are much oftener convinced than our reason. He had but little reading, and that tending to his pleasures more than to his instruction. In the library of a young prince the solemn folios are not much rumpled, books of a lighter digestion have the dog's ears.

Some pretend to be very precise in the time of his reconciling – the Cardinal de Retz, &c. I will not enter into it minutely, but whenever it was, it is observable that the Government of France did not think it advisable to discover it openly; upon which such obvious reflections may be made that I will not mention them.

Such a secret can never be put into a place which is so closely stopped that there shall be no chinks. Whispers went about; particular men had intimations; Cromwell had his advertisements in other things, and this was as well worth his paying for. There was enough said of it to startle a great many, though not universally diffused; so much, that if the Government here had not crumbled of itself, his right alone, with that and other clogs upon it, would hardly have thrown it down. I conclude that when he came into England he was as certainly a Roman Catholic as that he was a man of pleasure; both very consistent by visible experience.[2]

It is impertinent to give reasons for men's changing their religion. None can give them but themselves, as every man has quite a different way of arguing; a thing which may very well be accounted for. They are differing kinds of wit, to be quick to find a fault, and to be capable to find out a truth; there must be industry in the last, the first requires only a lively heat that catcheth hold of the weak side of anything, but to choose the strong one is another talent. The reason why men of wit are often the laziest in their enquiries is that their heat carrieth their thoughts so fast that they are apt to be tired, and they faint in the drudgery of a continued application. Have not men of great wit in all times permitted their understandings to give way to their first impressions? It taketh off from the diminution when a man doth not mind a thing, and the King had then other business; the inferior part of the man was then in possession, and the faculties of the brain, as to serious and painful enquiries, were laid asleep at least, though not extinguished. Careless men are most subject to superstition. Those who do not study reason enough to make it their guide have more unevenness; as they have neglects, so they have starts and frights; dreams will serve the turn, omens and sicknesses have violent and sudden effects upon them. Nor is the strength of an argument so effectual from its intrinsic force, as by its being well suited to the temper of the party.

The genteel part of the Catholic religion might tempt a Prince that had more of the fine gentleman than his governing capacity required; and the exercise of indulgence to sinners being more frequent in it than of inflicting penance might be some

2. It is now generally agreed that whatever his personal inclinations Charles postponed his conversion until he was on the point of death.

recommendation. Mistresses of that faith are stronger specifics in this case than any that are in physic.[3]

The Roman Catholics complained of his breach of promise to them very early. There were broad peepings out, glimpses so often repeated that to discerning eyes it was flaring; in the very first year there were such suspicions as produced melancholy shakings of the head, which were very significant. His unwillingness to marry a Protestant was remarkable, though both the Catholic and the Christian Crown would have adopted her.[4] Very early in his youth, when any German princess was proposed he put off the discourse with raillery. A thousand little circumstances were a kind of accumulative evidence, which in these cases may be admitted.

Men that were earnest Protestants were under the sharpness of his displeasure, expressed by raillery as well as by other ways. Men near him have made discoveries from sudden breakings out in discourse, &c. which showed there was a root.[5] It was not the least skilful part of his concealing himself, to make the world think he leaned towards an indifference in religion.

He had sicknesses before his death in which he did not trouble any Protestant divines; those who saw him upon his death-bed saw a great deal.

As to his writing those Papers,[6] he might do it. Though neither his temper nor education made him very fit to be an author, yet in this case – a known topic so very often repeated – he might write it all himself and yet not one word of it his own. That Church's argument doth so agree with men unwilling to take pains, the temptation of putting an end to all the trouble of enquiring is so great that

3. His two principal mistresses, Barbara Palmer, Countess of Castlemaine, and Louise de Kéroualle, Duchess of Portsmouth, were both Roman Catholics.

4. Spain (the Catholic Crown) certainly opposed the match with Portugal, which had rebelled against her rule in 1640, but France (the Christian Crown) had encouraged it.

5. When Halifax first became suspicious we cannot say, but when discussing the last few months of the reign Burnet wrote: 'Halifax discovered the King's inclinations to popery so plainly that I saw he was in great apprehensions. Many but little things began to break out which gave great suspicion', Foxcroft, *Supplement to Burnet's History* (1902), p. 138.

6. Early in his reign James II published two papers, supposed to have been found in his brother's study, which explained the reasons for his conversion.

it must be very strong reason that can resist; the King had only his mere natural faculties, without any acquisitions to improve them. So that it is no wonder, if an argument which gave such ease and relief to his mind made such an impression, that with thinking often of it (as men are apt to do of everything they like) he might, by the effect chiefly of his memory, put together a few lines with his own hand without any help at the time; in which there was nothing extraordinary, but that one so little inclined to write at all should prevail with himself to do it with the solemnity of a casuist.

II. *His* Dissimulation

One great objection made to him was the concealing himself, and disguising his thoughts. In this there ought to be a latitude given; it is a defect not to have it at all, and a fault to have it too much. Human nature will not allow the mean; like all other things, as soon as ever men get to do them well, they cannot easily hold from doing them too much. It is the case even in the least things, as singing, &c.

In France he was to dissemble injuries and neglects, from one reason; in England he was to dissemble too, though for other causes. A King upon the throne hath as great temptations (though of another kind) to dissemble as a King in exile. The King of France might have his times of dissembling as much with him, as he could have to do it with the King of France; so he was in a school.

No King can be so little inclined to dissemble but he must needs learn it from his subjects, who every day give him such lessons of it. Dissimulation is like most other qualities, it hath two sides; it is necessary, and yet it is dangerous too. To have none at all layeth a man open to contempt, to have too much exposeth him to suspicion, which is only the less dishonourable inconvenience. If a man doth not take very great precautions, he is never so much showed as when he endeavoureth to hide himself. One man cannot take more pains to hide himself than another will do to see into him, especially in the case of kings.

It is none of the exalted faculties of the mind, since there are chamber-maids will do it better than any prince in Christendom.

Men given to dissembling are like rooks[7] at play, they will cheat for shillings, they are so used to it. The vulgar definition of dissembling is downright lying; that kind of it which is less ill-bred cometh pretty near it. Only princes and persons of honour must have gentler words given to their faults than the nature of them may in themselves deserve.

Princes dissemble with too many not to have it discovered; no wonder then that he carried it so far that it was discovered. Men compared notes and got evidence, so that those whose morality would give them leave took it for an excuse for serving him ill. Those who knew his face fixed their eyes there and thought it of more importance to see than to hear what he said. His face was as little a blab as most men's, yet though it could not be called a prattling face it would sometimes tell tales to a good observer. When he thought fit to be angry he had a very peevish memory, there was hardly a blot that escaped him. At the same time that this showed the strength of his dissimulation it gave warning too; it fitted his present purpose, but it made a discovery that put men more upon their guard against him. Only self-flattery furnisheth perpetual arguments to trust again; the comfortable opinion men have of themselves keepeth up human society, which would be more than half destroyed without it.

III. *His* Amours, Mistresses, *&c.*

It may be said that his inclinations to love were the effects of health and a good constitution, with as little mixture of the seraphic part as ever man had; and though from that foundation men often raise their passions I am apt to think his stayed as much as any man's ever did in the lower region. This made him like easy mistresses. They were generally resigned to him while he was abroad, with an implied bargain. Heroic refined lovers place a good deal of their pleasure in the difficulty, both for the vanity of conquest and as a better earnest of their kindness.

After he was restored mistresses were recommended to him; which is no small matter in a Court, and not unworthy the thoughts

7. sc. card-sharpers.

even of a party. A mistress either dexterous in herself, or well-instructed by those that are so, may be very useful to her friends, not only in the immediate hours of her ministry, but by her influences and insinuations at other times. It was resolved generally by others whom he should have in his arms, as well as whom he should have in his councils. Of a man who was so capable of choosing, he chose as seldom as any man that ever lived.

He had more properly, at least in the beginning of his time, a good stomach to his mistresses, than any great passion for them. His taking them from others was never learnt in a romance, and indeed fitter for a philosopher than a knight errant. His patience for their frailties showed him no exact lover; it is a heresy according to a true lover's creed ever to forgive an infidelity, or the appearance of it. Love of ease will not do it, where the heart is much engaged; but where mere nature is the motive it is possible for a man to think righter than the common opinion, and to argue that a rival taketh away nothing but the heart, and leaveth all the rest.

In his latter times he had no love, but insensible engagements that made it harder than most might apprehend to untie them. The politics might have their part; a secret, a commission, a confidence in critical things, though it doth not give a lease for a precise term of years, yet there may be difficulties in dismissing them; there may be no love all the while, perhaps the contrary.

He was said to be as little constant as they were thought to be. Though he had no love he must have some appetite, or else he could not keep them for mere ease, or for the love of sauntering. Mistresses are frequently apt to be uneasy, they are in all respects craving creatures; so that though the taste of those joys might be flattened, yet a man who loved pleasure so as to be very unwilling to part with it might (with the assistance of his fancy, which doth not grow old so fast) reserve some supplemental entertainments, that might make their personal service be still of use to him. The definition of pleasure is, what pleaseth, and if that which grave men may call a corrupted fancy shall administer any remedies for putting off mourning for the loss of youth, who shall blame it?

The young men seldom apply their censure to these matters, and the elder have an interest to be gentle towards a mistake that seemeth to make some kind of amends for their decays.

He had wit enough to suspect, and he had wit enough too not to care. The ladies got a great deal more than would have been allowed to be an equal bargain in Chancery, for what they did for it, but neither the manner nor the measure of pleasure is to be judged by others.

Little inducements at first grew into strong reasons by degrees. Men who do not consider circumstances, but judge at a distance by a general way of arguing, conclude if a mistress in some cases is not immediately turned off it must needs be that the gallant is incurably subjected. This will by no means hold in private men, much less in princes, who are under more entanglements, from which they cannot so easily loosen themselves.

His mistresses were as different in their humours as they were in their looks. They gave matter of very different reflections. The last[8] especially was quite out of the definition of an ordinary mistress; the causes and the manner of her being first introduced were very different. A very peculiar distinction was spoken of, some extraordinary solemnities that might dignify though not sanctify her function.[9] Her chamber was the true Cabinet Council. The King did always by his councils as he did sometimes by his meals; he sat down out of form with the Queen, but he supped below stairs. To have the secrets of a king who happens to have too many is to have a king in chains. He must not only not part with her, but he must in his own defence dissemble his dislike; the less kindness he hath the more he must show. There is great difference between being muffled, and being tied; he was the first, not the last. If he had quarrelled at some times, besides other advantages this mistress had a powerful second[10] (one may suppose a kind of a guarantee); this to a man that loved his ease, though his age had not helped, was sufficient.

The thing called sauntering is a stronger temptation to princes

8. The Duchess of Portsmouth.

9. The reference is to a mock marriage ceremony held at Euston in Suffolk in 1671.

10. Louis XIV.

than it is to others. The being galled with importunities, pursued from one room to another with asking faces, the dismal sound of unreasonable complaints and ill-grounded pretences, the deformity of fraud ill-disguised; all these would make any man run away from them, and I used to think it was the motive for making him walk so fast. So it was more properly taking sanctuary. To get into a room where all business was to stay at the door, excepting such as he was disposed to admit, might be very acceptable to a younger man than he was, and less given to his ease. He slumbered after dinner, had the noise of the company to divert him, without their solicitations to importune him. In these hours where he was more unguarded no doubt the cunning men of the court took their times to make their observations, and there is as little doubt but he made his upon them too. Where men had chinks he would see through them as soon as any man about him. There was much more real business done there in his politic, than there was in his personal capacity, *stans pede in uno*;[11] and there was the French part of the government, which was not the least.

In short, without endeavouring to find more arguments, he was used to it. Men do not care to put off a habit, nor do often succeed when they go about it. His was not an unthinkingness; he did not perhaps think so much of his subjects as they might wish but he was far from being wanting to think of himself.

IV. *His* Conduct *to his* Ministers

He lived with his ministers as he did with his mistresses; he used them, but he was not in love with them. He showed his judgment in this, that he cannot properly be said ever to have had a Favourite, though some might look so at a distance. The present use he might have of them made him throw favours upon them which might lead the lookers on into that mistake; but he tied himself no more to them than they did to him, which implied a sufficient liberty on either side.

11. Horace, *Sermones*, iv, 10. It refers to the ability of Lucilius to write two hundred verses an hour standing on one foot; a proverbial expression for doing anything with indecent facility.

Perhaps he made dear purchases. If he seldom gave profusely but where he expected some unreasonable thing, great rewards were material evidences against those who received them.

He was free of access to them, which was a very gaining quality. He had at least as good a memory for the faults of his ministers as for their services, and whenever they fell the whole inventory came out; there was not a slip omitted.

That some of his Ministers seemed to have a superiority did not spring from his resignation to them, but to his ease. He chose rather to be eclipsed than to be troubled.

His brother[12] was a minister, and he had his jealousies of him. At the same time that he raised him, he was not displeased to have him lessened. The cunning observers found this out, and at the same time that he reigned in the cabinet he was very familiarly used at the private supper.

A minister turned off is like a lady's waiting woman, that knoweth all her washes, and hath a shrewd guess at her strayings; so there is danger in turning them off as well as in keeping them.

He had back stairs to convey informations to him, as well as for other uses; and though such informations are sometimes dangerous (especially to a Prince that will not take the pains necessary to digest them), yet in the main that humour of hearing everybody against anybody kept those about him in more awe than they would have been without it. I do not believe that ever he trusted any man or any set of men so entirely as not to have some secrets in which they had no share; as this might make him less well served, so in some degree it might make him the less imposed upon.

You may reckon under this article his female ministry; for though he had ministers of the Council, Ministers of the Cabinet and Ministers of the Ruelle,[13] the Ruelle was often the last appeal. Those who were not well there were used because they were necessary at the time, not because they were liked, so that their tenure was a little uncertain. His Ministers were to administer business to him as doctors do physic, wrap it up in something to make it less unpleasant; some skilful digressions were so far from being impertinent that they could not many times fix him to a fair audience

12. James, Duke of York, later King James II.

13. A ladies' salon.

without them. His aversion to formality made him dislike a serious discourse, if very long, except it was mixed with something to entertain him. Some, even of the graver sort too, used to carry this very far, and rather than fail, use the coarsest kind of youthful talk.

In general, he was upon pretty even terms with his ministers, and could as easily bear their being hanged as some of them could his being abused.

V. *Of his* WIT *and* CONVERSATION

His wit consisted chiefly in the quickness of his apprehension. His apprehension made him find faults, and that led him to short sayings upon them; not always equal, but often very good.

By his being abroad he contracted a habit of conversing familiarly which, added to his natural genius, made him very apt to talk; perhaps more than a very nice judgment would approve.

He was apter to make broad allusions upon anything that gave the least occasion than was altogether suitable with the very good breeding he showed in most other things. The company he kept whilst abroad had so used him to that sort of dialect, that he was so far from thinking it a fault or an indecency, that he made it a matter of raillery upon those who could not prevail upon themselves to join in it. As a man who hath a good stomach loveth generally to talk of meat, so in the vigour of his age he began that style, which by degrees grew so natural to him that after he ceased to do it out of pleasure he continued to do it out of custom. The hypocrisy of former times inclined men to think they could not show too great an aversion to it, and that helped to encourage this unbounded liberty of talking, without the restraints of decency which were before observed. In his more familiar conversations with the ladies even they must be passive, if they would not enter into it. How far sounds as well as objects may have their effects to raise inclination, might be an argument to him to use that style; or whether using liberty at its full stretch was not the general inducement, without any particular motives to it.

The manner of that time of telling stories had drawn him into it; being commended at first for the faculty of telling a tale well, he might insensibly be betrayed to exercise it too often. Stories are dangerous in this, that the best expose a man most by being oftenest repeated. It might pass for an evidence for the moderns against the ancients, that it is now wholly left off by all that have any pretence to be distinguished by their good sense.

He had the improvements of wine, &c., which made him pleasant and easy in company, where he bore his part, and was acceptable even to those who had no other design than to be merry with him.

The thing called wit a Prince may taste, but it is dangerous for him to take too much of it; it hath allurements which by refining his thoughts take off from their dignity, in applying them less to the governing part. There is a charm in wit which a Prince must resist, and that to him was no easy matter; it was contesting with Nature upon terms of disadvantage.

His wit was not so ill-natured as to put men out of countenance. In the case of a King especially, it is more allowable to speak sharply of them, than to them.

His wit was not acquired by reading; that which he had above his original stock by Nature was from company, in which he was very capable to observe. He could not so properly be said to have a wit very much raised, as a plain, gaining, well-bred, recommending kind of wit.

But of all men that ever liked those who had wit, he could the best endure those who had none. This leaneth more towards a satire than a compliment, in this respect, that he could not only suffer impertinence but at some times seemed to be pleased with it.

He encouraged some to talk a good deal more with him than one would have expected from a man of so good a taste. He should rather have ordered his Attorney-General to prosecute them for a misdemeanour in using commonsense so scurvily in his presence. However, if this was a fault it is arrogant for any of his subjects to object to it, since it would look like defying such a piece of indulgence. He must in some degree loosen the strength of his wit by his condescension to talk with men so very unequal to him. Wit must be used to some equality, which may give it exercise, or else it is apt either to languish or to grow a little vulgar, by reigning amongst men of a lower size, where there is no awe to keep a man upon his guard.

It fell out, rather by accident than choice, that his mistresses were such as did not care that wit of the best kind should have the precedence in their apartments. Sharp and strong wit will not always be so held in by good manners as not to be a little troublesome in a Ruelle. But wherever impertinence hath wit enough left to be thankful for being well used it will not only be admitted but kindly received; such charms everything hath that setteth us off by comparison.

His affability was a part, and perhaps not the least of his wit.

It is a quality that must not always spring from the heart. Men's pride, as well as their weakness, maketh them ready to be deceived by it; they are more ready to believe it a homage paid to their merit than a bait thrown out to deceive them. Princes have a particular advantage.

There was at first as much of art as nature in his affability, but by habit it became natural. It is an error of the better hand, but the universality taketh away a good deal of the force of it. A man that hath had a kind look seconded with engaging words whilst he is chewing the pleasure, if another in his sight should be received just as kindly, that equality would presently alter the relish. The pride of mankind will have distinction, till at last it cometh to smile for smile, meaning nothing of either side, without any kind of effect, mere drawing-room compliments; the bow alone would be better without them. He was under some disadvantages of this kind, that grew still in proportion as it came by time to be more known that there was less signification in those things than at first was thought.

The familiarity of his wit must needs have the effect of lessening the distance fit to be kept to him. The freedom used to him whilst abroad was retained by those who used it longer than either they ought to have kept it or he have suffered it, and others by their example learned to use the same. A King of Spain that will say nothing but *tiendro cuydado*[14] will to the generality preserve more respect; an engine[15] that will speak but sometimes, at the same time

14. Presumably *tendre cuidado*, 'I will take care'.

15. A mechanical toy; robot.

that it will draw the raillery of the few who judge well it will create respect in the ill-judging generality. Formality is sufficiently revenged upon the world for being so unreasonably laughed at; it is destroyed, it is true, but it hath the spiteful satisfaction of seeing everything destroyed with it.

His fine gentlemanship did him no good, encouraged in it by being too much applauded.

His wit was better suited to his condition before he was restored than afterwards. The wit of a gentleman and that of a crowned head ought to be different things. As there is a Crown Law, there is a Crown Wit too. To use it with reserve is very good, and very rare. There is a dignity in doing things seldom, even without any other circumstance. Where wit will run continually the spring is apt to fail; so that it groweth vulgar, and the more it is practised the more it is debased.

He was so good at finding out other men's weak sides that it made him less intent to cure his own; that generally happeneth. It may be called a treacherous talent, for it betrayeth a man to forget to judge himself, by being so eager to censure others; this doth so misguide men the first part of their lives, that the habit of it is not easily recovered when the greater ripeness of their judgment inclineth them to look more into themselves than into other men.

Men love to see themselves in the false looking-glass of other men's failings. It maketh a man think well of himself at the time, and by sending his thoughts abroad to get food for laughing they are less at leisure to see faults at home. Men choose rather to make the war in another country than to keep all well at home.

VI. *His* TALENTS, TEMPER, HABITS, *&c.*

He had a mechanical head, which appeared in his inclination to shipping and fortification, &c. This would make one conclude that his thoughts would naturally have been more fixed to business, if his pleasures had not drawn them away from it.

He had a very good memory, though he would not always make equal good use of it. So that if he had accustomed himself to direct his faculties to his business I see no reason why he might not have been a good deal master of it. His chain of memory was longer than his chain of thought; the first could bear any burden, the other was tired by being carried on too long; it was fit to ride a heat, but it had not wind enough for a long course.

A very great memory often forgetteth how much time is lost by repeating things of no use. It was one reason of his talking so much; since a great memory will always have something to say, and will be discharging itself, whether in or out of season, if a good judgment doth not go along with it, to make it stop and turn. One might say of his memory, that it was a *beauté journalière*;[16] sometimes he would make shrewd applications, &c., at others he would bring things out of it that never deserved to be laid in it.

He grew by age into a pretty exact distribution of his hours, both for his business, pleasures, and the exercise for his health, of which he took as much care as could possibly consist with some liberties he was resolved to indulge in himself. He walked by his watch, and when he pulled it out to look upon it skilful men would make haste with what they had to say to him.

He was often retained in his personal against his politic capacity. He would speak upon those occasions most dexterously against himself; Charles Stuart would be bribed against the King; and in the distinction he leaned more to his natural self than his character would allow. He would not suffer himself to be so much fettered by his character as was convenient; he was still starting out of it; the power of Nature was too strong for the dignity of his calling, which generally yielded as often as there was a contest.

It was not the best use he made of his backstairs to admit men to bribe him against himself, to procure a defalcation, help a lame accountant to get off, or side with the farmers against the improvement of the revenue.[17] The King was made the instrument to defraud the Crown, which is somewhat extraordinary.

That which might tempt him to it, probably, was his finding that those about him so often took money upon those occasions, so that

16. An inconstant beauty.

17. Halifax spent much of 1683 and 1684 trying to persuade Charles to re-allocate the Farm of the Excise, which explains his malice. His schemes were ill-advised.

he thought he might do well at least to be a partner. He did not take the money to hoard it; there were those at Court who watched those times as the Spaniards do for the coming in of the Plate Fleet.[18] The beggars of both sexes helped to empty his cabinet, and to leave room in them for a new lading upon the next occasion. These negotiators played double with him too, when it was for their purpose to do so. He knew it, and went on still; so he gained his present end at the time, he was less solicitous to enquire into the consequences.

He could not properly be said to be either covetous or liberal; his desire to get was not with an intention to be rich, and his spending was rather an easiness in letting money go than any premeditated thought for the distribution of it. He would do as much to throw off the burden of a present importunity as he would to relieve a want.

When once the aversion to bear uneasiness taketh place in a man's mind, it doth so check all the passions that they are damped into a kind of indifference; they grow faint and languishing, and come to be subordinate to that fundamental maxim, of not purchasing anything at the price of a difficulty. This made that he had as little eagerness to oblige as he had to hurt men; the motive of his giving bounties was rather to make men less uneasy to him than more easy to themselves; and yet no ill nature all this while. He would slide from an asking face, and could guess very well. It was throwing a man off from his shoulders that leaned upon them with his whole weight; so that the party was not gladder to receive, than he was to give. It was a kind of implied bargain, though men seldom kept it, being so apt to forget the advantage they had received that they would presume the King would as little remember the good he had done them so as to make it an argument against their next request.

This principle of making the love of ease exercise an entire sovereignty in his thoughts would have been less censured in a private man than might be in a Prince. The consequence of it to the public changeth the nature of that quality, or else a philosopher in his private capacity might say a great deal to justify it. The truth is,

18. The fleet which sailed once a year between Mexico and Spain carrying the bullion of the Indies.

a King is to be such a distinct creature from a man that their thoughts are to be put in quite a differing shape, and it is such a disquieting task to reconcile them that Princes might rather expect to be lamented than to be envied, for being in a Station that exposeth them if they do not do more to answer men's expectations than human nature will allow.

That men have the less ease for their loving it so much is so far from a wonder that it is a natural consequence, especially in the case of a Prince. Ease is seldom got without some pains, but it is yet seldomer kept without them. He thought giving would make men more easy to him, whereas he might have known it would certainly make them more troublesome.

When men receive benefits from Princes they attribute less to his generosity than to their own deserts, so that in their own opinion their merit cannot be bounded; by that mistaken rule, it can as little be satisfied. They would take it for a diminution to have it circumscribed. Merit hath a thirst upon it that can never be quenched by golden showers. It is not only still ready, but greedy to receive more. This King Charles found in as many instances as any Prince that ever reigned, because the easiness of access introducing the good success of their first request, they were the more encouraged to repeat those importunities, which had been more effectually stopped in the beginning by a short and resolute denial. But his nature did not dispose him to that method, it directed him rather to put off the troublesome minute for the time, and that being his inclination he did not care to struggle with it.

I am of an opinion, in which I am every day more confirmed by observation, that gratitude is one of those things that cannot be bought. It must be born with men, or else all the obligations in the world will not create it. An outward show may be made to satisfy decency, and to prevent reproach; but a real sense of a kind thing is a gift of nature, and never was, nor can be acquired.

The love of ease is an opiate, it is pleasing for the time, quieteth the spirits, but it hath its effects that seldom fail to be most fatal. The immoderate love of ease maketh a man's mind pay a passive obedience to anything that happeneth, it reduceth the thoughts from having desire to be content.

It must be allowed he had a little over-balance on the well-natured side, not vigour enough to be earnest to do a kind thing, much less to do a harsh one; but if a hard thing was done to another man he did not eat his supper the worse for it. It was rather a deadness than severity of Nature, whether it proceeded from a dissipation of spirits or by the habit of living in which he was engaged.

If a King should be born with more tenderness than might suit with his office he would in time be hardened. The faults of his subjects make severity so necessary, that by the frequent occasions given to use it it comes to be habitual, and by degrees the resistance that Nature made at first groweth fainter, till at last it is in a manner quite extinguished.

In short, this Prince might more properly be said to have gifts than virtues, such as affability, easiness of living, inclinations to give and to forgive; qualities that flowed from his nature rather than from his virtue.

He had not more application to anything than the preservation of his health; it had an entire preference to anything else in his thoughts, and he might be said without aggravation to study that with as little intermission as any man in the world. He understood it very well, only in this he failed, that he thought it was more reconcilable with his pleasures than it really was. It is natural to have such a mind to reconcile these, that it is the easier for any man that goeth about it to be guilty of that mistake.

This made him overdo in point of nourishment, the better to furnish to those entertainments; and then he thought by great exercise to make amends, and to prevent the ill effects of his blood being too much raised. The success he had in this method whilst he had youth and vigour to support him in it encouraged him to continue it longer than Nature allowed. Age stealeth so insensibly upon us, that we do not think of suiting our way of reasoning to the several stages of life; so insensibly that not being able to pitch upon any precise time when we cease to be young, we either flatter ourselves that we always continue to be so, or at least forget how much we are mistaken in it.

VII. Conclusion

After all this, when some rough strokes of the pencil have made several parts of the picture look a little hard, it is justice that would be due to every man, much more to a Prince, to make some amends, and to reconcile men as much as may be to it by the last finishing.

He had as good a claim to a kind interpretation as most men. First as a Prince, living and dead, generous and well-bred men will be gentle to them; next as an unfortunate Prince in the beginning of his time, and a gentle one in the rest.

A Prince neither sharpened by his misfortunes whilst abroad nor by his power when restored is such a shining character that it is a reproach not to be so dazzled with it as not to be able to see a fault in its full light. It would be a scandal in this case to have an exact memory. And if all who are akin to his vices should mourn for him, never Prince would be better attended to his grave. He is under the protection of common frailty, that must engage men for their own sakes not to be too severe where they themselves have so much to answer.

What therefore an angry philosopher would call lewdness, let frailer men call a warmth and sweetness of the blood, that would not be confined in the communicating itself; an overflowing of good nature, of which he had such a stream that it would not be restrained within the banks of a crabbed and unsociable virtue.

If he had sometimes less firmness than might have been wished, let the kindest reason be given; and if that should be wanting, the best excuse. I would assign the cause of it to be his loving at any rate to be easy, and his deserving the more to be indulged in it by his desiring that everybody else should be so.

If he sometimes let a servant fall, let it be examined whether he did not weigh so much upon his master as to give him a fair excuse. That yieldingness, whatever foundations it might lay to the disadvantage of posterity, was a specific to preserve us in peace for his own time. If he loved too much to lie upon his own down bed of ease, his subjects had the pleasure during his reign of lolling and stretching upon theirs. As a sword is sooner broken upon a feather bed than upon a table, so his pliantness broke the blow of a present mischief much better than a more immediate resistance would perhaps have done.

Ruin saw this, and therefore removed him first to make way for further overturnings.[19]

If he dissembled, let us remember first, that he was a King, and that dissimulation is a jewel of the crown; next, that it is very hard for a man not to do sometimes too much of that which he concludeth necessary for him to practice. Men should consider that as there would be no false dice if there were no true ones, so if dissembling is grown universal it ceaseth to be foul play, having an implied allowance by the general practice. He that was so often forced to dissemble in his own defence might the better have the privilege sometimes to be the aggressor, and to deal with men at their own weapon.

Subjects are apt to be as arbitrary in their censure as the most assuming Kings can be in their power. If there might be matter for objections, there is not less reason for excuses; the defects laid to his charge are such as may claim indulgence from mankind.

Should nobody throw a stone at his faults but those who are free from them, there would be but a slender shower.

What private man will throw stones at him because he loved? Or what Prince, because he dissembled?

If he either trusted or forgave his enemies, or in some cases neglected his friends more than could in strictness be allowed, let not those errors be so arraigned as take away the privilege that seemeth to be due to princely frailties. If Princes are under the misfortune of being accused to govern ill their subjects have the less right to fall hard upon them, since they generally so little deserve to be governed well.

The truth is, the calling of a King, with all its glittering, hath such an unreasonable weight upon it, that they may rather expect to be lamented than to be envied for being set upon a pinnacle, where they are exposed to censure if they do not do more to answer men's expectations than corrupted nature will allow.

19. A conclusive demonstration that this work was composed after the Revolution of 1688.

It is but justice therefore to this Prince to give all due softenings to the less shining parts of his life; to offer flowers and leaves to hide, instead of using aggravations to expose them.

Let his royal ashes then lie soft upon him, and cover him from harsh and unkind censures; which though they should not be unjust can never clear themselves from being indecent.

THE LADY'S NEW YEAR'S GIFT;
OR,
ADVICE TO A DAUGHTER

EDITORIAL INTRODUCTION

This treatise was addressed to his daughter Elizabeth, later Countess of Chesterfield, and mother of the famous 4th earl. It was published in January 1688, when she was twelve years of age. According to Horace Walpole, she kept her father's gift on her dressing table always, but he also reveals that her husband wrote in it 'wasted effort!', for she was an abominable shrew. Be this as it may, *Advice to a Daughter* was easily Halifax's most popular work; it was in print for most of the following century in various editions, and it was translated into French (1692, 1748, 1752 and 1757) and Italian (1734).[1]

1. For further details, see Foxcroft, ii, 379ff.

THE LADY'S NEW YEAR'S GIFT;
OR,
ADVICE TO A DAUGHTER

DEAR DAUGHTER,
I find that even our most pleasing thoughts will be unquiet; they *will* be in motion, and the mind can have no rest whilst it is possessed by a darling passion. You are at present the chief object of my care as well as of my kindness, which sometimes throweth me into visions of your being happy in the world that are better suited to my partial wishes than to my reasonable hopes for you. At other times, when my fears prevail, I shrink as if I was struck at the prospect of danger to which a young woman must be exposed. But how much the more lively, so much the more liable you are to be hurt, as the finest plants are the soonest nipped by the frost. Whilst you are playing, full of innocence, the spiteful world will bite, except you are guarded by your caution. Want of care therefore, my dear child, is never to be excused, since as to this world it hath the same effect as want of virtue. Such an early-sprouting wit requireth so much the more to be sheltered by some rules, like something strewed on tender flowers to preserve them from being blasted.

You must take it well to be pruned by so kind a hand as that of a father. There may be some bitterness in mere obedience; the natural love of liberty may help to make the commands of a parent harder to go down. Some inward resistance there will be where power and not choice maketh us move, but when a father layeth aside his authority and persuadeth only by his kindness, you will never answer it to good nature if it hath not weight with you.

A great part of what is said in the following discourse may be above the present growth of your understanding, but that, becoming every day taller, will in a little time reach up to it, so as to make it easy to you. I am willing to begin with you before your mind is quite formed, that being the time in which it is most capable of receiving a colour that will last when it is mixed with it. Few things are well learnt but by early precepts; those well infused, make them natural, and we are never sure of retaining what is valuable till by a continued habit we have made it a piece of us.

Whether my skill can draw the picture of a fine woman may be a question; but it can be none, that I have drawn that of a kind father. If you will take an exact copy, I will so far presume upon my workmanship as to undertake you shall not make an ill figure. Give me so much credit as to try, and I am sure that neither your wishes nor mine shall be disappointed by it.

RELIGION

The first thing to be considered is Religion. It must be the chief object of your thoughts, since it would be a vain thing to direct your behaviour in the world and forget that which you are to have towards him who made it. In a strict sense, it is the only thing necessary; you must take it into your mind and from thence throw it into your heart, where you are to embrace it so close as never to lose the possession of it.

But then it is necessary to distinguish between the reality and the pretence. Religion doth not consist in believing the legend of the nursery, where children with their milk are fed with the tales of witches, hobgoblins, prophecies and miracles. We suck in so greedily these early mistakes that our riper understanding hath much ado to cleanse our minds from this kind of trash. The stories are so entertaining that we do not only believe them but relate them, which makes the discovery of the truth somewhat grievous, when it makes us lose such a field of impertinence[1] where we might have diverted ourselves, besides the throwing some shame upon us for having ever received them. This is making the world a jest, and imputing to God Almighty that the province he assigneth to the Devil is to play at blindman's buff, and show[2] tricks with mankind; and is so far from being religion that it is not sense, and hath right only to be called that kind of devotion of which ignorance is the undoubted mother, without competition or dispute. These mis-

1. foolishness. 2. This may be a misprint for 'share'.

takes are therefore to be left off with your hanging sleeves,[3] and you ought to be as much out of countenance to be found with them about you as to be seen playing with babies[4] at an age when other things are expected from you.

The next thing to be observed to you is that religion doth as little consist in loud answers and devout convulsions at church, or praying in an extraordinary manner. Some ladies are so extreme stirring at church that one would swear the worm in their conscience made them so unquiet. Others will have such a divided face between a devout goggle and an inviting glance that the unnatural mixture maketh even the best looks to be at that time ridiculous. These affected appearances are ever suspected, like very strong perfumes, which are generally thought no very good symptoms in those that make use of them. Let your earnestness therefore be reserved for your closet, where you may have God Almighty to yourself; in public be still and calm, neither indecently careless, nor affected in the other extreme.

It is not true devotion to put on an angry zeal against those who may be of a differing persuasion. Partiality to ourselves makes us often mistake it for a duty to fall hard upon others in that case; and being pushed on by self-conceit, we strike without mercy, believing that the wounds we give are meritorious, and that we are fighting God Almighty's quarrel, when the truth is we are only setting out ourselves. Our devotion too often breaketh out into that shape which most agreeth with our particular temper. The choleric grow into a hardened severity against all who dissent from them, snatch at all the texts of Scripture that suit with their complexion, and because God's wrath was some time kindled they conclude that anger is a divine virtue, and are so far from imagining their ill natured zeal requireth an apology that they value themselves upon it, and triumph in it. Others, whose nature is more credulous than ordinary, admit no bounds or measure to it; they grow as proud of extending their faith as princes are of enlarging their dominions, not considering that our faith like our stomach, is capable of being over-charged, and that as the last is destroyed by taking in more than it can digest, so our reason may be extinguished by oppressing

3. baby clothes; we would say 'rompers'. 4. dolls.

it with the weight of too many strange things; especially if we are forbidden to chew what we are commanded to swallow. The melancholy and the sullen are apt to place a great part of their religion in dejected or ill-humoured looks, putting on an unsociable face, and declaiming against the innocent entertainments of life with as much sharpness as they could bestow upon the greatest crimes. This generally is only a vizard,[5] there is seldom anything real in it. No other thing is the better for being sour, and it would be hard that religion should be so, which is the best of things. In the meantime it may be said with truth, that this surly kind of devotion hath perhaps done little less hurt in the world by frighting, than the most scandalous examples have done by infecting it.

Having told you in these few instances, to which many more might be added, what is not true religion, it is time to describe to you what is so. The ordinary definitions of it are no more like it, than the common sign posts[6] are like the princes they would represent. The unskilful daubers in all ages have generally laid on such ill colours, and drawn such harsh lines, that the beauty of it is not easily to be discerned. They have put in all the forbidding features that can be thought of, and in the first place have made it an irreconcilable enemy to nature, when in reality they are not only friends but twins, born together at the same time, and it is doing violence to them both, to go about to have them separated. Nothing is so kind and so inviting as true and unsophisticated religion: instead of imposing unnecessary burdens upon our nature, it easeth us of the greater weight of our passions and mistakes; instead of subduing us with rigour it redeemeth us from the slavery we are in to ourselves, who are the most severe masters whilst we are under the usurpation of our appetites let loose and not restrained.

Religion is a cheerful thing, so far from being always at cuffs with good humour that it is inseparably united to it. Nothing unpleasant belongs to it, though the spiritual cooks have done their unskilful part to give an ill relish to it. A wise epicure would be religious for the sake of pleasure; good sense is the foundation of both, and he is a bungler who aimeth at true luxury but where they are joined.

5. mask. 6. inn signs.

Religion is exalted reason, refined and sifted from the grosser parts of it; it dwelleth in the upper region of the mind, where there are fewest clouds or mists to darken or offend it; it is both the foundation and the crown of all virtues; it is morality improved and raised to its height by being carried nearer heaven, the only place where perfection resideth; it cleanseth the understanding and brusheth off the earth that hangeth about our souls. It doth not want the hopes and the terrors which are made use of to support it; neither ought it to descend to the borrowing any argument out of itself, since there we may find everything that should invite us. If we were to be hired to religion, it is able to out-bid the corrupted world, with all it can offer to us, being so much the richer of the two in everything where reason is admitted to be a judge of the value.

Since this is so, it is worth your pains to make religion your choice, and not make use of it only as a refuge. There are ladies who, finding by the too visible decay of their good looks that they can shine no more by that light, put on the varnish of an affected devotion, to keep up some kind of figure in the world. They take sanctuary in the church when they are pursued by growing contempt, which will not be stopped, but followeth them to the altar. Such late penitence is only a disguise for the tormenting grief of being no more handsome; that is the killing thought which draweth the sighs and tears, that appear outwardly to be applied to a better end.

There are many who have an aguish devotion, hot and cold fits, long intermissions, and violent raptures. This uneveness is by all means to be avoided. Let your method be a steady course of good life, that may run like a smooth stream, and be a perpetual spring to furnish to the continued exercise of virtue. Your devotion may be earnest, but it must be unconstrained, and like other duties you must make it your pleasure too, or else it will have very little efficacy. By this rule you may best judge of your own heart. Whilst those duties are joys it is an evidence of their being sincere; but when they are a penance it is a sign that your nature maketh some resistance; and whilst that lasteth you can never be entirely secure of yourself.

If you are often unquiet, and too nearly touched by the cross accidents of life, your devotion is not of the right standard; there is too much alloy in it. That which is right and unmixed taketh away the sting of everything that would trouble you; it is like a healing balm that extinguisheth the sharpness of the blood; so this softeneth and dissolveth the anguish of the mind. A devout mind hath the privilege of being free from passions, as some climates are from all venomous kind of creatures. It will raise you above the little vexations to which others for want of it will be exposed, and bring you to a temper, not of stupid indifference, but of such a wise resignation that you may live in the world so as it may hang about you like a loose garment, and not tied too close to you.

Take heed of running into that common error of applying God's judgments upon particular occasions. Our weights and measures are not competent to make the distribution either of his mercy or his justice; he hath thrown a veil over these things, which makes it not only an impertinence but a kind of sacrilege for us to give sentence in them without his commission.

As to your particular faith, keep to the religion that is grown up with you, both as it is the best in itself, and that the reason of staying in it upon that ground is somewhat stronger for your sex than it will perhaps be allowed to be for ours; in respect that the voluminous inquiries into the truth, by reading, are less expected from you. The best of books will be direction enough to you not to change; and whilst you are fixed and sufficiently confirmed in your own mind, you will do best to keep vain doubts and scruples at such a distance that they may give you no disquiet.

Let me recommend to you a method of being rightly informed, which can never fail. It is in short this: get understanding, and practise virtue. And if you are so blessed as to have those for your share, it is not surer that there is a God, than it is that by him all necessary truths will be revealed to you.

HUSBAND

That which challengeth the next place in your thoughts is how to live with a husband. And though that is so large a word that few rules can be fixed to it which are unchangeable, the methods being as various as the several tempers of men to which they must be suited, yet I cannot omit some general observations, which, with the help of your own, may the better direct you in the part of your life upon which your happiness most dependeth.

It is one of the disadvantages belonging to your sex that young women are seldom permitted to make their own choice; their friends' care and experience are thought safer guides to them than their own fancies, and their modesty often forbiddeth them to refuse when their parents recommend, though their inward consent may not entirely go along with it. In this case there remaineth nothing for them to do but to endeavour to make that easy which falleth to their lot, and by a wise use of everything they may dislike in a husband turn that by degrees to be very supportable which, if neglected, might in time beget an aversion.

You must first lay it down for a foundation in general, that there is inequality in the sexes, and that for the better economy of the world the men, who were to be the lawgivers, had the larger share of reason bestowed upon them; by which means your sex is the better prepared for the compliance that is necessary for the better performance of those duties which seem to be most properly assigned to it. This looks a little uncourtly at the first appearance, but upon examination it will be found that nature is so far from being unjust to you that she is partial on your side. She hath made you such large amends by other advantages for the seeming injustice of the first distribution that the right of complaining is come over to our sex. You have it in your power not only to free yourselves but to subdue your masters, and without violence throw both their natural and legal authority at your feet. We are made of differing tempers, that our defects may the better be mutually supplied: your sex wanteth our reason for your conduct, and our strength for your protection; ours wanteth your gentleness to soften and to entertain us. The first part of our life is a good deal subjected to you in the nursery, where you reign without competition, and by that means have the advantage of giving the first impressions. Afterwards you have stronger influences, which, well managed, have more force in your behalf than all our privileges and jurisdictions can pretend to have against you. You have more strength in your looks than we have in our laws, and more power by your tears than we have by our arguments.

It is true that the laws of marriage run in a harsher style towards your sex. Obey is an ungenteel word, and less easy to be digested by making such an unkind distinction in the words of the contract, and so very unsuitable to the excess of good manners which generally goes before it. Besides, the universality of the rule seemeth to be a grievance, and it appeareth reasonable that there might be an exemption for extraordinary women from ordinary rules, to take away the just exception that lieth against the false measure of general equality.

It may be alleged by the counsel retained by your sex, that as there is in all other laws an appeal from the letter to the equity, in cases that require it, it is as reasonable that some court of a larger jurisdiction might be erected, where some wives might resort and plead specially, and in such instances where Nature is so kind as to raise them above the level of their own sex they might have relief, and obtain a mitigation in their own particular of a sentence which was given generally against womankind. The causes of separation are now so very coarse that few are confident enough to buy their liberty at the price of having their modesty so exposed. And for disparity of minds, which above all other things requireth a remedy, the laws have made no provision, so little refined are numbers of men by whom they are compiled. This and a great deal more might be said to give a colour to the complaint.

But the answer to it in short is, that the institution of marriage is too sacred to admit a liberty of objecting to it; that the supposition of yours being the weaker sex having without all doubt a good foundation maketh it reasonable to subject it to the masculine dominion; that no rule can be so perfect as not to admit some exceptions, but the law presumeth there would be so few found in this case who would have a sufficient right to such a privilege that it is safer some injustice should be connived at in a very few instances than to break into an establishment upon which the order of human society doth so much depend.

You are therefore to make your best of what is settled by law and custom, and not vainly imagine that it will be changed for your sake. But that you may not be discouraged, as if you lay under the weight of an incurable grievance; you are to know that by a wise and dexterous conduct it will be in your power to relieve yourself from anything that looketh like a disadvantage in it. For your better direction I will give a hint of the most ordinary causes of dissatisfaction between man and wife, that you may be able by such a warning to live so upon your guard that when you shall be married you may know how to cure your husband's mistakes and to prevent your own.

First then, you are to consider you live in a time which hath rendered some kind of frailties so habitual that they lay claim to large grains of allowance. The world in this is somewhat unequal, and our sex seemeth to play the tyrant in distinguishing partially for ourselves, by making that in the utmost degree criminal in the woman which in a man passeth under a much gentler censure. The root and the excuse of this injustice is the preservation of families from any mixture which may bring a blemish to them; and whilst the point of honour continues to be so placed, it seems unavoidable to give your sex the greater share of the penalty. But if in this it lieth under any disadvantage, you are more than recompensed by having the honour of families in your keeping. The consideration so great a trust must give you maketh full amends, and this power the world hath lodged in you can hardly fail to restrain the severity of an ill husband and to improve the kindness and esteem of a good one. This being so, remember that next to the danger of committing the fault yourself the greatest is that of seeing it in your husband. Do not seem to look or hear that way: if he is a man of sense he will reclaim himself, the folly of it is of itself sufficient to cure him; if he is not so, he will be provoked but not reformed. To expostulate in these cases looketh like declaring war, and preparing reprisals, which to a thinking husband would be a dangerous reflexion.

Besides, it is so coarse a reason which will be assigned for a lady's too great warmth upon such an occasion that modesty no less than prudence ought to restrain her, since such an indecent complaint makes a wife more ridiculous that the injury that provoketh her to it. But it is yet worse, and more unskilful, to blaze[7] it in the world, expecting it should rise up in arms to take her part; whereas she will find it can have no other effect than that she will be served up in all companies as the reigning jest at that time; and will continue to be the common entertainment till she is rescued by some newer folly that cometh upon the stage, and driveth her away from it. The impertinence[8] of such methods is so plain that it doth not deserve the pains of being laid open. Be assured that in these cases your discretion and silence will be the most prevailing reproof. An affected ignorance, which is seldom a virtue, is a great one here; and when your husband seeth how unwilling you are to be uneasy there is no stronger argument to persuade him not to be unjust to you. Besides, it will naturally make him more yielding in other things; and whether it be to cover or redeem his offence, you may have the good effects of it whilst it lasteth, and all that while have the most reasonable ground that can be of presuming such a behaviour will at last entirely convert him. There is nothing so glorious to a wife as a victory so gained; a man so reclaimed is for ever after subjected to her virtue, and her bearing for a time is more than rewarded by a triumph that will continue as long as her life.

The next thing I will suppose is, that your husband may love wine more than is convenient. It will be granted that though there are vices of a deeper dye, there are none that have greater deformity than this, when it is not restrained. But with all this, the same custom which is the more to be lamented for its being so general should make it less uneasy to everyone in particular who is to suffer by the effects of it. So that in the first place it will be no new thing if you should have a drunkard for your husband; and there is by too frequent examples evidence enough that such a thing may happen, and yet a wife may live too without being miserable. Self-love dictateth aggravating words to everything we feel; ruin and misery are the terms we apply to whatever we do not like, forget-

7. publish or blazon. 8. folly.

ting the mixture allotted to us by the condition of human life, by which it is not intended we should be quite exempt from trouble. It is fair if we can escape such a degree of it as would oppress us, and enjoy so much of the pleasant part as may lessen the ill taste of such things as are unwelcome to us. Everything hath two sides, and for our own ease we ought to direct our thoughts to that which may be least liable to exception. To fall upon the worst side of a drunkard giveth so unpleasant a prospect that it is not possible to dwell upon it; let us pass then to the more favourable part, as far as a wife is concerned in it.

I am tempted to say (if the irregularity of the expression could in strictness be justified) that a wife is to thank God her husband hath faults. Mark the seeming paradox, my dear, for your own instruction, it being intended no further. A husband without faults is a dangerous observer, he hath an eye so piercing, and seeth everything so plain, that it is exposed to his full censure. And though I will not doubt but that virtue will disappoint the sharpest inquiries, yet few women can bear the having all they say or do represented in the clear glass of an understanding without faults. Nothing softeneth the arrogance of our nature like a mixture of some frailties; it is by them we are best told; that we must not strike too hard upon others, because we ourselves do so often deserve blows. They pull our rage by the sleeve, and whisper gentleness to us in our censures, even when they are rightly applied. The faults and passions of husbands bring them down to you, and make them content to live upon less unequal terms than faultless men would be willing to stoop to, so haughty is mankind till humbled by common weaknesses and defects, which in our corrupted state contribute more towards the reconciling us to one another than all the precepts of the philosophers and divines. So that where the errors of our nature make amends for the disadvantages of yours it is more your part to make use of the benefit than to quarrel at the fault.

Thus in case a drunken husband should fall to your share, if you will be wise and patient his wine shall be of your side; it will throw a veil over your mistakes, and will set out and improve everything you do that he is pleased with. Others will like him less, and by that means he may perhaps like you the more. When after having dined too well he is received at home without a storm, or so much as a reproaching look, the wine will naturally work out all in kindness, which a wife must encourage, let it be wrapped up in never so much impertinence.[9] On the other side it would boil up into rage if the mistaken wife should treat him roughly, like a certain thing called a kind shrew, than which the world, with all its plenty, cannot show a more senseless, ill-bred, forbidding creature. Consider that where the man will give such frequent intermissions of the use of his reason the wife insensibly getteth a right of governing in the vacancy, and that raiseth her character and credit in the family to a higher pitch than perhaps could be done under a sober husband, who never putteth himself into an incapacity of holding the reins. If these are not entire consolations, at least they are remedies to some degree. They cannot make drunkenness a virtue, nor a husband given to it a felicity; but you will do yourself no ill office in the endeavouring by these means to make the best of such a lot, in case it should happen to be yours, and by the help of a wise observation to make that very supportable which would otherwise be a load that would oppress you.

The next case I will put is that your husband may be choleric or ill-humoured. To this it may be said, that passionate men generally make amends at the foot of the account. Such a man, if he is angry one day without any sense, will the next day be as kind without any reason. So that by marking how the wheels of such a man's head are used to move you may easily bring over all his passion to your party. Instead of being struck down by his thunder, you shall direct it where and upon whom you shall think it best applied. Thus are the strongest poisons turned to the best remedies; but then there must be art in it, and a skilful hand, else the least bungling maketh it mortal. There is a great deal of nice care requisite to deal with a man of this complexion. Choler proceedeth from pride, and maketh a man so partial to himself that he swelleth against contradiction, and thinketh he is lessened if he is opposed. You must in this case take heed of increasing the storm by an unwary word, or kindling the fire whilst the wind is in a corner which may blow it

9. folly.

in your face; you are dextrously to yield everything till he beginneth to cool, and then by slow degrees you may rise and gain upon him. Your gentleness well timed will like a charm dispel his anger ill placed; a kind smile will reclaim when a shrill, pettish answer would provoke him. Rather than fail upon such occasions, when other remedies are too weak a little flattery may be admitted, which by being necessary will cease to be criminal.

If ill-humour and sullenness, and not open and sudden heat, is his disease, there is a way of treating that too, so as to make it a grievance to be endured. In order to it, you are first to know that naturally good sense hath a mixture of surly in it, and there being so much folly in the world, and for the most part so triumphant, it giveth frequent temptations to raise the spleen of men who think right. Therefore that which may generally be called ill-humour is not always a fault; it becometh one when either it is wrong applied, or that it is continued too long when it is not so. For this reason you must not too hastily fix an ill name upon that which may perhaps not deserve it; and though the case should be that your husband might too sourly resent anything he disliketh, it may so happen that more blame shall belong to your mistake than to his ill-humour. If a husband behaveth himself sometimes with an indifference that a wife may think offensive, she is in the wrong to put the worst sense upon it if by any means it will admit a better. Some wives will call it ill-humour if their husbands change their style from that which they used whilst they made their first addresses to them; others will allow no intermission or abatement in the expressions of kindness to them, not enough distinguishing times, and forgetting that it is impossible for men to keep themselves up all their lives to the height of some extravagant moments. A man may at some times be less careful in little things, without any cold or disobliging reason for it; as a wife may be too expecting in smaller matters without drawing upon herself the inference of being unkind. And if your husband should be really sullen, and have such frequent fits as might take away the excuse of it, it concerneth you to have an eye prepared to discern the first appearances of cloudy weather, and to watch when the fit goeth off, which seldom lasteth long if it is let alone. But whilst the mind is sore everything galleth it, and that maketh it necessary to let the black humour begin to spend itself before you come in and venture to undertake it.

If in the lottery of the world you should draw a covetous husband, I confess it will not make you proud of your good luck; yet even such a one may be endured too, though there are few passions more intractable than that of avarice. You must first take care that your definition of avarice may not be a mistake. You are to examine every circumstance of your husband's fortune, and weigh the reason of everything you expect from him before you have right to pronounce that sentence. The complaint is now so general against all husbands that it giveth great suspicion of its being often ill-grounded; it is impossible they should all deserve that censure, and therefore it is certain that it is many times misapplied. He that spareth in everything is an inexcusable niggard; he that spareth in nothing is as inexcusable a madman. The mean is, to spare in what is least necessary, to lay out more liberally in what is more required in our several circumstances. Yet this will not always satisfy. There are wives who are impatient of the rules of economy, and are apt to call their husband's kindness in question if any other measure is put to their expense than that of their own fancy. Be sure to avoid this dangerous error, such a partiality to yourself, which is so offensive to an understanding man that he will very ill bear a wife's giving herself such an injurious preference to all the family, and whatever belongeth to it.

But to admit the worst, and that your husband is really a close-handed wretch, you must in this, as in other cases, endeavour to make it less afflicting to you; and first you must observe seasonable hours of speaking. When you offer anything in opposition to this reigning humour a third hand and a wise friend may often prevail more than you will be allowed to do in your own cause. Sometimes you are dexterously to go along with him in things where you see that the niggardly part of his mind is most predominant, by which you will have the better opportunity of persuading him in things where he may be more indifferent. Our passions are very unequal, and are apt to be raised or lessened according as they work upon different objects; they are not to be stopped or restrained in those things where our mind is more particularly engaged. In other matters they are more tractable, and will sometimes give reason a hearing and admit a fair dispute. More than that, there are few men, even in this instance of avarice, so entirely abandoned to it that at some hours and upon some occasions will not forget their natures, and for that time turn prodigal. The same man who will grudge himself what is necessary, let his pride be raised and he shall be profuse; at another time his anger shall have the same effect; a fit of vanity, ambition, and sometimes of kindness, shall open and enlarge his narrow mind; a dose of wine will work upon this tough humour, and for the time dissolve it. Your business must be, if this case happeneth, to watch these critical moments, and not let one of them slip without making your advantage of it; and a wife may be said to want skill if by these means she is not able to secure herself in a good measure against the inconveniences this scurvy quality in a husband might bring upon her, except he should be such an incurable monster as I hope will never fall to your share.

The last supposition I will make, is, that your husband should be weak,[10] and incompetent to make use of the privileges that belong to him. It will be yielded that such a one leaveth room for a great many objections. But God Almighty seldom sendeth a grievance without a remedy, or at least such a mitigation as taketh away a great part of the sting and the smart of it. To make such a misfortune less heavy, you are first to bring to your observation that a wife very often maketh the better figure for her husband's making no great one, and there seemeth to be little reason why the same lady that chuseth a waiting-woman with worse looks may not be content with a husband with less wit; the argument being equal from the advantage of the comparison. If you will be more ashamed in some cases of such a husband, you will be less afraid than you would perhaps be of a wise one. His unseasonable weakness may no doubt sometimes grieve you, but then set against this, that it giveth you the dominion if you will make the right use of it. It is next to his being dead, in which case the wife hath right to administer; therefore, be sure, if you have such an idiot, that none except yourself may have the benefit of the forfeiture. Such a fool is a dangerous beast if others have the keeping of him, and you must be very

10. feeble-minded.

undexterous if when your husband shall resolve to be an ass, you do not take care he may be *your* ass. But you must go skilfully about it, and above all things take heed of distinguishing in public what kind of husband he is. Your inward thoughts must not hinder the outward payment of the consideration that is due to him; your slighting him in company, besides that it would to a discerning by-stander give too great encouragement for the making nearer applications to you, is in itself such an indecent way of assuming that it may provoke the tame creature to break loose, and to show his dominion for his credit which he was content to forget for his ease. In short, the surest and the most approved method will be to do like a wise minister to an easy prince; first give him the orders you afterwards receive from him.

With all this, that which you are to pray for is a wise husband, one that by knowing how to be a master for that very reason will not let you feel the weight of it; one whose authority is so softened by his kindness that if giveth you ease without abridging your liberty; one that will return so much tenderness for your just esteem of him that you will never want[11] power, though you will seldom care to use it. Such a husband is as much above all the other kinds of them as a rational subjection to a prince great in himself is to be preferred before the disquiet and uneasiness of unlimited liberty.

Before I leave this head, I must add a little concerning your behaviour to your husband's friends, which requireth the most refined part of your understanding to acquit yourself well of it. You are to study how to live with them with more care than you are to apply to any other part of your life; especially at first, that you may not stumble at the first setting out. The family into which you are grafted will generally be apt to expect, that like a stranger in a foreign country you should conform to their methods, and not bring in a new model by your own authority. The friends in such a case are tempted to rise up in arms as against an unlawful invasion, so that you are with the utmost caution to avoid the least appearances of anything of this kind. And that you may with less difficulty afterwards give your directions, be sure at first to receive them from

11. lack.

your husband's friends. Gain them to you by early applying to them, and they will be so satisfied, that as nothing is more thankful than pride, when it is complied with, they will strive which of them shall most recommend you; and when they have helped you to take root in your husband's good opinion you will have less dependence upon theirs, though you must not neglect any reasonable means of preserving it. You are to consider, that a man governed by his friends is very easily inflamed by them; and that one who is not so will yet for his own sake expect to have them considered. It is easily improved to a point of honour in a husband, not to have his relations neglected; and nothing is more dangerous than to raise an objection which is grounded upon pride. It is the most stubborn and lasting passion we are subject to, and where it is the first cause of the war, it is very hard to make a secure peace. Your caution in this is of the last importance to you.

And that you may the better succeed in it, carry a strict eye upon the impertinence of your servants; take heed that their ill-humour may not engage you to take exceptions, or their too much assuming in small matters raise consequences which may bring you under great disadvantage. Remember that in the case of a royal bride those about her are generally so far suspected to bring in a foreign interest that in most countries they are insensibly reduced to a very small number, and those of so low a figure that it doth not admit the being jealous of them. In little and in the proportion, this may be the case of every new married woman, and therefore it may be more advisable for you to gain the servants you find in a family than to tie yourself too fast to those you carry into it.

You are not to overlook these small reflections because they may appear low and inconsiderable; for it must be said, that as the greatest streams are made up of the small drops at the head of the springs from whence they are derived, so the greater circumstances of your life will be in some degree directed by these seeming trifles, which having the advantages of being the first acts of it, have a greater effect than singly in their own nature they could pretend to.

I will conclude this article with my advice, that you would as much as nature will give you leave endeavour to forget the great indulgence you have found at home. After such a gentle discipline as you have been under, everything you dislike will seem the harsher to you. The tenderness we have had for you, my dear, is of another nature, peculiar to kind parents, and differing from that which you will meet with first in any family into which you shall be transplanted; and yet they may be very kind too, and afford no justifiable reason to you to complain. You must not be frighted with the first appearances of a differing scene; for when you are used to it you may like the house you go to better than that you left; and your husband's kindness will have so much advantage of ours that we shall yield up all competition, and as well as we love you, be very well contented to surrender to such a rival.

HOUSE, FAMILY and CHILDREN

You must lay before you, my dear, that there are degrees of care to recommend yourself to the world in the several parts of your life. In many things, though the doing them well may raise your credit and esteem, yet the omission of them would draw no immediate reproach upon you; in others, where your duty is more particularly applied, the neglect of them is amongst those faults which are not forgiven, and will bring you under a censure which will be a much heavier thing than the trouble you would avoid. Of this kind is the government of your house, family and children, which since it is the province allotted to your sex, and that the discharging it well will for that reason be expected from you, if you either desert it out of laziness or manage it ill for want of skill, instead of a help you will be an encumbrance to the family where you are placed.

I must tell you, that no respect is lasting but that which is produced by our being in some degree useful to those that pay it. Where that faileth the homage and the reverence go along with it, and fly to others where something may be expected in exchange for them. And upon this principle the respects even of the children and the servants will not stay with one that doth not think them worth their care, and the old housekeeper shall make a better figure in the family than the lady with all her fine clothes, if she wilfully relinquishes her title to the government. Therefore take heed of carrying your good breeding to such a height as to be good for nothing, and to be proud of it. Some think it hath a great air to be above troubling their thoughts with such ordinary things as their house and family; others dare not admit cares for fear they should hasten wrinkles; mistaken pride maketh some think they must keep themselves up, and not descend to these duties, which do not seem enough refined for great ladies to be employed in, forgetting all this while that it is more than the greatest princes can do, at once to preserve respect and to neglect their business. No age ever erected altars to insignificant gods; they had all some quality applied to them to draw worship from mankind. This maketh it the more unreasonable for a lady to expect to be considered, and at the same time resolve not to deserve it. Good looks alone will not do, they are not such a lasting tenure as to be relied upon; and if they should stay longer than they usually do it will by no means be safe to depend upon them; for when time hath abated the violence of the first liking, and that the nap is a little worn off, though still a good degree of kindness may remain, men recover their sight which before might be dazzled, and allow themselves to object as well as to admire.

In such a case, when a husband seeth an empty, airy thing sail up and down the house to no kind of purpose, and look as if she came thither only to make a visit; when he findeth that after Her Emptiness hath been extreme busy about some very senseless thing, she eats her breakfast half an hour before dinner, to be at greater liberty to afflict the company with her discourse, then calleth for her coach that she may trouble her acquaintance, who are already cloyed with her; and having some proper dialogues ready to display her foolish eloquence at the top of the stairs, she setteth out like a ship out of the harbour laden with trifles, and cometh back with them; at her return she repeateth to her faithful waiting-woman the triumphs of that day's impertinence,[12] then, wrapped up in flattery and clean linen, goeth to bed so satisfied that it throweth her into pleasant dreams of her own felicity. Such a one is seldom serious but with her tailor; her children and family may now and

12. foolery.

then have a random thought, but she never taketh aim but at something very impertinent—I say, when a husband, whose province is without doors, and to whom the economy of the house would be in some degree indecent, findeth no order nor quiet in his family, meeteth with complaints of all kinds springing from this root, the mistaken lady who thinketh to make amends for all this by having a well-chosen petticoat will at last be convinced of her error, and with grief be forced to undergo the penalties that belong to those who are wilfully insignificant. When this scurvy hour cometh upon her she first groweth angry; then when the time of it is past would perhaps grow wiser, not remembering that we can no more have wisdom than grace whenever we think fit to call for it. There are times and periods fixed for both, and when they are too long neglected, the punishment is that they are irrecoverable, and nothing remaineth but an useless grief for the folly of having thrown them out of our power. You are to think what a mean figure a woman maketh when she is so degraded by her own fault, whereas there is nothing in those duties which are expected from you that can be a lessening to you, except your want of conduct makes it so.

You may love your children without living in the nursery, and you may have a competent and discreet care of them, without letting it break out upon the company, or exposing yourself by turning your discourse that way, which is a kind of laying children to the parish, and it can hardly be done anywhere that those who hear it will be so forgiving as not to think they are overcharged with them. A woman's tenderness to her children is one of the least deceitful evidences of her virtue, but yet the way of expressing it must be subject to the rules of good breeding; and though a woman of quality ought not to be less kind to them than mothers of the meanest rank are to theirs, yet she may distinguish herself in the manner, and avoid the coarse methods, which in women of a lower size might be more excusable. You must begin early to make them love you, that they may obey you. This mixture is nowhere more necessary than in children. And I must tell you that you are not to expect returns of kindness from yours, if ever you have any, without grains of allowance; and yet it is not so much a defect in their good nature as a shortness of thought in them. Their first insufficiency maketh them lean so entirely upon their parents for what is necessary that the habit of it maketh them continue the same expectations for what is unreasonable, and as often as they are denied, so often they think they are injured; and whilst their desires are strong, and their reasons yet in the cradle, their anger looketh no farther than the thing they long for and cannot have, and to be displeased for their own good is a maxim they are very slow to understand. So that you may conclude the first thoughts of your children will have no small mixture of mutiny, which being so natural, you must not be angry, except you would increase it. You must deny them as seldom as you can, and when there is no avoiding it you must do it gently; you must flatter away their ill humour, and take the next opportunity of pleasing them in some other things before they either ask or look for it. This will strengthen your authority, by making it soft to them, and confirm their obedience, by making it their interest. You are to have as strict a guard upon yourself amongst your children as if you were amongst your enemies. They are apt to make wrong inferences, to take encouragement from half words, and misapply what you may say or do so as either to lessen their duty or to extend their liberty farther than is convenient. Let them be more in awe of your kindness than of your power. And above all, take heed of supporting a favourite child in its impertinence, which will give right to the rest of claiming the same privilege. If you have a divided number, leave the boys to the father's more peculiar[13] care, that you may with the greater justice pretend to a more immediate jurisdiction over those of your own sex. You are to live so with them that they may never choose to avoid you except when they have offended; and then let them tremble, that they may distinguish. But their penance must not continue so long as to grow too sour upon their stomachs, that it may not harden instead of correcting them. The kind and severe part must have their several turns seasonably applied; but your indulgence is to have the broader mixture, that love rather than fear may be the root of their obedience.

Your servants are in the next place to be considered; and you must remember not to fall into the mistake of thinking that because

13. particular.

they receive wages, and are so much inferior to you, therefore they are below your care to know how to manage them. It would be as good reason for a master workman to despise the wheels of his engines, because they are made of wood. These are the wheels of your family; and let your directions be never so faultless, yet if these engines stop or move wrong the whole order of your house is either at a stand or discomposed. Besides, the inequality which is between you must not make you forget that nature maketh no such distinction, but that servants may be looked upon as humble friends, and that returns of kindness and good usage are as much due to such of them as deserve it, as their service is due to us when we require it. A foolish haughtiness in the style of speaking, or in the manner of commanding them, is in itself very indecent; besides that it begetteth an aversion in them of which the least ill effect to be expected is that they will be slow and careless in all that is enjoined them; and you will find it true by your experience that you will be so much the more obeyed as you are less imperious. Be not too hasty in giving your orders, nor too angry when they are not altogether observed; much less are you to be loud, and too much disturbed. An evenness in distinguishing when they do well or ill is that which will make your family move by a rule, and without noise, and will the better set out your skill in conducting it with ease and silence, that it may be like a well disciplined army, which knoweth how to anticipate the orders that are fit to be given them. You are never to neglect the duty of the present hour to do another thing, which though it may be better in itself is not to be unseasonably preferred. Allot well chosen hours for the inspection of your family, which may be so distinguished from the rest of your time that the necessary cures may come in their proper place, without any influence upon your good humour, or interruption to other things. By these methods you will put yourself in possession of being valued by your servants, and then their obedience will naturally follow.

I must not forget one of the greatest articles belonging to a family, which is the expense. It must not be such as by failing either in the time or measure of it may rather draw censure than gain applause. If it was well examined, there is more money given to be laughed at than for any one thing in the world, though the purchasers do not think so. A well stated rule is like the Line, when that is once passed we are under another Pole; so the first straying from a rule is a step towards making that which was before a virtue to change its nature, and to grow either into a vice or at least an impertinence. The art of laying out money wisely is not attained to without a great deal of thought, and it is yet more difficult in the case of a wife, who is accountable to her husband for her mistakes in it. It is not only his money, his credit too is at stake, if what lieth under the wife's care is managed either with indecent thrift or too loose profusion. You are therefore to keep the mean between these two extremes, and it being hardly possible to hold the balance exactly even, let it rather incline towards the liberal side, as more suitable to your quality and less subject to reproach. Of the two, a little money misspent is sooner recovered than the credit which is lost by having it unhandsomely saved; and a wise husband will less forgive a shameful piece of parsimony than a little extravagance, if it be not too often repeated. His mind in this must be your chief direction; and his temper, when once known, will in great measure justify your part in the management, if he is pleased with it.

In your clothes avoid too much gaudy. Do not value yourself upon an embroidered gown, and remember that a reasonable word or an obliging look will gain you more respect than all your fine trappings. This is not said to restrain you from a decent compliance with the world, provided you take the wiser and not the foolisher part of your sex for your pattern. Some distinctions are to be allowed whilst they are well suited to your quality and fortune, and in the distribution of the expense it seemeth to me that a full attendance,[14] and well chosen ornaments for your house, will make you a better figure than too much glittering in what you wear, which may with more ease be imitated by those that are below you. Yet this must not tempt you to starve everything but your own appartment; or in order to more abundance there, give just cause to the least servant you have to complain of the want of what is necessary. Above all, fix it in your thoughts as an unchangeable maxim, that nothing is truly fine but what is fit and that just so much as is proper for your circumstances of their several kinds is

14. of servants.

much finer than all you can add to it. When you once break these bounds you launch into a wide sea of extravagance. Everything will become necessary, because you have a mind to it; and you have a mind to it, not because it is fit for you, but because somebody else hath it. This lady's logic setteth reason upon its head, by carrying the rule from things to persons, and appealing from what is right to every fool that is in the wrong. The word 'necessary' is miserably applied, it disordereth families and overturneth governments by being so abused. Remember that children and fools want everything because they want wit to distinguish; and therefore there is no stronger evidence of a crazy understanding than the making too large a catalogue of things necessary, when in truth there are so very few things that have a right to be placed in it. Try everything first in your judgment, before you allow it a place in your desire, else your husband may think it as necessary for him to deny as it is for you to have whatever is unreasonable; and if you shall too often give him that advantage the habit of refusing may perhaps reach to things that are not unfit for you.

There are unthinking ladies who do not enough consider how little their own figure agreeth with the fine things they are so proud of. Others when they have them will hardly allow them to be visible; they cannot be seen without light, and that is many times so saucy and so prying that like a too forward gallant it is to be forbid the chamber. Some, when you are ushered into their dark Ruelle,[15] it is with such solemnity that a man would swear there was something in it, till the unskilful lady breaketh silence, and beginneth a chat, which discovereth it is a puppet-play with magnificent scenes. Many esteem things rather as they are hard to be gotten than that they are worth getting; this looketh as if they had an interest to pursue that maxim because a great part of their own value dependeth upon it. Truth in these cases would be often unmannerly, and might derogate from the prerogative great ladies would assume to themselves of being distinct creatures from those of their sex which are inferior and of less difficult access.

In other things, too, your condition must give the rule to you, and therefore it is not a wife's part to aim at more than a bounded

15. salon.

liberality; the farther extent of that quality (otherwise to be commended) belongeth to the husband, who hath better means for it. Generosity wrong placed becometh a vice. It is no more a virtue when it groweth into an inconvenience, virtues must be enlarged or restrained according to differing circumstances; a princely mind will undo a private family. Therefore things must be suited or else they will not deserve to be commended, let them in themselves be never so valuable; and the expectations of the world are best answered when we acquit ourselves in that manner which seemeth to be prescribed to our several conditions, without usurping upon those duties which do not so particularly belong to us.

I will close the consideration of this article of expense with this short word. Do not fetter yourself with such a restraint in it as may make you remarkable, but remember that virtue is the greatest ornament, and good sense the best equipage.

BEHAVIOUR and CONVERSATION

It is time now to lead you out of your house into the world. A dangerous step, where your virtue alone will not secure you except it is attended with a great deal of prudence. You must have both for your guard, and not stir without them. The enemy is abroad, and you are sure to be taken, if you are found straggling. Your behaviour is therefore to incline strongly towards the reserved part; your character is to be immoveably fixed upon that bottom, not excluding a mixture of greater freedom as far as it may be innocent and well timed. The extravagancies of the age have made caution more necessary; and by the same reason that the too great licence of ill men hath by consequence in many things restrained the lawful liberty of those who did not abuse it, the unjustifiable freedoms of some of your sex have involved the rest in the penalty of being reduced. And though this cannot so alter the nature of things as to make that criminal which in itself is indifferent, yet if it maketh it dangerous that alone is sufficient to justify the restraint. A close behaviour is the fittest to receive virtue for its constant guest, because there, and there only, it can be secure. Proper reserves are the outworks, and must never be deserted by those who intend to keep the place; they keep off the possibilities not only of being taken but of being attempted; and if a woman seeth danger, though at never so remote a distance, she is for that time to shorten her line of liberty. She who will allow herself to go to the utmost extent of everything that is lawful is so very near going farther that those who lie at watch will begin to count upon her.

Mankind, from the double temptation of vanity and desire, is apt to turn everything a woman doth to the hopeful side; and there are few who dare make an impudent application till they discern something which they are willing to take for an encouragement. It is safer therefore to prevent such forwardness than to go about to cure it. It gathereth strength by the first allowances, and claimeth a right from having been at any time suffered with impunity. Therefore nothing is with more care to be avoided than such a kind of civility as may be mistaken for invitation; and it will not be enough for you to keep yourself free from any criminal engagements, for if you do that which either raiseth hopes or createth discourse there is a spot thrown upon your good name; and those kind of stains are the harder to be taken out, being dropped upon you by the man's vanity as well as by the woman's malice.

Most men are in one sense platonic lovers, though they are not willing to own that character. They are so far philosophers as to allow that the greatest part of pleasure lieth in the mind; and in pursuance of that maxim there are few who do not place the felicity more in the opinion of the world of their being prosperous lovers than in the blessing itself, how much soever they appear to value it. This being so, you must be very cautious not to gratify these chameleons at the price of bringing a cloud upon you reputation, which may be deeply wounded though your conscience is unconcerned.

Your own sex too will not fail to help the least appearance that giveth a handle to be ill-turned. The best of them will not be displeased to improve their own value by laying others under a disadvantage, when there is a fair occasion given for it. It distinguisheth them still the more; for their own credit is more exalted and, like a picture set off with shades, shineth more when a lady either less innocent or less discreet is set near, to make them appear so much the brighter. If these lend their breath to blast such as are so unwary as to give them this advantage, you may be sure there will be a stronger gale from those who, besides malice or emulation, have an interest too, to strike hard upon a virtuous woman. It seemeth to them that their load of infamy is lessened by throwing part of it upon others; so that they will not only improve it when it lieth in their way but take pains to find out the least mistake an innocent woman committeth, in revenge of the injury she doth in leading a life which is a reproach to them. With these you must be extreme wary, and neither provoke them to be angry nor invite them to be intimate.

To the men you are to have a behaviour which may secure you without offending them. No ill-bred, affected shyness, nor a roughness unsuitable to your sex and unnecessary to your virtue, but a way of living that may prevent all coarse railleries or unmannerly freedoms; looks that forbid without rudeness and oblige without invitation, or leaving room for the saucy inferences men's vanity suggesteth to them upon the least encouragements. This is so very nice, that it must engage you to have a perpetual watch upon your eyes, and to remember that one careless glance giveth more advantage than a hundred words not enough considered, the language of the eyes being very much the most significant, and the most observed.

Your civility, which is always to be preserved, must not be carried to a compliance which may betray you into irrecoverable mistakes. This French ambiguous word *complaisance* hath led your sex into more blame than all other things put together. It carrieth them by degrees into a certain thing called 'a good kind of woman', an easy idle creature, that doth neither good nor ill but by chance, hath no choice, but leaveth that to the company she keepeth. Time, which by degrees addeth to the signification of words, hath made her according to the modern style little better than one who thinketh it a rudeness to deny when civilly required either her service in person, or her friendly assistance to those who would have a meeting or want a confidant. She is a certain thing always at hand, an easy companion, who hath ever great compassion for distressed lovers; she censureth nothing but rigour, and is never without a plaster for a wounded reputation, in which chiefly lieth her skill in chirurgery. She seldom hath the propriety of any particular gallant, but liveth upon brokerage, and waiteth for the scraps her friends are content to leave her.

There is another character, not quite so criminal yet not less ridiculous; which is that of 'a good-humoured woman', one who thinketh she must always be in a laugh, or a broad smile, because good humour is an obliging quality, thinketh it less ill-manners to talk impertinently than to be silent in company. When such a prating engine rideth Admiral,[16] and carrieth the lantern in a circle of fools – a cheerful coxcomb coming in for a recruit – the chattering of monkeys is a better noise than such a concert of senseless merriment. If she is applauded in it she is so encouraged that, like a ballad singer who if commended breaketh his lungs, she letteth herself loose, and overfloweth upon the company. She conceiveth that mirth is to have no intermission, and therefore she will carry it about with her, though it be to a funeral; and if a man should put a familiar question she doth not know very well how to be angry, for then she would be no more that pretty[17] thing called a good humoured woman. This necessity of appearing at all times to be so infinitely pleased is a grievous mistake, since in a handsome woman that invitation is unnecessary, and in one who is not so, ridiculous. It is not intended by this that you should forswear laughing; but remember that, fools being always painted in that posture, it may fright those who are wise from doing it too frequently, and going too near a copy which is so little inviting; and much more from doing it loud, which is an unnatural sound and looketh so much like another sex that few things are more offensive. That boisterous kind of jollity is as contrary to wit and good manners as it is to modesty and virtue. Besides, it is a coarse kind of quality, that throweth a woman into a lower form, and degradeth her from the rank of those who are more refined. Some ladies speak loud and make a noise to be the more minded, which looketh as if they beat their drums for volunteers, and if by mis-

16. The 'Admiral', or flag-ship, carried a lantern at night.
17. 'Pretty' was usually used in a derogatory sense.

fortune none come in to them, they may, not without reason, be a good deal out of countenance.

There is one thing yet more to be avoided, which is the example of those who intend nothing farther than the vanity of conquest, and think themselves secure of not having their honour tainted by it. Some are apt to believe their virtue is too obscure, and not enough known except it is exposed to a broader light, and set out to its best advantage by some public trials. These are dangerous experiments, and generally fail, being built upon so weak a foundation as that of a too great confidence in ourselves. It is as safe to play with fire as to dally with gallantry. Love is a passion that hath friends in the garrison, and for that reason must by a woman be kept at such a distance that she may not be within the danger of doing the most usual thing in the world, which is conspiring against herself. Else the humble gallant who is only admitted as a trophy very often becometh the conqueror; he putteth on the style of victory, and from an admirer groweth into a master, for so he may be called from the moment he is in possession. The first resolutions of stopping at good opinion and esteem grow weaker by degrees against the charms of courtship skilfully applied. A lady is apt to think a man speaketh so much reason whilst he is commending her that she has much ado to believe him in the wrong when he is making love to her; and when besides the natural inducements your sex hath to be merciful, she is bribed by well-chosen flattery, the poor creature is in danger of being caught like a bird listening to the whistle of one that hath a snare for it. Conquest is so tempting a thing that it often maketh woman mistake men's submissions, which with all their fair appearance have generally less respect than art in them. You are to remember that men who say extreme things many times say them most for their own sakes; and that the vain gallant is often as well pleased with his own compliments as he could be with the kindest answer. Where there is not that ostentation you are to suspect there is design. And as strong perfumes are seldom used but where they are necessary to smother an unwelcome scent, so excessive good words leave room to believe they are strewed to cover something which is to gain admittance under a disguise. You must therefore be upon your guard, and consider that of the two, respect is more dangerous than anger. It puts even the best understandings out of their place for the time, till their second thoughts restore them; it stealeth upon us insensibly, throweth down our defences, and maketh it too late to resist after we have given it that advantage. Whereas railing goeth away in sound; it hath so much noise in it that by giving warning it bespeaketh caution. Respect is a slow and a sure poison, and like poison swelleth us within ourselves. Where it prevaileth too much it groweth to be a kind of apoplexy in the mind, turneth it quite round, and after it hath once seized the understanding becometh mortal to it. For these reasons, the safest way is to treat it like a sly enemy, and to be perpetually upon the watch against it.

I will add one advice to conclude this head, which is that you will let every seven years make some alteration in you towards the graver side, and not be like the girls of fifty who resolve to be always young, whatever time with his iron teeth hath determined to the contrary. Unnatural things carry a deformity in them never to be disguised; the liveliness of youth in a riper age looketh like a new patch upon an old gown, so that a gay matron, a cheerful old fool, may be reasonably put into the list of the tamer kind of monsters. There is a certain creature called a grave hobby-horse, a kind of a she numps,[18] that pretendeth to be pulled to a play, and must needs go to Bartholomew Fair to look after the young folks, whom she only seemeth to make her care; in reality she taketh them for her excuse. Such an old butterfly is of all creatures the most ridiculous, and the soonest found out. It is good to be early in your caution, to avoid anything that cometh within distance of such despicable patterns, and not like some ladies, who defer their conversion till they have been so long in possession of being laughed at that the world doth not know how to change their style when they are reclaimed from that which gave the first occasion for it.

The advantages of being reserved are too many to set down; I will only say, that it is a guard to a good woman, and a disguise to an ill one. It is of so much use to both, that those ought to use it as an artifice who refuse to practise it as a virtue.

18. she-fool.

FRIENDSHIPS

I must in a particular manner recommend to you a strict care in the choice of your friendships. Perhaps the best are not without their objections, but however, be sure that yours may not stray from the rules which the wiser part of the world hath set to them. The leagues offensive and defensive seldom hold in politics, and much less in friendships. The violent intimacies, when once broken, of which they scarce ever fail, make such a noise; the bag of secrets untied, they fly about like birds let loose from a cage, and become the entertainment of the town. Besides, these great dearnesses by degrees grow injurious to the rest of your acquaintance, and throw them off from you. There is such an offensive distinction when the Dear Friend cometh into the room that it is flinging stones at the company, who are not apt to forgive it.

Do not lay out your friendship too lavishly at first, since it will, like other things, be so much the sooner spent. Neither let it be of too sudden a growth, for as the plants which shoot up too fast are not of that continuance as those which take more time for it, so too swift a progress in pouring out your kindness is a certain sign that by the course of nature it will not be long lived. You will be responsible to the world if you pitch upon such friends as at the time are under the weight of any criminal objection. In that case you will bring yourself under the disadvantages of their character, and must bear your part of it. Choosing implieth approving, and if you fix upon a lady for your friend against whom the world shall have given judgment, is not so well natured as to believe you are altogether averse to her way of living, since it doth not discourage you from admitting her into your kindness. And resemblance of inclinations being thought none of the least inducements to friendship, you will be looked upon at least as a well-wisher if not a partner with her in her faults. If you can forgive them in another, it may be presumed you will not be less gentle to yourself; and therefore you must not take it ill, if you are reckoned a *croupière*,[19]

19. gambling partner.

and condemned to pay an equal share with such a friend of the reputation she hath lost.

If it happeneth that your friend should fall from the state of innocence after your kindness was engaged to her, you may be slow in your belief in the beginning of the discovery; but as soon as you are convinced by a rational evidence you must, without breaking too roughly, make a far and a quick retreat from such a mistaken acquaintance; else by moving too slowly from one that is so tainted, the contagion may reach you so far as to give you part of the scandal, though not of the guilt. This matter is so nice, that as you must not be too hasty to join in the censure upon your friend when she is accused, so you are not on the other side to defend her with too much warmth; for if she should happen to deserve the report of common fame, besides the vexation that belongeth to such a mistake you will draw an ill appearance upon yourself, and it will be thought you pleaded for her not without some consideration of yourself. The anger which must be put on to vindicate the reputation of an injured friend may incline the company to suspect you would not be so zealous if there was not a possibility that the case might be your own. For this reason you are not to carry your dearness so far as absolutely to lose your sight where your friend is concerned. Because malice is too quick sighted, it doth not follow that friendship must be blind; there is to be a mean between these two extremes, else your excess of good nature may betray you into a very ridiculous figure, and by degrees you may be preferred to such offices as you will not be proud of. Your ignorance may lessen the guilt, but will improve the jest upon you, who shall be kindly sollicitous to procure a meeting, and innocently contribute to the ills you would avoid; whilst the contriving lovers, when they are alone, shall make you the subject of their mirth, and perhaps (with respect to the Goddess of Love be it spoken) it is not the worst part of their entertainment – at least it is the most lasting – to laugh at the believing friend who was so easily deluded.

Let the good sense of your friends be a chief ingredient in your choice of them, else let your reputation be never so clear, it may be clouded by their impertinence.[20] It is like our houses being in the

20. folly.

power of a drunken or a careless neighbour, only so much worse, as that there will be no insurance here to make you amends as there is in the case of fire.

To conclude this paragraph: if formality is to be allowed in any instance, it is to be put on to resist the invasion of such forward women as shall press themselves into your friendship, where if admitted they will either be a snare or an incumbrance.

CENSURE

I will come next to the consideration, how you are to manage your censure, in which both care and skill will be a good deal required. To distinguish is not only natural but necessary, and the effect of it is that we cannot avoid giving judgment in our minds, either to absolve or to condemn as the case requireth. The difficulty is, to know when and where it is fit to proclaim the sentence. An aversion to what is criminal, a contempt of what is ridiculous, are the inseparable companions of understanding and virtue; but the letting them go farther than our own thoughts hath so much danger in it, that though it is neither possible nor fit to suppress them entirely, yet it is necessary they should be kept under very great restraints. An unlimited liberty of this kind is little less than sending a herald and proclaiming war to the world, which is an angry beast when so provoked. The contest will be unequal, though you are never so much in the right, and if you begin against such an adversary it will tear you in pieces, with this justification, that it is done in its own defence. You must therefore take heed of laughing, except in company that is very sure. It is throwing snowballs against bullets and it is the disadvantage of a woman that the malice of the world will help the brutality of those who will throw a slovenly untruth upon her. You are for this reason to suppress your impatience for fools, who besides that they are too strong a party to be unnecessarily provoked, are of all others the most dangerous in this case. A blockhead in his rage will return a dull jest that will lie heavy, though there is not a grain of wit in it. Others will do it with more art, and you must not think yourself secure because your reputation may perhaps be out of the reach of ill-will; for if it findeth that part guarded it will seek one which is more exposed. It flieth, like a corrupt humour in the body, to the weakest part. If you have a tender side, the world will be sure to find it, and to put the worst colour upon all you say or do, give an aggravation to everything that may lessen you, and a spiteful turn to everything that might recommend you. Anger layeth open those defects which friendship would not see and civility might be willing to forget. Malice needeth no such invitation to encourage it, neither are any pains more superfluous than those we take to be ill spoken of. If envy, which never dyeth and seldom sleepeth, is content sometimes to be in a slumber, it is very unskilful to make a noise to awake it.

Besides, your wit will be misapplied if it is wholly directed to discern the faults of others, when it is so necessary to be often used to mend and prevent your own. The sending our thoughts too much abroad hath the same effect as when a family never stayeth at home; neglect and disorder naturally followeth; as it must do within ourselves if we do not frequently turn our eyes inwards to see what is amiss with us, where it is a sign we have an unwelcome prospect when we do not care to look upon it, but rather seek our consolations in the faults of those we converse with.

Avoid being the first in fixing a hard censure, let it be confirmed by the general voice before you give into it. Neither are you then to give sentence like a magistrate, or as if you had a special authority to bestow a good or ill name at your discretion. Do not dwell too long upon a weak side, touch and go away; take pleasure to stay longer where you can commend, like bees that fix only upon those herbs out of which they may extract the juice of which their honey is composed. A virtue stuck with bristles is too rough for this age, it must be adorned with some flowers, or else it will be unwillingly entertained; so that even where it may be fit to strike, do it like a lady, gently; and assure yourself, that where you care to do it you will wound others more and hurt yourself less by soft strokes than by being harsh or violent.

The triumph of wit is to make your good nature subdue your censure; to be quick in seeing faults, and slow in exposing them. You are to consider that the invisible thing called a good name is made up of the breath of numbers that speak well of you; so that if by a disobliging word you silence the meanest, the gale will be less strong which is to bear up your esteem. And though nothing is so vain as the eager pursuit of empty applause, yet to be well thought of and to be kindly used by the world is like a glory about a woman's head; it is a perfume she carrieth about with her, and leaveth wherever she goeth; it is a charm against ill-will. Malice may empty her quiver, but cannot wound; the dirt will not stick, the jests will not take. Without the consent of the world a scandal doth not go deep; it is only a slight stroke upon the injured party and returneth with the greater force upon those that gave it.

VANITY AND AFFECTATION

I must with more than ordinary earnestness give you caution against vanity, it being the fault to which your sex seemeth to be the most inclined; and since affectation for the most part attendeth it, I do not know how to divide them. I will not call them twins, because more properly vanity is the mother and affectation is the darling daughter; vanity is the sin, and affectation is the punishment; the first may be called the root of self-love, the other the fruit. Vanity is never at its full growth till it spreadeth into affectation, and then it is complete.

Not to dwell any longer upon the definition of them, I will pass to the means and motives to avoid them. In order to it, you are to consider that the world challengeth the right of distributing esteem and applause, so that where any assume by their single authority to be their own carvers it groweth angry, and never faileth to seek revenge. And if we may measure a fault by the greatness of the penalty, there are few of a higher size than vanity, as there is scarce a punishment which can be heavier than that of being laughed at.

Vanity maketh a woman tainted with it, so top full of herself that she spilleth it upon the company. And because her own thoughts are entirely employed by self-contemplation, she endeavoureth, by a cruel mistake, to confine her acquaintance to the same narrow circle of that which only concerneth her Ladyship, forgetting that she is not of half that importance to the world that she is to herself, so mistaken she is in her value by being her own appraiser. She will fetch such a compass in discourse to bring in her beloved self, and rather than fail, her fine petticoat, that there can hardly be a better scene than such a trial of ridiculous ingenuity. It is a pleasure to see her angle for commendations, and rise so dissatisfied with the ill-bred company, if they will not bite. To observe her throwing her eyes about to fetch in prisoners, and go about cruising like a privateer, and so out of countenance if she return without booty, is no ill piece of comedy. She is so eager to draw respect[21] that she always misseth it, yet thinketh it so much her due that when she faileth she groweth waspish, not considering that it is impossible to commit a rape upon the will, that it must be fairly gained, and will not be taken by storm; and that in this case the tax ever riseth highest by a benevolence.[22] If the world, instead of admiring her imaginary excellencies, taketh the liberty to laugh at them, she appealeth from it to herself, for whom she giveth sentence and proclaimeth it in all companies. On the other side, if encouraged by a civil word she is so obliging, that she will give thanks for being laughed at in good language. She taketh a compliment for a demonstration, and setteth it up as an evidence even against her looking glass. But the good lady, being all this while in a most profound ignorance of herself, forgetteth that men would not let her talk upon them, and throw so many senseless words at their head, if they did not intend to put her person to fine and ransom for her impertinence. Good words of any other lady are so many stones thrown at her, she can by no means bear them, they make her so uneasy that she cannot keep her seat, but up she riseth and goeth home half burst with anger and strait-lacing. If by great chance she saith anything that hath sense in it, she expecteth such an excessive rate of commendations that to her thinking the company ever riseth in her debt. She looketh upon rules as things made for the common people, and not for persons of her rank; and this opinion sometimes tempteth her to extend her prerogative to the dispensing with the Commandments. If by great fortune she happeneth in spite of her

21. attention.
22. A benevolence was a medieval levy which was in theory quite voluntary.

vanity to be honest, she is so troublesome with it, that as far as in her lieth she maketh a scurvy thing of it. Her bragging of her virtue looketh as if it cost her so much pains to get the better of herself that the inferences are very ridiculous. Her good humour is generally applied to the laughing at good sense. It would do one good to see how heartily she despiseth anything that is fit for her to do. The greatest part of her fancy is laid out in choosing her gown, as her discretion is chiefly employed in not paying for it. She is faithful to the fashion, to which not only her opinion but her senses are wholly resigned. So obsequious she is to it, that she would be ready to be reconciled even to virtue with all its faults, if she had her dancing master's word that it was practised at court.

To a woman so composed, when affectation cometh in to improve her character it is then raised to the highest perfection. She first setteth up for a fine thing, and for that reason will distinguish herself, right or wrong, in everything she doth. She would have it thought that she is made of so much the finer clay, and so much more sifted than ordinary, that she hath no common earth about her. To this end she must neither move nor speak like other women, because it would be vulgar; and therefore must have a language of her own, since ordinary English is too coarse for her. The looking glass in the morning dictateth to her all the motions of the day, which by how much the more studied are so much the more mistaken. She cometh into a room as if her limbs were set on with ill-made screws, which maketh the company fear the pretty thing should leave some of its artificial person upon the floor. She doth not like herself as God Almighty made her, but will have some of her own workmanship; which is so far from making her a better thing than a woman that it turneth her into a worse creature than a monkey. She falleth out with nature, against which she maketh war without admitting a truce, those moments excepted in which her gallant may reconcile her to it. When she hath a mind to be soft and languishing there is something so unnatural in that affected easiness that her frowns could not be by many degrees so forbidden. When she would appear unreasonably humble, one may see she is so excessively proud that there is no enduring it. There is such an impertinent smile, such a satisfied simper, when she faintly disowneth some fulsome commendation a man happeneth to bestow upon her against his conscience, that her thanks for it are more visible under such a thin disguise than they could be if she should print them. If a handsomer woman taketh any liberty of dressing out of the ordinary rules the mistaken lady followeth, without distinguishing the unequal pattern, and maketh herself uglier by an example misplaced; either forgetting the privilege of good looks in another, or presuming without sufficient reason upon her own. Her discourse is a senseless chime of empty words, a heap of compliments so equally applied to differing persons that they are neither valued nor believed. Her eyes keep pace with her tongue, and are therefore always in motion. One may discern that they generally incline to the compassionate side, and that notwithstanding her pretence to virtue she is gentle to distressed lovers and ladies that are merciful. She will repeat the tender part of a play so feelingly, that the company may guess without injustice, she was not altogether a disinterested spectator. She thinketh that paint and sin are concealed by railing at them. Upon the latter she is less hard, and being divided between the two opposite prides of her beauty and her virtue, she is often tempted to give broad hints that somebody is dying for her; and of the two she is less unwilling to let the world think she may be sometimes profaned than that she is never worshipped.

Very great beauty may perhaps so dazzle for a time that men may not so clearly see the deformity of these affectations. But when the brightness goeth off, and that the lover's eyes are by that means set at liberty to see things as they are, he will naturally return to his senses, and recover the mistake into which the lady's good looks had at first engaged him, and being once undeceived, ceaseth to worship that as a goddess which he seeth is only an artificial shrine moved by wheels and springs, to delude him. Such women please only like the first opening of a scene, that hath nothing to recommend it but the being new. They may be compared to flies, that have pretty shining wings for two or three hot months, but the first cold weather maketh an end of them. So the latter season of these fluttering creatures is dismal; from their nearest friends they receive a very faint respect, from the rest of the world the utmost degree of contempt.

Let this picture supply the place of any other rules which might be given to prevent your resemblance to it; the deformity of it, well considered, is instruction enough; from the same reason that the sight of a drunkard is a better sermon against that vice than the best that was ever preached upon that subject.

PRIDE

After having said this against vanity, I do not intend to apply the same censure to pride, well placed and rightly defined. It is an ambiguous word; one kind of it is as much a virtue as the other is a vice, but we are naturally so apt to choose the worst that it is become dangerous to commend the best side of it.

A woman is not to be proud of her fine gown; nor when she hath less wit than her neighbours, to comfort herself that she hath more lace. Some ladies put so much weight upon ornaments that if one could see into their hearts it would be found that even the thought of death is made less heavy to them by the contemplation of their being laid out in state, and honourably attended to the grave. One may come a good deal short of such an extreme, and yet still be sufficiently impertinent,[23] by setting a wrong value upon things which ought to be used with more indifference. A lady must not appear solicitous to engross respect[24] to herself, but be content with a reasonable distribution, and allow it to others, that she may have it returned to her. She is not to be troublesomely nice, nor distinguish herself by being too delicate, as if ordinary things were too coarse for her; this is an unmannerly and an offensive pride, and where it is practised deserveth to be mortified, of which it seldom faileth. She is not to lean too much upon her quality, much less to despise those who are below it. Some make quality an idol, and then their reason must fall down and worship it. They would have the world think that no amends can ever be made for the want of a great title or an ancient coat of arms; they imagine that with these advantages they stand upon the higher ground, which

23. foolish. 24. attention.

maketh them look down upon merit and virtue as things inferior to them. This mistake is not only senseless but criminal too, in putting a greater price upon that which is a piece of good luck than upon things which are valuable in themselves. Laughing is not enough for such a folly, it must be severely whipped, as it justly deserves. It will be confessed, there are frequent temptations given by pert upstarts to be angry, and by that to have our judgments corrupted in these cases. But they are to be resisted; and the utmost that is to be allowed is, when those of a new edition will forget themselves so as either to brag of their weak side, or to endeavour to hide their meanness by their insolence, to cure them by a little seasonable raillery, a little sharpness well placed, without dwelling too long upon it.

These and many other kinds of pride are to be avoided.

That which is to be recommended to you, is an emulation to raise yourself to a character by which you may be distinguished; an eagerness for precedence in virtue, and all such other things as may gain you a greater share of the good opinion of the world. Esteem to virtue is like a cherishing air to plants and flowers, which maketh them blow and prosper; and for that reason it may be allowed to be in some degree the cause as well as the reward of it. That pride which leadeth to a good end cannot be a vice, since it is the beginning of a virtue; and to be pleased with just applause is so far from a fault that it would be an ill symptom in a woman who should not place the greatest part of her satisfaction in it. Humility is no doubt a great virtue, but it ceaseth to be so when it is afraid to scorn an ill thing. Against vice and folly it is becoming your sex to be haughty, but you must not carry the contempt of things to arrogance towards persons, and it must be done with fitting distinctions, else it may be inconvenient by being unseasonable. A pride that raiseth a little anger to be out-done in anything that is good, will have so good an effect that it is very hard to allow it to be a fault.

It is no easy matter to carry even between these differing kinds so described, but remember that it is safer for a woman to be thought too proud than too familiar.

DIVERSIONS

The last thing I shall recommend to you is a wise and a safe method of using diversions. To be too eager in the pursuit of pleasure whilst you are young is dangerous, to catch at it in riper years is grasping a shadow; it will not be held. Besides that, by being less natural it groweth to be indecent. Diversions are the most properly applied to ease and relieve those who are oppressed by being too much employed. Those that are idle have no need of them, and yet they above all others give themselves up to them. To unbend our thoughts, when they are too much stretched by our cares, is not more natural than it is necessary, but to turn our whole life into a holiday is not only ridiculous but destroyeth pleasure instead of promoting it. The mind, like the body, is tired by being always in one posture; too serious breaketh it, and too diverting looseneth it. It is variety that giveth the relish, so that diversions too frequently repeated grow first to be indifferent and at last tedious. Whilst they are well chosen and well timed they are never to be blamed, but when they are used to an excess, though very innocent at first they often grow to be criminal, and never fail to be impertinent.

Some ladies are bespoken for merry meetings, as Bessus was for duels.[25] They are engaged in a circle of idleness, where they turn round for the whole year, without the interruption of a serious hour. They know all the players' names, and are intimately acquainted with all the booths in Bartholomew Fair. No soldier is more obedient to the sound of his captain's trumpet than they are to that which summoneth them to a puppet play or a monster. The spring that bringeth out flies and fools maketh them inhabitants in Hyde Park; in the winter they are an encumbrance to the play house and the ballast of the drawing room. The streets all this while are so weary of these daily faces, that men's eyes are over-laid with them. The sight is glutted with fine things, as the stomach with sweet ones, and when a fair lady will give too much of herself to

25. Bessus was a character in Beaumont and Fletcher's *King and No King* who pretended at one stage to be committed to 212 duels.

the world she groweth luscious,[26] and oppresseth instead of pleasing. These jolly ladies do so continually seek diversion that in a little time they grow into a jest, yet are unwilling to remember that if they were seldomer seen they would not be so often laughed at. Besides, they make themselves cheap, than which there cannot be an unkinder word bestowed upon your sex.

To play sometimes, to entertain company or to divert yourself, is not to be disallowed, but to do it so often as to be called a gamester is to be avoided, next to the things that are most criminal. It hath consequences of several kinds not to be endured; it will engage you into a habit of idleness and ill hours, draw you into ill-mixed company, make you neglect your civilities abroad and your business at home, and impose into your acquaintance such as will do you no credit.

To deep play there will be yet greater objections. It will give occasion to the world to ask spiteful questions. How you dare venture to lose, and what means you have to pay such great sums? If you pay exactly, it will be enquired from whence the money cometh? If you owe, and especially to a man, you must be so very civil to him for his forbearance that it layeth a ground of having it further improved if the gentleman is so disposed, who will be thought no unfair creditor, if where the estate faileth he seizeth upon the person. Besides, if a lady could see her own face upon an ill game, at a deep stake, she would certainly forswear anything that could put her looks under such a disadvantage.

To dance sometimes will not be imputed to you as a fault, but remember that the end of your learning it was, that you might the better know how to move gracefully. It is only an advantage so far. When it goeth beyond it one may call it excelling in a mistake, which is no very great commendation. It is better for a woman never to dance, because she hath no skill in it, than to do it too often because she doth it well. The easiest as well as the safest method of doing it is in private companies, amongst particular friends, and then carelessly, like a diversion, rather than with solemnity, as if it was a business, or had anything in it to deserve a month's preparation by serious conference with a dancing-master.

26. over-ripe.

Much more might be said to all these heads, and many more might be added to them. But I must restrain my thoughts, which are full of my dear child, and would overflow into a volume, which would not be fit for a new year's gift. I will conclude with my warmest wishes for all that is good to you: that you may live so as to be an ornament to your family, and a pattern to your sex; that you may be blessed with a husband that may value, and with children that may inherit your virtue; that you may shine in the world by a true light, and silence envy by deserving to be esteemed; that wit and virtue may both conspire to make you a great figure. When they are separated, the first is so empty and the other so faint that they scarce have right to be commended. May they therefore meet and never part; let them be your guardian angels, and be sure never to stray out of the distance of their joint protection. May you so raise your character that you may help to make the next age a better thing, and leave posterity in your debt for the advantage it shall receive by your example.

Let me conjure you, my dearest, to comply with this kind ambition of a father, whose thoughts are so engaged in your behalf that he reckoneth your happiness to be the greatest part of his own.

SELECTED LETTERS

EDITORIAL INTRODUCTION

These letters are intended to cover aspects of Halifax's life which are not covered in his works. Those addressed to his brother Henry Savile, Envoy in Paris, are from *The Savile Correspondence*, ed. W. D. Cooper (Camden Society 1858).[1] The letters to Gilbert Burnet were edited by Dorothy Lane Poole and published in the *English Historical Review*, xxvi (1911),[2] they are in answer to letters from Burnet edited by H. C. Foxcroft and published in *Camden Miscellany XI* (1907). The letters to William of Orange are from Sir John Dalrymple's *Memoirs of Great Britain and Ireland.* (2 vols. 1771–3), vol. II, pt. 2.[3] The spelling and punctuation have been modernised.

1. Cited as '*SC*'.
2. Cited as '*EHR*'.
3. Cited as Dalrymple'.

SELECTED LETTERS

I

To Henry Savile.

1 May 1679.

It seemeth you had the knowledge of my preferment[4] before I could tell it you, so little did I apprehend myself to be likely to be readmitted into the state of grace, as you might perceive by the style of my last, in which I assure you I did not dissemble with you. To undertake the being useful to my friends in the station I am in, would be a piece of arrogance very unfit for a councillor of a new edition; but if ever such a miracle should come to pass, as that from such a degree of disfavour as I have lain under I should come to have any credit, no doubt but our envoy in France might rely upon a friend at Court....

I suppose Harry[5] may now be with you if no accident has made his journey slower. I have confined him to ten days or a fortnight's stay in Paris; in which time you will be able to search him, so as to send me his perfect character along with him. And pray take some pains in it, it being of some moment to me that I should not mistake his humour, which is less discoverable by a father than by any other man less concerned.

I cannot blame you for fearing a journey with a court;[6] I know few things would give me more terror. But it must be done, and I dare rely upon you for making it as easy to you as the matter will bear. We are here every day upon high points: God send us once at an end of them! Impeachments of ministers, trials of peers for their life, discourses and votes too, concerning the heir presumptive, are the only things our thoughts are employed about. And I that have dreamt this half year of the silence and retirement of old

4. He had been re-admitted to the Privy Council on 21 April.
5. The Hon. Henry Savile, Halifax's eldest son.
6. Louis XIV's intended state progress was, in fact, cancelled.

Rufford, find myself engaged in an active and an angry world, and must rather take my part in it with grief than avoid it with scandal. . . .

My Lord Sunderland is very kind, and I value his being so to the degree I ought. I need not tell you how much you owe him, but remember it is no small thing for men at court to speak kindly of their friends when they are at a distance. . . .

SC. pp. 84–5.

II

To Henry Savile.

17 July 1679.

I had sent you the first news of the dissolution of the Parliament,[7] but that Henry Thynne promised to do it, so that I relied upon him, and I suppose he did not fail you. It is to be presumed you make comments upon it at Paris, as we do at London, though not just the same; and you may be sure that those who are near the King have their share of the censure that ever attendeth things of this nature.

You would think it a strange thing to have it from other hands, and not from mine, that the King, resolving to add my Lord Robartes and my Lord Gerrard to the earls' bench, hath thought fit to let me keep them company. I keep the same name still, and intend your nephew shall take that of the barony, which is Eland; if any young woman that is a good match may be found that can be fool enough to like him the better for it, this piece of preferment hath something in it, else it is to me of very little moment more than as it is a mark of the King's favour, which maketh everything valuable.

I am often at Windsor, where much of the time is taken up about your friend my Lord Lauderdale,[8] who is defending himself against the Scotch lords, who have brought up their lawyers to

7. On 12 July. This was the First Exclusion Parliament, which had met in March.

8. Halifax was being sarcastic; Henry Savile had fallen into deep disgrace in 1677 for voting against Lauderdale, the King's High Commissioner in Scotland.

report their complaints; and, though perhaps after the hearing they have had all things will not proceed so as they might expect in relation to their own particulars, yet it is believed they will have the satisfaction of seeing their great adversary removed, but when and in what manner is a thing of more uncertainty....

SC. pp. 109–10.

III

To Thomas Thynne.

31 July 1679.

Besides your kindness to me in prevailing against your own inclinations at my request, which I must put amongst a thousand other obliging evidences you have given me of your friendship, you are doing the most public service that can be to the nation, by making use of your interest to get reasonable men chosen for the Parliament, and if the rest of England had as good a prospect of elections as you have for two counties, I durst almost undertake that notwithstanding all the discouraging circumstances we live under, things might be brought to such a settlement, as that we might at least sleep secure from any sudden destruction.

The world is at present a good deal heated, and I have just interest enough at Court to entitle me to a part of the fury of the coffee houses; I need not tell you that they are encouraged by some of my small friends[9] which I need not describe to you. My method shall be to let the storm have its course, and when we grow calm again, I do not doubt but I shall be able to wipe off the dirt that hath been thrown upon me.

Foxcroft, i, 180.

IV

To Henry Savile.

8 January 1680.

I do not know what you have done to your nephew, but he is full of kindness for you, and presumeth much upon yours, which maketh him not only willing to go from hence, but impatient till he

9. Antony Ashley Cooper, Earl of Shaftesbury, the Opposition leader, who was sho rt in stature.

is with you, and I do with less difficulty comply with him since the Parliament is put off, which would have been an entertainment of some use as well as pleasure to him. I hope that when he is left to himself without the encumbrance of a governor, he will make a good use of that liberty, and think himself so much the more obliged to improve, to avoid miscarrying under his own conduct; though I presume he will not think fit to insist so much upon his right to dispose of himself as not to give it up to you whenever you will be so kind as to advise him.

Our world here is so over-run with the politics, the fools' heads so heated, and the knaves so busy, that a wasps' nest is a quieter place to sleep in than this town is to live in, which maketh me so weary of it that you must not wonder if you hear that, notwithstanding my passion for London, that hath been little inferior to yours for Paris, I go very early this spring into the country, where, besides other invitations, I shall have that of seeing my small works at Rufford, having yet only had the pleasure of disbursing for them.[10] I confess I dream of the country, as men do of small beer when they are in a fever, and at this time poor old Rufford with all its wrinkles hath more charms for me than anything London can show me....

SC. pp. 133–4.

V

To Henry Savile.

Rufford, 2 February 1680.

I am once more got to my old tenement, which I had not seen since I had given order to renew and repair it. It looketh now somewhat better than when you was last here; and, besides the charms of your native soil, it hath something more to recommend itself to your kindness than when it was so mixed with the old ruins of the abbey that it looked like a medley of superstition and sacrilege, and, though I have still left some decayed part of old building, yet there are none of the rags of Rome remaining. It is now all heresy, which in my mind looketh pretty well, and I have at least as much reverence for it now as I had when it was encumbered with those sanctified

10. He went the last week in January.

ruins. In short, with all the faults that belong to such a misshapen building patched up at so many several times, and notwithstanding the forest hath not its best clothes at this time of the year, I find something here which pleaseth me, whether it be the general disease of loving home, or whether for the sake of variety, since I have been so long absent as to make my own house a new thing to me, or by comparing it to other places where one is less at ease, I will not determine. The best reason I can give is, that I grow every day fitter for a coal fire and a country parlour, being come now to the worst part of my elder brothership in having so much a greater share of years than you that it may make amends for the inequality of the division in other respects.

The greatest pleasure I have now to hope for dependeth much upon the good advice you will give your nephew, who never shall have any injunctions from me but such as he ought for his own sake to impose upon himself. I think him so capable of succeeding well in the world that it is pity he should miscarry by a wrong setting out at first; therefore pray let us have a care of his launching, for there is the greatest danger for young men in this age. . . .

I have great reason to be pleased with your kindness to him, but you have drawn an unnecessary encumbrance upon yourself by taking him into your house. Pray make him no compliments that give you any trouble, and therefore let him be in some lodging near you, where he may be enough under your eye without giving you the inconvenience of an inmate. It may be a real kindness to inform him sometimes of such things as pass through your hands as are not great secrets, and yet may give him a taste and quicken his appetite to know what passeth in the world. He promised me to read books of treaties and negotiations, in which you may not only encourage but direct him very much to his advantage. It is a great matter for a growing man to apply himself to read what may be of some use, which may be done with as much pleasure at least as in losing time upon *nouvelles* and *entretiens*, things only fit for young fellows and their wenches to read till the hour of assignation cometh for a more substantial entertainment.

You may believe I do not disapprove your raptures in commendation of a retired life, but I will not betray you so far as to encourage you to go beyond the bare speculation till your circumstances are better fitted to put your philosophy in practice. Your company would not have been unwelcome at Sir William Coventry's, where we could have entertained you a little of things that have passed in our world, to make you a return to the account you would have given us of France, but amongst the other disadvantages of life it ever happeneth that friends are separated when at the same time we are crowded by our enemies; or, which is almost as bad, by those who are tedious, or at the best indifferent. The Duke of Newcastle[11] is just coming in, so I take my leave.

SC. pp. 137–9.

VI

To Gilbert Burnet.

31 July 1680.

I must lament the loss of my Lord of Rochester, though the manner of his leaving us maketh it an unkind thing to him to be sorry for it; but our grief in these cases is always for ourselves, and I swear I am touched with the kind words of a dying man, who, though he showed some decay of his senses in speaking too well of me, yet it seemeth you did not think his end was so near when you left him.[12] My gratitude to his memory must make me very glad of the commission he hath given you; he hath sat to you, and I am sure you will make him like, that he may live a little longer amongst us, and being drawn by so good a hand, the beauty of such a penitent may draw all men's eyes and thoughts to it, and make them forget everything in him, but what is fit to be followed and esteemed.[13]

11. His near neighbour, at Welbeck Abbey.

12. John Wilmot, Earl of Rochester, the notorious rake, died on 26 July, having been ministered unto by Burnet in his last illness, during which he expressed deep piety and penitence. When told that Halifax had inquired after him (he was a great friend of Henry Savile), 'he bid me [Burnet] tell you that he returned his humble thanks to you, and added, that you were the man in the world he valued most; he believed you were melancholy on account of the public'.

13. Rochester commissioned Burnet to write an account of his conversion and death, which was published before the end of the year.

I am not pleased that we at St Martin's must despair of you, for I am still for myself, yet for your sake I congratulate the appearance there is, of your succeeding in Covent Garden, which I should not do if I did not think it a step to better things;[14] I believe I shall be tempted to a piece of nonconformity, and stray sometimes from my own parish, a sin you are to absolve me for, when you are the occasion of it.

EHR, p. 537.

VII

To Gilbert Burnet.

9 August 1680.

... I will not lose the hope of seeing you better established, though the appearances at present seem to discourage you; merit is a long way about, but it is a very sure one, and upon that foundation you may, without breach of your modesty, expect any advancement the Church can give in England, but I believe your friends will be more impatient in your behalf, than you will be for yourself; and in the meantime you need not envy anybody having the pleasure of employing your time in that which doth not only give you a present satisfaction, but will raise you higher by a preferment of your own creating than you can be made by any other hand,[15] though never so liberal, or more properly, never so just to you. I assure you my long stay in the country hath not made me weary of it; my absence from better company hath made me grow down to it, so that I doubt whether I am now fit for any other place; but I think the time of the year, and some small affairs I am to look after, will bring me up the next month.

EHR, p. 538.

14. Halifax had hoped that Burnet would be made rector of St Martin's in the Fields on the incumbent's appointment to a bishopric; instead Simon Patrick was transferred from St Paul's, Covent Garden, which also eluded Burnet's grasp.

15. He refers to Burnet's *History of the Reformation*, of which the first volume was published the following month.

VIII

To Gilbert Burnet.

Rufford, 23 August 1680.

I congratulate with you the pleasure you must have in finishing a work the world is in so great expectation of,[16] and the hearing it reviveth my impatience till I see it, in the meantime you will I suppose entertain yourself with giving some account of my Lord Rochester, concerning which, do not think it impertinent that I give you this caution, which is, that it is not possible for you to write on a subject that requireth more care, and therefore though it looketh like a slight thing, and such a one as you would rather play with, than spend much either of your time or thoughts upon it, let me beg of you to be exactly careful in it, and to file it over oftener than you have ever done anything that hath come from you. I will allow you to laugh at this unnecessary tenderness of mine, provided you will not take it ill of me. The Parliament being now prorogued to October, in a manner that maketh it believed, all men's thoughts will be upon it, with exclusion to anything else, and I hope sometime the next month to know your conjectures, which will be necessary to direct so ignorant a man, as my long absence hath made me.

EHR, pp. 538–9.

IX

To Thomas Thynne.

5 October 1680.

This will find you returned to Drayton, where you are so great a stranger that you ought to forfeit it for non-residence, and now that the Parliament sitteth, you are likely to leave it again for a good while, which I am very glad of for my own sake, since I am for the winter settled in town again.

I believe that though I found at my arrival a new scene in state

16. *The History of the Reformation.*

matters, yet it is the same as when you left the town, so that I shall not be able to give any information that is new to you, but I confess I was a little surprised to see such a change in some of the Court in relation to the Duke;[17] I am told there is now as much anger against him at Whitehall as there can be at the other end of the town, so industrious his Highness hath been to spoil his own business; the waves beat so high against him, that great part of the world will not hear of anything less than exclusion. For my own part I neither am nor will be under any obligations that might restrain the freedom of my opinion concerning him; but yet if there is any possibility of making ourselves safe by lower expedients, I had rather use them, than venture upon so strong a remedy as the disinheriting the next heir of the Crown. Upon this occasion I have been thinking what is proper for a friend to advise you as to your own particular. If you do not come at the first sitting, the country party will be angry and perhaps treat you as roughly as they have done some of your friends. If you do come, in all probability the first business will be to proceed against the Duke, and if you have the same tenderness you used to have in point of decency towards him you will be in great difficulties to know how to behave yourself. For my own sake I wish you here for a thousand reasons, but as things are, I do not know whether it may not be advisable for you to hearken a little for a week or ten days, whilst the Parliament sitteth, after their method of proceeding, and upon that form your resolutions of coming up; and though others may do it better, I shall not omit to give you the best lights I can. In the meantime I can tell you, the town sayeth as confidently the King will quit his brother as those of his party say the contrary: a fine world, and a happy prospect of things, when our remedies are little less to be feared than our disease.

Foxcroft, i, 241.

17. of York.

X

To Henry Savile.

13 December 1680.

You will before this have one of mine which giveth you some account of my late preferment in the House of Commons, who were pleased to make me a man of more importance than I am, the better to entitle me to the honour of being addressed against.[18] I am not worth the notice they have been pleased to take of me, and I do not doubt of outliving the disadvantage this may seem to throw upon me, being resolved to give such evidence of myself, if I should continue to have any part in the public business, as shall cure the suspicions men may have taken of me in a heat, for differing with them in some of their darling points, to which they are at present so wedded that no reason can be admitted in contradiction to them. Your kindness maketh this appear a heavier thing than either it is in itself, or than I apprehend it; the circumstances that attended it are more than the thing itself and yet I have borne it without much disquiet. I must only cast about for a new set of friends, for my old ones have been so very zealous for the public that some of them thought it as meritorious to persecute me as others believed it excusable to desert me; the history of it I reserve till I see you, and in the meantime whatever may be said from any other hand to lay any blame upon me, let it not find any great credit with you, for I dare undertake when you hear all you shall not need to make use of any partiality to incline you to judge of my side.

SC, pp. 170–71.

XI

To Henry Savile.

6 January 1681.

Your answer to mine by Mr Nelson is in a style that of all others ought to be the most welcome to me. I like kindness best when it is in so plain a dress, and to be told by a brother, and, which is

18. See Introduction, p. 13 above.

more, by a friend, what the world sayeth or thinketh of me; though their censures of me may be mistaken, yet I cannot be so in judging your part to proceed only from true and perfect kindness, which I assure you is not thrown away upon me. Your opinion that I am in the right may be too partial, but that I think myself so, you may undertake for me, and I shall not deceive you, and if the points lately in question are errors on my side I have this to say in my excuse, that I have hardly one friend that was not till very lately of that very opinion which is now accounted a mortal heresy; so that if by a greater measure of grace than I pretend to they have outrun me by their sudden conversion, they ought to have been gentler to a weak brother than I have found them. If I could tell you the several steps of their behaviour to me, you would wonder they do not turn Papists, since there is no other church in the world charitable enough to give them absolution for it. I would not much doubt of satisfying you in the great objections made against me if I had time to discourse with you, but a letter cannot be made long enough to give you a clear light into things of this kind. You will I am sure give me some kind of credit when I tell you I am not such a volunteer in philosophy as to provoke such a storm as hath fallen upon me from a mistaken principle of bravery, to do a thing only because it is dangerous; but when upon inquiry I think myself in the right, I confess I have an obstinate kind of morality, which I hope may make amends for my want of devotion. It seems the foreign ministers have had my picture drawn by their correspondents not very much to my advantage. I guess who were the painters, and think I am not mistaken in it.

Where all this will end, either in relation to myself or to the public, God in Heaven only knoweth. I am at this hour threatened with more thunder from the House of Commons tomorrow; whether it will be so or in what manner I do not yet know, but where there is infinite anger there is reason to expect the worst; for which I have recourse still to my small philosophy, and have not only the comfort of innocence to support me, but the impossibility of avoiding any strokes of this kind without such indecencies (to give no worse term) as I can never digest: and, though I agree with you this is not an age for a man to follow the strict morality of better times, yet sure mankind is not yet so debased but that there will ever be found some few men who will scorn to join in concert with the public voice, when it is not well grounded, and even that popular fury which may now blow in my face will perhaps with a little patience not only abate, but turn against these very men that now appear against me. I am interrupted, and so can only tell you I am for ever yours. *SC*, pp. 172–4.

XII

To Henry Savile.

20 January 1681.

You have given full evidence of your kindness by your fears for me, which I suppose may increase when you hear of the dissolution of a Parliament. You may believe me when I tell you, this is not to be imputed to me, though I am far from arraigning the better judgments of those with whom I may differ in this particular. If it should happen, which is not unlikely, that I should go down to Rufford, you will be further convinced in this matter; and if I could talk with you, I should as little doubt of doing it in that of my Lord Stafford, in which you are possessed I see by the powerful majority, which is not at all times found to be in the right.[19] A man must never hope a pardon for small sins if he will digest great ones, and where blood is in the case there is not, or at least ought not to be, any room for prudence. That an honest man is a very scurvy calling I agree with you; but having used it so long I do not know how to change, but must be content to keep to it with all its hazards and inconveniences. By what you say concerning my late friends, I find a statesman hath as much charity out of interest as a Christian hath from his religion, and is as easily reconciled to his enemies whenever the scene changeth, and that it suiteth well with his affairs. I confess I, who am slow to anger, when I am once thoroughly injured, am apt enough to retain it, not so far as to revenge myself, but only to remember, and not easily to trust again . . . *SC*, p. 176.

19. Lord Stafford was impeached of high treason and condemned on the flimsiest of evidence in December 1680. Halifax was in the minority of peers which voted for his acquittal.

XIII

To Henry Savile.

25 January 1681.

Your kind repeated earnestness to rescue me from the dangers you apprehend I am in from the general anger that hath of late been raised against me, coming from the warmth of your heart, as I am sure it doth, is a welcome though an unnecessary evidence of your mind towards me, and though I cannot absolutely agree to your prescriptions of a looser morality in things that relate to the public, yet I am enough convinced, and was so even before my late experience, that there is a good deal of hazard in opposing the torrent of a House of Commons; but on the other side, it being the only definition of an honest man to be a lover of justice with all its inconveniences, I do not very well know how things of this kind are to be avoided, but by such means as would lie heavier upon me than all the votes or addresses an angry Parliament can throw upon me. I have had the good luck to have every unpopular thing imputed to me in the first place, and by going a strait way without any bias, or engaging in any faction, one part of the world hath been much more violent against me than the other hath been in my defence. All these disadvantages did not move me so as to quit my ground whilst the Parliament sat. I thought myself restrained by a necessary point of honour not to do that by compulsion which perhaps in itself was the thing in the world I most desired; but now that the Parliament is dissolved,[20] I am going down to Rufford to breathe a little, and enjoy some quiet, which will be a very welcome thing to me, and when we meet again at Oxford I must venture to go into the storm, and receive the shot once more of an angry House of Commons, except they should by a miracle grow into a better temper than is naturally expected from them. I shall at least have some respite, though I assure you it was not my choice. I am for ever yours.

SC, pp. 177–8.

20. On 18 January. Another was summoned to meet at Oxford on 21 March.

XIV

To Gilbert Burnet.

21 February 1681.

I received yours yesterday with the sermon[21] which I assure you from such an author is a very acceptable present to me, and I made haste to read it, though I had heard one in the morning. For out of Parliament I am a very good Protestant, notwithstanding that dull fiction of my journey to Cornburgh,[22] and many others of the same size, which show God's judgement upon malice, or else my noble friends might have been happier in their invention. Sure your style did not please some of the auditors, for to me it appeareth there is a part of your discourse cometh very close to what they are now adoing; so that I expect shortly to hear you are a fallen angel, and though I should not rejoice at a friend's disgrace, yet self-interest will not allow me to be sorry for anything that will make you fitter company for me, who am so hardened by being railed at that the spears and arrows which come out of some men's mouths cannot pierce me; and that I may not be discomposed with the melancholy prospects you mention, I can wink and resolve not to see mine till it cometh so near as to save the trouble of taking care to avoid it; so I hope that in spite of the storm that threateneth us, I shall have calm enough to read and enjoy your second volume,[23] for which I have expectations big enough to lessen if not destroy the pleasure I shall take in it if it came from any other hand than one where I am secure not to be disappointed. The things you tell me give occasion for many comments, but they must be sad and unpleasing, and therefore not fit to entertain you with. . . .

EHR, p. 539.

21. 'A Sermon before the Aldermen of the City of London at St Lawrence Church, 30 January, being the day of the Martyrdom of King Charles I.'

22. Presumably Cornbury, Oxfordshire, the seat of the Church Tory leader the 2nd Earl of Clarendon.

23. Of *The History of the Reformation*, which appeared the following month.

XV

To Gilbert Burnet.

Rufford, 5 March 1681.

I must thank you for your book, and should do it more, if you had not restrained me by your preface; I swear I must chide you, at the same time that others are angry at the compliments you bestow upon me,[24] for though I should not be displeased with your partiality to me, confined within reasonable bounds, yet to raise me to a character I am as little able to make good as I am desirous to pretend to it, doth but expose me the more to censure, which at this time is not very necessary, and getteth anger to yourself from those who, as much as they are your friends, will not easily forgive you so great a mistake. It is a very difficult style I am to use in this case; for between expressing myself so as may look like the anger of a lady that teareth a love letter, though she liketh it, and the omitting anything that is fit to be said in return to what is kindly intended, I am so puzzled that I dare not venture to say anymore, how much soever the subject may require it. I can with more liberty tell you how sensible I am of your kind advice, about my going to Oxford,[25] where I have no temptations that can persuade me to like the journey, but on the other side I do not know how to indulge myself so far as to excuse my attendance in Parliament, especially at such a time as this, and going as I shall do with the intentions of contributing all I can in my little capacity to a better composure of things, in which I hope I am so fixed that the douceurs I expect from some of my noble friends shall not be able to shake me. Besides, I am unwilling to give them the handle of saying I avoid them, for I am sure their gentleness is such as would give everything that I do the worst interpretation; those very men who perhaps might be content I stayed at home, would, if I did so,

24. In the preface to the second volume of his *History of the Reformation* Burnet mentioned 'the right honourable the Earl of Halifax, whom if I reckon among the greatest persons this age has produced I am sure all that know him will allow that I speak modestly of him'.

25. Where Parliament was to meet on 21 March.

impute it to fear or guilt, and instead of allowing it to be a merit in me, would make it a trophy to themselves. I must not gratify them at this price, but this I will say, that let them come to Parliament as men ought to do, with no schemes ready drawn, nor resolutions taken beforehand, let there be no Lords of the Articles[26] to exclude the consideration of anything they do not propose, and then let all men be tried and judged whether they do not in their several stations promote everything that may tend to healing and reconcilement; upon this measure I am content to receive my sentence, and I cannot make a better wish for the public, than that every member of both houses might come with as good a meaning as I do to Oxford. Things lie in a wide compass, but[27] raiseth difficulties, and anger keepeth them up, so that, God knoweth, my hopes can by no means keep pace with my wishes, and I begin to be more solicitous to seek out arguments to persuade me to bear being undone, than to find out remedies to prevent it. You see how a man's retired thoughts do naturally warp towards the more melancholy and despairing side, so you must take them with that allowance, and not receive them as grounds to discourage you from hoping better things, but however you may be disappointed in that, I am sure you shall never be so in believing me, Your (etc.)

EHR, pp. 539–40.

XVI

To Henry Savile.

28 July 1681.

I have yours by Sir Richard Mason,[28] and have seen that which you wrote to Secretary Jenkins, and they both afford considerable matter of reflexion; and for what you direct more particularly to

26. The Lords of the Articles controlled the agenda of the Scots Estates at Edinburgh.

27. There is a word missing here; perhaps 'jealousy', in the sense of 'suspicion'.

28. In his letter to Jenkins, dated 22 July, Savile described the mounting persecution of the French Protestants, and urged that the English Government publicly offer them asylum. In his letter to his brother, which has not survived, he clearly added some private warning or request.

myself I need not tell you how kindly I take it; and, though perhaps my suspicions may not be altogether so strong as yours, yet sure there is ground enough for me to have my cautions, being under such circumstances as I am, and having enemies of so many several colours; I know no better expedient to secure myself against all events than to build upon the same foundation and live by the same maxims I have ever done since my being in business, and to take care that in all my actions there may be so much of the Protestant and the Englishman as may silence the objections of my being a Papist or a pensioner. In particular I shall endeavour to justify my Protestantship by doing all that is in my power towards the encouragement of those that shall take sanctuary here out of France; though even in that, our present condition considered, there is great tenderness to be used in the manner of it, that we may give no occasion for a higher persecution against them there, or by disputing a prince's power over his own subjects draw a question upon us which would hardly be decided in our favour; and we are not strong enough to support our having the wrong end of an argument. Upon this occasion I must give you a hint to be wary in your expressions, without abating anything of your due zeal for religion. . . .

SC, pp. 211–12.

XVII

To William of Orange.

18 January 1687.

Your Highness will give me leave to acknowledge your goodness to my son,[29] in giving him such favourable admittance, which hath made him yet more ambitious to deserve the countenance you have been pleased to afford him. I hope you will put him in the list of those who are to be disposed of by you, since it is a tenure by which I and mine shall ever hold. He is so full of his veneration for your Highness, that he doth himself a very good office with me, by such an effect of his judgement; yet I will not answer for it so far,

29. Lord William Savile, Halifax's second son, who was returning from the Grand Tour via Holland.

but that he may have been guilty in the manner of paying his respects, in which if he hath failed, his youth and his good intentions must be his excuse. He will bring your commands carefully to me, which will be so much the more welcome, by giving me the assurance that I still retain the same place in your Highness's thoughts, though I have not of late had so frequent opportunities of recommending myself to them.

In one thing I have had the luck to guess right, and not to mislead you by a wrong conjecture; that is, about the meeting of the Parliament, which you see is to be prorogued,[30] notwithstanding the positive discourses to the contrary. The motion of public things at present hath not only variety but some kind of contradiction in it. It is very rapid, if looked upon on one side, if on the other, it is as slow; for though there appeareth the utmost vigour to pursue the design which hath been so long laid, there seemeth to be no less firmness in the nation, and aversion to change; so that conversions are so thin, and those which are, so little fit to be examples,[31] that the prevailing party is not a little discountenanced by making no quicker progress; for that reason it is believed they will mend their pace; and if so, every day will give more light to what is intended, though it is already no more a mystery. Whatever happeneth, nothing must ever alter my resolutions of being devoted to your Highness's service.

Dalrymple, pp. 186-7

XVIII

To William of Orange.

31 May 1687.

I deferred my thanks for the honour of your Highness's letter[32] till I could pay them by the same hand that brought it. Having had the opportunity of discoursing frequently, and at large, with Monsieur Dykveldt, it would be less proper now to enter into particulars, or

30. From February to April. It had not met since 1685.
31. The kind of people involved were Obadiah Walker, Master of University College, Oxford, Nell Gwynne, and the eccentric Earl of Peterborough.
32. None of the Prince's letters to Halifax are extant.

to make repetitions of that which he will be so much better able to explain. I shall, therefore, only put your Highness in mind, that my conjectures about the meeting of the Parliament have not hitherto been disappointed; and if I may be allowed to continue them, I am of opinion there will be none in November, neither this nor a new one, though that is threatened, upon a supposition that it shall be made up of Dissenters, and that they will comply with whatever shall be expected of them. Neither of these will be found true, in my opinion, if the trial should be made; there are a great many circumstances which make such a scheme very impracticable, and the more they consider it the more they will be discouraged from attempting it. Besides, the case in short is this; the great design cannot be carried on without numbers; numbers cannot be had without converts, the old stock not being sufficient; converts will not venture till they have such a law to secure them as hath no exception to it; so that an irregularity, or any degree of violence to the law, would so entirely take away the effect of it that men would as little run the hazard of changing their religion after the making it as before. This reason alone fixeth my opinion, though other arguments are not wanting, and upon this foundation I have no kind of apprehension that the legislative power can ever be brought to pursue the present designs. But our affairs here depend so much upon what may be done abroad, that our thoughts, though never so reasonable, may be changed by what we may hear by the next post. A war in Germany, and much more if one nearer to us, will have such an influence here, that our counsels must be fitted to it; and whether or no we shall have an avowed part in it, it is pretty sure we shall have a leaning to one of the parties; and our resolutions at home are to be suited to the interest abroad which we shall happen to espouse. Men's jealousies here are so raised, that they can hardly believe the King of France's journey to Luxembourg to have no more in it than bare curiosity to see it; but your Highness hath your eyes so open, and your thoughts so intent upon everything that moveth, that no doubt you either see there is no mystery, or if there is you have searched to the bottom of it. Monsieur Dykveldt will entertain your Highness with all his observations, which he hath made with great diligence, having conversed with men of all complexions, and by that means he knoweth a great deal of the present state of our affairs. The opportunities he hath had will make him the more welcome here again, whenever there shall be a fair occasion of bringing him. His free way of conversing giveth him an easier admittance than he would have if he was too reserved; and his being known to be a creature of your Highness encourageth men to talk to him with less restraint. May your Highness continue well and safe.

Dalrymple, pp. 196-7.

XIX

To William of Orange.

25 August 1687.

It would be unnecessary to give your Highness a recommending character of my Lord of Shrewsbury,[33] who hath already so good a one established and allowed in the world. I shall only say in short, that he is, without any competition, the most considerable man of quality that is growing up amongst us; that he hath right thoughts for the public and a most particular veneration for your Highness; he is loose and untied from any faction that might render him partial, or give a wrong bias to his opinion; and I do not doubt but upon the first discourse you shall have with him you will be encouraged to treat him without any manner of reserve.

There is so little alteration here since Monsieur Dykveldt left us that I can hardly acquaint you with anything of moment which would be new to you. I have told my Lord Shrewsbury my thoughts, who is very well able to improve and explain them to your Highness. It is not to be imagined but that a certain design will still go on; all that is to be hoped is, that it will be so crippled with the difficulties it every day meeteth with, that it will be disabled from making so swift a progress as is necessary for the end it aimeth at. There are some things that can never prevail upon men's minds, if they have time allowed to consider them; this may be the present case, the whole kingdom being now so well informed that all men

33. Charles Talbot, 12th Earl, then aged 27. Later Secretary of State to William III, etc.

are settled in their dislike of the unwelcome thing that is endeavoured to be imposed on them. This consideration alone freeth me in a great measure from the fears I might otherwise have. Not that it throweth me into such a security as to make me neglect the means that shall from time to time be thought most reasonable for our preservation, towards which your Highness seemeth to me to be in the best method that can be imagined, in being firm to your true interest, unmoveable in everything that is essential, and cautious to give no advantage which might, with any colour of reason, be made use of against you. This conduct being continued, can hardly fail, there being so many things that concur to make it succeed. I find by Monsieur Zuylestein,[34] that your Highness is inclined to believe there will be a Parliament, upon which, being encouraged in my good luck in guessing right hitherto upon the same subject, I take the liberty to tell you that I do not think any will be called till by some sudden accident it shall become necessary and unavoidable: my reasons for it will be better repeated by my Lord of Shrewsbury, so that I shall not now give your Highness the trouble of them.

We are full of the news from Hungary, which is not equally welcome to the several Princes in Christendom.[35] We think it may have a considerable influence upon this part of the world, and if the season was not too far advanced, we are apt to believe France might this very year give some trouble to its neighbours. What part we here might have in it I cannot tell, but suppose we shall be slow to engage in a war which, besides the expense, to which we cannot furnish, is liable to so many accidents that we shall not easily be persuaded to run the hazard of it. Your Highness hath your thoughts intent upon every new thing that ariseth in the world, and knoweth better than anybody how to improve every conjuncture, and turn it to the advantage of that interest of which you are the chief support; and as your care and skill will never be wanting,

34. Who had come in July, ostensibly on a formal mission of condolence on the death of James's mother-in-law, Duchess Laura of Modena.

35. The Emperor's successes against the Turks, especially the fall of Buda that summer, made it likely that he would soon be able to turn to the West. This was unwelcome, of course, to Louis XIV.

so, I hope, they will meet with their just reward of good success, which is the top of my wishes, as it is the utmost of my ambition to be serviceable to a Prince to whom I am eternally devoted.

Dalrymple, pp. 207-8.

XX

To William of Orange.

12 April 1688.

I avoid giving your Highness unnecessary trouble, and though this hath a good conveyance, yet it may perhaps be so long in its way to you that it will not be pertinent to repeat what you will have had from other hands.

There hath been little that is new this great while, since either the old methods have continued, or else what appeareth to be new is at least not strange, being produced by a natural consequence, and therefore to be reasonably expected and foreseen. In some particulars, to men at a distance, the engine seemeth to move fast, but by looking nearer one may see it doth not stir upon the whole matter, so that here is a rapid motion without advancing a step, which is the only miracle that Church hath yet showed to us. Every atempt turneth back upon them. They change the magistracy in the corporations, and still for the worse as to their own designs. The irregular methods have spent themselves without effect; they have run so fast that they begin to be out of breath, and the exercise of extraordinary powers, both ecclesiastical and civil, is so far from fixing the right of them, that men are more united in objecting to them. The world is still where it was, with this only difference, that it groweth every day more averse to that which is endeavoured to be imposed upon them. The very Papists who have estates act unwillingly like pressed men, and have such an eye to what may happen in a revolution[36] that their present advantages hardly make amends for their fears. Upon the whole, they are so divided between the fear of losing their opportunity by delay, or spoiling it with too much haste, that their steps are wavering and

36. Any change of government; not 'revolution' in our sense.

uncertain, and distrusting the very instruments they use, they are under great mortifications, notwithstanding the appearance of carrying everything without opposition. Being thus discouraged by their ill success in their attempts, some say they are altering their scheme, and not finding their expectations answered by the Dissenters, they have thoughts of returning to their old friends, the high churchmen; but the truth is, the Papists have of late been so hard and fierce upon them, that the very species of those formerly mistaken men is destroyed; they have so broken that loom in pieces, that they cannot set it up again to work upon it. In the meantime the men at the helm are certainly divided amongst themselves, which will produce great effects if men will let it work, and not prevent the advantages that may be expected by being too unquiet, or doing things out of season; the great thing to be done now, is to do nothing, but wait for the good consequences of their divisions and mistakes. Unseasonable stirrings, or anything that looketh like the Protestants being the aggressors, will tend to unite them, and by that means will be a disappointment to those hopes which otherwise can hardly fail. Nothing, therefore, in the present conjuncture can be more dangerous than unskilful agitators, warm men who would be active at a wrong time, and want patience to keep their zeal from running away with them.[37]

It is said by some that there is an intention of making a new attempt to beget a better understanding with your Highness; that in order to it, the present envoy,[38] as less acceptable, is to be removed, and another sent, who, if he should be less known, may perhaps for that very reason be the more dangerous. If this should be true, and that softer proposals should be made from hence, it will deserve all your caution to receive them so as neither to give advantage by rejecting them too roughly on one side, or on the other, by giving any colour for them to pretend there is a consent given to anything that may be inconvenient. After the reports

37. The reference is perhaps to Gilbert Burnet, whose pamphlets roused James II to disproportionate rage, or Burnet's nephew James Johnstone, now in London stirring up trouble.

38. Sir Ignatius White, marquis d'Albeville, James's envoy to The Hague, was an Irish adventurer who was *persona non grata* to William.

raised here, without any manner of ground, first of your Highness being a Papist, then of your being desirous to have the test repealed, there is nothing of that kind which may not be thought possible; so that if there should now be any nearer treaty,[39] it might perhaps be made use of with more advantage by them, to mislead men at a distance into a wrong belief. In lower instances, it hath not been unusual in such cases to set proposals on foot of which no other effect is expected than to bring men under doubts and suspicions from their own friends. The instruments that shall be made use of, their interests and dependencies being well considered and examined, will give a great deal of light, if anything of this kind should be attempted; and it happeneth well, that they will have to do with one who knoweth so well how to judge of men and things as not to be within the danger of being easily surprised, neither by any upon this occasion, nor by any other of our countrymen who speak what is dictated to them by men of several interests, or endeavour to value themselves upon their correspondencies and influences here, which I doubt have seldom foundation strong enough for your Highness to build upon. There can be nothing better recommended to you than the continuance of the method which you practise; neither to comply in anything that is unfit, nor to provoke further anger by any act that is unnecessary. This will not, perhaps, be sufficient to prevent ill-will, but it will in a great measure secure you from the ill effects of it.

Your Highness must allow me to applaud my good fortune in not having hitherto made a wrong conjecture about the sitting of the Parliament. Notwithstanding the discourse that have been made by the great men, with the greatest assurance, that it would meet one time after another, I ever thought it impracticable, considering the measures that are taken, and I am now as much an unbeliever for October, as I was for April, which was the time prefixed for the meeting. With all this your Highness must expect that it will still be given out there will be one; it is not perhaps thought convenient, neither indeed would it be so, that all foreign Princes and States should conclude there never will be a Parliament in England in this King's reign; a great deal would depend upon such an opinion

39. negotiation.

received, which would have an influence upon their manner of treating with us. But according to the most rational conjecture, how extraordinary soever many things may appear which have been done, the letting a Parliament meet as matters now stand would so undo them all, that it is hardly to be supposed possible.

The other great point which at present maketh the discourse is, whether England will have a war with the States; in this, the more thinking sort of men are of opinion there will be none. There is disposition enough for it, for reasons which need not to be explained; but there are so many discouraging circumstances, and the prejudice from ill success would be so much greater than the utmost which can be hoped in case of prospering, that the men in power must go against all the common methods of arguing if they venture upon an experiment which may be so destructive to them.

I have tired your Highness so long, that it is time for me to close with my wishes for your own and the Princess's health, which are of that consequence to the world, that nothing can be desperate whilst you are well and safe. For myself, I must ever be unalterably devoted to you.

Dalrymple, pp. 219-22.

XXI

To William of Orange.

25 July 1688.

So many things have happened of late that it is reasonable enough to conclude upon the first apprehension of them that they should produce great alterations in reference to the public, and yet with all this, upon a strict observation of all circumstances, I see nothing to raise more hopes on one side, or to incline the other to despair. I find that every new attempt bringeth a fresh disadvantage upon the great design, which is exposed and disappointed by so many repeated mistakes; the world is so much confirmed, that there is every day less danger of being overrun; the several parties, though differing never so much in other things, seem to agree in their resolution of preserving by all legal means the securities of their religion and their laws. The late business concerning the bishops hath such an effect that it is hardly to be imagined; the consequences are not seen to their full extent by the men in power, though they are not a little mortified by the ill success of it. I look upon it as that which hath brought all the Protestants together, and bound them up into a knot that cannot easily be untied. It is one of those kind of faults that can never be repaired; all that can be done to mend it will probably make it worse, as is seen already by every step that hath been since made to recover the reputation they have lost by it. It is given out that there will be yet some further proceedings against the bishops; but in that I am an unbeliever, as well as concerning the meeting of the Parliament, my opinion being still the same as I gave your Highness in my last; the continuance of the discourse of it, and even by those who are presumed to know best, doth not at all make me alter my judgement. A Parliament can never be an indifferent thing, and therefore it is a very weak argument to say that it will be tried, and if it doth not comply, it shall be dissolved. Things of this kind are not to be so handled; the consequences may be too great to make the experiment without better grounds to expect success than at present appear. In short, I still remain persuaded that there is no effectual progress made towards the great design; and even the thing[40] that party relyeth upon is subject to so many accidents and uncertainties that according to human probability we are secure, notwithstanding the ill appearances, which fright most when they are least examined. I wish your Highness all happiness, and to myself the continuance of your good opinion, which cannot be more valued by any man living, than it is by your most devoted servant.

Dalrymple, pp. 235-6.

40. The birth of the Prince of Wales, on 10 June.

APPENDIX

'OBSERVATIONS UPON A LATE LIBEL'

In 1940 Hugh Macdonald published a new edition of a pamphlet of 1681, *Observations upon a Late Libel called 'A Letter from a Person of Quality to his Friend concerning the King's Declaration* ... [etc.][1] He argued that this was an undiscovered work of Halifax's, because it was so attributed by a pencil annotation in the Trinity Library copy, because of the use of the archaic third-person singular ending '-eth'. (as in 'sayeth', 'speaketh'), which was one of Halifax's idiosyncrasies, and because of a certain likeness of style, less easy to define. Foxcroft accepted this,[2] but it is not unfair to point out that she was then in her eighties, that pencil annotations in college copies of seventeenth-century pamphlets mean nothing either way, and that Halifax was not the only man who used the '-eth' ending, though not regularly. The similarities of style are no more than similarities, but the clinching point is that whereas in every other work of his Halifax falls over backward to avoid personal allusions,[3] here he positively wallows in them; the whole work is an indictment of the Exclusionist Whigs by name, and many other men are dragged in on the flimsiest of excuses. In my opinion this is not Halifax's work, and on any unbiased assessment thc verdict must be 'not proven'.

1. Cambridge University Press, 1940. Macdonald also provides an exact bibliography of Halifax's other works.

2. *Character*, p. 137.

3. See above, p. 27.

MORE ABOUT PENGUINS AND PELICANS

Penguin Book News, which appears every month, contains details of all the new books issued by Penguins as they are published. From time to time it is supplemented by *Penguins in Print* – a complete list of all our available titles. (There are well over three thousand of these.)

A specimen copy of *Penguin Book News* will be sent to you free on request, and you can become a subscriber for the price of the postage – 4s. for a year's issues (including the complete lists). Just write to Dept EP, Penguin Books Ltd, Harmondsworth, Middlesex, enclosing a cheque or postal order, and your name will be added to the mailing list.

Some other books published by Penguins are described on the following pages.

Note: *Penguin Book News* and *Penguins in Print* are not available in the U.S.A. or Canada

Pelican Classics

THE ORIGIN OF SPECIES

DARWIN

Edited by J. W. Burrow

The Origin of Species is at the root of man's present attitude to himself and the universe: no one book since the *Summa* of Thomas Aquinas has made a comparable impact. Written for the general public of the 1850s, it remains, in the words of Dr Burrow's helpful and entertaining introduction, 'easily the most readable and approachable of the great revolutionary works of the scientific imagination'.

Pelican Classics

LEVIATHAN

HOBBES

Edited by C. B. Macpherson

From the turmoil of the English Civil War, when life was truly 'nasty, brutish, and short', Hobbes's *Leviathan* (1651) speaks directly to the twentieth century. In its over-riding concern for peace, its systematic analysis of power, and its elevation of politics to the status of a science, it mirrors much modern thinking. And despite its contemporary notoriety – Pepys called it 'a book the Bishops will not let be printed again' – it was also, as Dr Macpherson shows, a convincing apologia for the emergent seventeenth-century market society.

REFLECTIONS ON THE REVOLUTION IN FRANCE

BURKE

Edited by Conor Cruise O'Brien

Burke's *Reflections* (1790) detonated the great debate on the French Revolution. But Burke's conservatism was more radical than is often admitted by those who see him as the father of modern conservatism. Traditionalism, for him, involved a return to an earlier humanity and even his counter-revolutionary prescriptions were revolutionary in their way. Added to this, Burke was an Irishman: and this fact, argues Dr O'Brien, entails a wholly new evaluation of the man.

ON WAR

CLAUSEWITZ

Edited by Anatol Rapoport

In his famous treatise *On War* (1832) Carl von Clausewitz may be said to have distilled Napoleon into theory. He is best remembered for his pronouncement that war is a continuation of politics by other means and for his observations on total war: but modern strategists who profess to apply his doctrines would do well to read him again. For Clausewitz, as Professor Rapoport contends, made a distinction between judicious and injudicious war, and the relationship he detected between war and politics really means that war can only be waged in certain circumstances.